World Music Pedagogy, Volume III

World Music Pedagogy, Volume III: Secondary School Innovations provides a rationale and a resource for the implementation of World Music Pedagogy in middle and high school music classes, grades 7–12 (ages 13–18). Such classes include secondary general music, piano, guitar, songwriting, composition/improvisation, popular music, world music, music technology, music production, music history, and music theory courses. This book is not a depository of ready-made lesson plans but rather a tool to help middle and high school teachers to think globally in the music classroom.

Strategies and techniques of World Music Pedagogy are promoted by discussions of a multicultural music education, descriptive vignettes of realistic teaching environments, conversations with culture-bearers/pedagogues, and prompts for self-reflection. This volume approaches important issues of multicultural education and social justice that are often neglected in music education texts—proving to be a valuable resource for both nascent music educators and veteran practitioners alike.

Listening Episode music examples can be accessed on the eResource site from the Routledge catalog page.

Karen Howard is Assistant Professor of Music Education at the University of St. Thomas.

Jamey Kelley is Assistant Professor of Choral Music Education at the University of North Texas.

Routledge World Music Pedagogy Series

Series Editor: Patricia Shehan Campbell, University of Washington

The **Routledge World Music Pedagogy Series** encompasses principal cross-disciplinary issues in music, education, and culture in six volumes, detailing theoretical and practical aspects of World Music Pedagogy in ways that contribute to the diversification of repertoire and instructional approaches. With the growth of cultural diversity in schools and communities and the rise of an enveloping global network, there is both confusion from and a clamoring by teachers for music that speaks to the multiple heritages of their students, as well as to the spectrum of expressive practices in the world that constitute the human need to sing, play, dance, and engage in the rhythms and inflections of poetry, drama, and ritual.

Volume I: Early Childhood Education
Sarah H. Watts

Volume II: Elementary Music Education
J. Christopher Roberts and Amy C. Beegle

Volume III: Secondary School Innovations
Karen Howard and Jamey Kelley

Volume IV: Instrumental Music Education
Mark Montemayor, William J. Coppola, and Christopher Mena

Volume V: Choral Music Education
Sarah J. Bartolome

Volume VI: School-Community Intersections
Patricia Shehan Campbell and Chee-Hoo Lum

World Music Pedagogy

Secondary School Innovations

Volume III

Karen Howard
University of St. Thomas

Jamey Kelley
University of North Texas

Routledge
Taylor & Francis Group

NEW YORK AND LONDON

First published 2018
by Routledge
711 Third Avenue, New York, NY 10017

and by Routledge
2 Park Square, Milton Park, Abingdon, Oxon, OX14 4RN

Routledge is an imprint of the Taylor & Francis Group, an informa business

Library of Congress Cataloging-in-Publication Data
The Library of Congress has cataloged the combined volume edition as follows:
Names: Roberts, J. Christopher, author. | Beegle, Amy C., author.
Title: World music pedagogy.
Description: New York ; London : Routledge, 2018– | Includes bibliographical
    references and index.
Identifiers: LCCN 2017050640 (print) | LCCN 2017054487 (ebook) |
    ISBN 9781315167589 () | ISBN 9781138052727 | ISBN
    9781138052727q(v.2 : hardback) | ISBN 9781138052796q(v.2 : pbk.)
Subjects: LCSH: Music—Instruction and study.
Classification: LCC MT1 (ebook) | LCC MT1. W92 2018 (print) |
    DDC 780.71—dc23
LC record available at https://lccn.loc.gov/2017050640

ISBN: 978-1-138-04112-7 (hbk)
ISBN: 978-1-138-04113-4 (pbk)
ISBN: 978-1-315-17465-5 (ebk)

Typeset in Times New Roman
by Apex CoVantage, LLC

Visit the eResource: www.routledge.com/9781138041134

Contents

Chapter 3   **Participatory Musicking**   **50**

Chapter 4   **Performing World Music**   **80**

Chapter 5   Creating World Music   110

Chapter 6   Integrating World Music   137

Series Foreword

Turning and turning in the widening gyre
The falcon cannot hear the falconer;
Things fall apart; the centre cannot hold;
Mere anarchy is loosed upon the world . . .
(from "The Second Coming," W. B. Yeats)

There is a foreboding tone to the stanza above, which at first may seem out of sync
with a book on the pedagogy of world music. After all, music education is an intact
phenomenon, arguably innocent and pure, that envelops teachers and their students in
the acts of singing, playing, and dancing, and this field is decidedly not about falcons.
Instead, music education conjures up long-standing images of spirited high school
bands, choirs, orchestras, of young adolescents at work in guitar and keyboard classes,
of fourth-grade xylophone and recorder players, of first-grade rhythm bands, and of
toddlers accompanied by parents playing small drums and shakers. At a time of demographic diversity, with a wide spectrum of students of various shapes, sizes, and hues
laid wide open, music education can press further, as the field has the potential to hold
court in a child's holistic development as a core avenue for the discovery of human
cultural heritage and the celebration of multiple identities based upon race, ethnicity,
gender, religion, and socioeconomic circumstance.

Yet there is a correspondence of the stanza, and the disquiet that Yeats commu-
nicates, with this book and with the book series, *World Music Pedagogy in School
and Community Practice*. I refer the reader to the start of the third line, and also to
the title of a novel by Nigerian author Chinua Achebe. A landmark in the world's
great literature, *Things Fall Apart* has been very much in mind through the

conception of this project, its design and development by a team of authors, and its thematic weave in these tempestuous times. Achebe's writing of cultural misunderstanding, of the arrogance and insensitivity of Western colonizers in village Africa, of competing cultural systems, is relevant.

We raise questions relative to music teaching and learning: Do things fall apart, or prove ineffective, when they do not reflect demographic change; do they not respond to cultural variation; and do they not reasonably reform to meet the needs of a new era? Can music education remain relevant and useful through the full-scale continuation of conventional practices, or is there something prophetic in the statement that things fall apart, particularly in music education, if there are insufficient efforts to revise and adapt to societal evolution? There is hard-core documentation of sparkling success stories in generations of efforts to musically educate children. Yet there is also evidence of frayed, flailing, and failing programs that are the result of restrictive music selections and exclusive pedagogical decisions that leave out students, remain unlinked to local communities, and ignore a panorama of global expressions. There is the sinking feeling that music education programs exclusively rooted in Western art styles are insensitive and unethical for 21st-century schools and students, and that choices of featured music are statements on people we choose to include and exclude from our world.

Consider many school programs for their long-standing means of musically educating students within a Western framework, featuring Western school-based music, following Western literate traditions of notation, Western teacher-directed modes of learning, and Western fixed rather than flexible and spontaneously inventive musicking potentials. These approaches are all good for particular times and places, and yet they are arguably unethical in the exclusion of music and music-makers in the world. Certainly, all practices deserve regular review, upgrades, and even overhauls. Today's broad population mix of students from everywhere in the world press on diversifying the curriculum, and the discoveries of "new" music-culture potentials are noteworthy and necessary in making for a more inclusive music education.

So, the Nigerian author selected the Irish poet's phrase as meaningful to his seminal work, much as we might reflect upon its meaning so to muster a response to the societal disruption and contestation across the land and in the world. The practice of musically educating children, youth, and adults may not at first appear to be the full solution to the challenges of local schools and societies, nor essential to meeting mandates in cultural and multicultural understanding. But music is as powerful as it is pan-human; musicking is musical involvement in what is humanly necessary; and the musical education of children and youth benefit their thoughts, feelings, and behaviors. When things fall apart, or seem to be on the brink of breaking up, of serving fewer students and to a lesser degree than they might be served, we look to ways in which the music of many cultures and communities can serve to grow the musicianship of our students as well as their understanding of heritage and humanity, of people and places. Thus, from cynicism springs hope, and from darkness comes light, as this book and book series rises up as a reasoned response to making music relevant and multiply useful in the lives of learners in schools and communities.

THE SERIES

Each of the six volumes in the **World Music Pedagogy Series** provides a sweep of teaching-learning encounters that lead to the development of skills, understandings, and values that are inherent within a diversity of the world's musical cultures. Written for professionally active teachers as well as students in undergraduate and certification programs on their way to becoming teachers, these volumes encompass the application of the World Music Pedagogy (WMP) process from infancy and toddlerhood through late adolescence and into the community.

The books are unified by conceptualizations and format, and of course by the Series aim of providing theoretical frameworks for and practical pedagogical experiences in teaching the world's musical cultures. Individual WMP volumes are organized by music education context (or class type) and age/grade level.

For every volume in the WMP Series, common elements are intended to communicate with coherence the means by which learners can become more broadly musical and culturally sensitive to people close by and across the world. All volumes include seven chapters that proceed from an introduction of the particular music education context (and type), to the play-out of the five dimensions, to the reflective closing of how WMP contributes to meeting various musical and cultural goals, including those of social justice through music as well as issues of diversity, equity, and inclusion.

There are scatterings of music notations across each volume, mostly meant to assist the teacher who is preparing the orally based lessons rather than to suggest their use with students. Many of the chapters launch from vignettes, real-life scenarios of teachers and students at work in the WMP process, while chapters frequently close on interviews with practicing music educators and teaching musicians who are devoting their efforts to effecting meaningful experiences for students in the world's musical cultures. Authors of several of the volumes provide commentaries on published works for school music ensembles, noting what is available of notated scores of selected world music works, whether transcribed or arranged, and how they can be useful alongside the adventures in learning by listening.

LISTENING LINKS FOR THE SERIES

Of central significance are the listening links for recordings that are featured in teaching-learning episodes. These episodes are lesson-like sequences that run from 3 minutes to 30 minutes, depending upon the interest and inclination of the teacher, which pay tribute to occasions for brief or extended listening experiences that may be repeated over a number of class sessions. The listening links are noted in the episode descriptions as well as at each chapter's end, and users can connect directly to the recordings (audio as well as video recordings) through the Routledge eResource site for each of the Series' volumes, linked to the catalog page of each volume on www.routledge.com/Routledge-World-Music-Pedagogy-Series/book-series/WMP.

All volumes recommend approximately 20 listening links, and Chapters 2–6 in each volume provide illustrations of the ways in which these listening selections can develop into experiences in the five WMP dimensions. From the larger set of recommended listening tracks, three selections continue to appear across the chapters as keystone selections, which are intended to show the complete pathways of how these three recordings can be featured throughout the five dimensions. These learning pathways are noted in full in Appendix I, so that the user can see in one fell swoop the flow of teaching-learning from Attentive Listening to Engaged Listening, Enactive Listening, Creating World Music, and Integrating World Music. A second

Appendix (II) provides recommended resources for further reading, listening, viewing, and development of the ways of WMP.

***

As a collective of authors, and joined by many of our colleagues in the professional work of music teachers and teaching musicians, we reject the hateful ideologies that blatantly surface in society. We are vigilant of the destructive choices that can be made in the business of schooling young people, and which may result from racism, bigotry, and prejudice. Hate has no place in society or its schools, and we assert that music is a route to peace, love, and understanding. We reject social exclusion, anti-Semitism, white supremacy, and homophobia (and other insensitive, unfeeling, or unbalanced perspectives). We oppose the ignorance or intentional avoidance of the potentials for diversity, equity, and inclusion in curricular practice. We support civility and "the culture of kindness," and hold a deep and abiding respect for people across the broad spectrum of our society. We are seeking to develop curricular threads that allow school music to be a place where all are welcome, celebrated, and safe; where every student is heard; and where cultural sensitivity can lead to love.

ACKNOWLEDGMENTS

This collective of authors is grateful to those who have paved the way to teaching music with diversity, equity, and inclusion in mind. I am personally indebted to the work of my graduate school mentors, William M. Anderson, Terry Lee Kuhn, and Terry M. Miller, and to Halim El-Dabh and Virginia H. Mead, all of whom committed themselves to the study of music as a worldwide phenomenon, and who paved the way for me and many others to perform, study, and teach music with multicultural, intercultural, and global aims very much in mind. I am eternally grateful to Barbara Reeder Lundquist for her *joie de vivre* in the act of teaching music and in life itself. This work bears the mark of treasured University of Washington colleagues, then and now, who have helped to lessen the distance between the fields of ethnomusicology and music education, especially Steven J. Morrison, Shannon Dudley, and Christina Sunardi. Many thanks to the fine authors of the books in this Series: Sarah J. Bartolome, Amy Beegle, William J. Coppola, Karen Howard, Jamey Kelley, Chee Hoo Lum, Chris Mena, Mark Montemayor, J. Christopher Roberts, and Sarah J. Watts. They are "the collective" who shaped the course of the Series, and who toiled to fit the principles of World Music Pedagogy into their various specialized realms of music education. We are grateful to Constance Ditzel, music editor at Routledge, who caught the idea of the Series and enthusiastically encouraged us to write these volumes, and to her colleague, Peter Sheehy, who carried it through to its conclusion.

As in any of these exciting though arduous writing projects, I reserve my unending gratitude for my husband, Charlie, who leaves me "speechless in Seattle" in his support of my efforts. Once again, he gave me the time it takes to imagine a project, to write, read, edit, and write some more. It could not have been done without the time and space that he spared me, busying himself with theories behind "the adsorption of deuterated molecular benzene," while I helped to shape, with the author-team, these ideas on World Music Pedagogy.

Patricia Shehan Campbell
December 2017

Acknowledgments

First and foremost, the authors would like to thank Patricia Shehan Campbell for the invitation to participate in the series, and her endless support throughout the process. Also, many thanks to the following people for their support and assistance in the preparation of this book: Leanna Kelley Fuller, Christopher Roberts, Christian Gaylord, Alison Farley, Bryan Nichols, Candice Davenport, Bill Longo, Kate Longo, Michelle Alexander, Sonia Chintha, David Aarons, Kathy Armstrong, Sarah Minette, and Joko Sutrisno.

Episodes

Listening Episode examples can be accessed on the eResource site from the Routledge catalog page.

1

Teaching and Learning in Context

Music of the world's cultures can be a captivating musical adventure—and the many fine musical expressions of our world are accessible with just a few clicks of the mouse or taps on a screen. With an Internet connection, one can travel to the other side of the globe in a matter of seconds and experience the rich musical heritage of geographically distant cultures. This is an unprecedented time in human history, where communication with culture-bearers and artist-musicians is literally at one's fingertips. In mere seconds, one can be transported to the East African country of Tanzania where ululations ring out as Wagogo women sing, move, and play hand drums, building sonic layers atop each other. On this virtual journey, one can witness artistic collaboration as world-renowned cellist Yo-Yo Ma plays Saint-Saens' "The Swan" right alongside the improvised movement of Lil Buck, a dancer who specializes in an African American street-style form known as "jookin'"—a compelling experience to watch for (and listen to) in the deeply expressive dance reflection of the music's melody, rhythm, phrasing, articulation, and dynamics. A listener can experience the Yoshida Brothers playing "Kodo" on the traditional Japanese *shamisen*, a three-stringed instrument, with lightning speed and accuracy. The musical world of secondary school students can also be explored at a glance via a Minneapolis-based group of children performing their own rap lyrics about their favorite snacks, *Hot Cheetos and Takis*. Similarly, the strident tones and dissonant chord clusters of a Bulgarian women's choir are ready for the listening ear. There are infinite possibilities for learning musical concepts and skills as they are expressed around the world within the secondary school music classroom, needing a music teacher who is brave enough to embark on the journey.

The purpose of this book is to enable the understanding by secondary school students, under the tutelage and facilitation by music teachers, of people of a diversity of cultures through experiences with their music. This book is meant to serve as a resource for the implementation of World Music Pedagogy (WMP) by teachers within secondary school music classes of various innovative performance, creative, and academic emphases, and to suggest ways in which social justice is put into play through a musical education that encompasses the expressive knowledge and values of diverse cultures and pursues an equity agenda. The descriptor "secondary school music" as used here refers to grade levels 6 through 12 (approximately ages 12–18) as conceived by the U.S. education system, with attention to students (and their teachers) in schools referred to as "high school" and "middle school." The book is subtitled "Secondary School Music Innovations" to suggest the focus of this volume is on music teachers and their students in secondary school music courses other than the long-standing instrumental and choral ensembles (which are the targeted topics of Volumes IV and V). This volume centers on the distinct music experiences of secondary students in diverse settings, such as class piano, guitar, music theory, and those courses growing in popularity like digital music production, songwriting, mariachi, composition, popular music ensembles, and world percussion ensembles.

Of note is our attempt to consider how non-standard music courses may fill the needs and meet the interests of an extensive population of secondary school students who are not drawn to standard music study but are keen to know music, to play it, sing it, listen to it, create it, and move it into their lives beyond school. The insertion of a broad set of musical experiences from local and global cultures can tune students into their family cultures, the cultures of their friends, and the world of cultures into which they will one day graduate.

The following chapters are not intended as a depository of ready-made lesson plans, although there are exemplar descriptions and illustrations of pedagogical components throughout the chapters. Rather, they are meant to function as a tool to aid music teachers in thinking globally, culturally, and socioculturally as they design music courses in middle and high schools in urban, suburban, rural, and small-town settings. The material contained within this book is cued to WMP strategies and techniques through discussions of the essence of multicultural education and ethnomusicological considerations in and through music, depictions of WMP in action through descriptive vignettes of realistic secondary school teaching environments, and conversations with culture-bearers, artist-musicians, and master teachers.

The content of this book is organized by the five dimensions of WMP as designed by Patricia Shehan Campbell (2004) as they pertain to the learning and development of secondary school music students. Each chapter focuses on essential experiences that encourage musical development and cultural understandings, from deep listening through to composing in the style of particular world music cultures. In this chapter, secondary school music innovations will be explored as a suitable and necessary environ for the implementation of WMP. After examining types of secondary school music as well as the students within them, critical issues and philosophies related to WMP will be proffered for consideration.

Secondary School Music Innovations

Ms. Harmon is starting her fourth year as a music teacher at Morrison Middle School. She is a graduate, with honors, from a local university and well-versed in the methods of instrumental and choral ensemble instruction. Despite her conventional training in a music education teacher program, her job responsibilities do not include large traditional performance ensembles. Her teaching schedule includes one section of piano class, two sections of guitar, a survey class of world music traditions, and a new addition to the course catalog, the World Rhythms Percussion Ensemble. This elective course is open to all students enrolled at Morrison and features a different world music culture every eight weeks.

In addition to providing quality musical experiences within her classroom, Ms. Harmon strives to facilitate meaningful interactions between her students and the community that highlight the social and cultural connections created by music-making. Working with the cultural commission at Morrison Middle School, an organization of parents and school faculty, an annual fundraiser supports the hiring of culture-bearers and artist-musicians to work with students in the development of a performance assembly for the school. This year, a New York–based group specializing in the performance of traditional Japanese percussion music known as Taiko will soon be in residence. Ms. Harmon makes it a point each year to connect the resident music culture with the lesson content in one or more of her classes.

As the artist-in-residence group for the coming term features taiko drumming, shakuhachi (Japanese flute), and folk dance, she decides that her World Rhythms Percussion Ensemble is the appropriate course in which to integrate lessons about Japanese musical traditions. While she also briefly prepares the students in her other courses and ensembles for the upcoming music residency, she wants to create plans for her percussion ensemble that will take the students deep into the music culture via meaningful listening experiences. Two months before the guest musicians arrive, Ms. Harmon e-mails the director of the Japanese music group. She explains her intention to work with her percussion ensemble students on taiko rhythms and asks for guidance in appropriate materials. The director is excited to speak with a music teacher so keen on sharing his music culture. He sends her some brochures that he has prepared for his own students that indicate basic taiko rhythm drills. He also includes suggestions for reading material, audio clips, and online videos that he feels are of high quality for repeated attentive listening and beginning attempts at engaging with the new sounds. Ms. Harmon readily implements the materials in her class, guiding students through listening and opening the ear to the sounds of Japanese taiko. She also presents information about how these new musical sounds they are exploring function within contemporary Japanese culture.

Because she does not have actual taiko drums, Ms. Harmon decides that the school's supply of congas and djembes can be substituted for the Japanese drums. She practices diligently on her own leading up to the lessons with her percussion ensemble so that she will feel comfortable teaching the rhythms to her ensemble. On the day of the first lesson in taiko with her percussion ensemble, the students enter the music room to a recording of a taiko group from Japan. The virtuosic flow of pitches from the fue (bamboo flute), the bachi (drumsticks) striking the tile floor, the dry cracking sound of the drums, and the players' shouts of encouragement fill the room. The students' eyes go wide with excitement as they find their way to a drum.

Ms. Harmon exemplifies a secondary school music teacher looking for paths into teaching world music cultures. She collaborated with a culture-bearer to develop meaningful lessons that reflect important features of the music culture. She understood the reality of learning circumstances in a classroom setting rather than within a specialized program of taiko study in Japan, and she readily adapted her teaching by using the instruments available to her. She also demonstrated an understanding of the time she needed to put in with her own research into the music culture, practicing the music that was new to her, and thinking of effective teaching and learning experiences for her percussion ensemble students to listen and respond to the music.

Over the past 50 years, secondary music programs have extended the learning opportunities open to students by offering classes beyond the familiar ensemble experiences found in band, choir, orchestra, and even jazz band. Many secondary music programs now offer courses in guitar, keyboard, beginning and advanced theory, popular music, songwriting, digital music production, and an array of globally oriented courses that may reflect the musical activity of the local community, student interests, the expertise of the music teacher, or a particular music culture or genre. Progressive music programs have insisted on providing music experiences that are more relevant to the students' lives and that emphasize the development of skills in individuals, rather than group performance in high-stakes concerts. Freed from performance and festival schedules, students can experience music deeply, through intentional listening episodes, participatory music-making, as well as studying music as culture, in knowing its context and purpose.

We use the term Secondary School Music Innovations in an inclusive manner to reflect unique teaching and learning scenarios that feature the phases of WMP. Secondary school music offerings, including a wide array of courses offering varied musical experiences to adolescent learners, are also included. These course suggestions are meant to open the circle of curricular offerings to a fuller, more comprehensive, and more democratically expansive representation of musical potentials and student interests. Throughout this book, teaching and learning examples as well as descriptive vignettes will be used to illustrate how WMP can be employed in a panoply of secondary music classrooms.

In many secondary schools, especially those at the middle school level, music classes outside of the realm of performing ensembles have been designated as "general music." With about 40 years of use in some regions, the label of "secondary general music" is variously defined, is sometimes inclusive and sometimes not, and comes with assumptions or misconceptions. Often, "secondary general music" teachers are given very little guidance as to what should be included within a so-called general music curriculum. This lack of direction may lead to course offerings that consist of a hodge-podge of music experiences. Some teachers use rotations to structure their courses, such as exploring ukuleles, piano, steel band, and composition, each for a quarter of the school year. Other music teachers conceptualize secondary general music as an extension of the type of experiences students have had in elementary music classes: a variety of activities in singing, note-reading, and playing instruments. Such a description of secondary school music does not encapsulate the diverse music course offerings that are possible in secondary schools, nor does it suggest learning experiences tuned to adolescent student interests and needs. Courses classified as secondary school music may share some of the same intended goals of those courses grouped within the label of "secondary general music," but they are markedly different in organization, content, and execution with an aim toward equity in a broad representation of people, music, and cultures. Secondary school music is already pressing toward a broader array of possibilities for musical study, all of them angled to allow students to have participatory experiences in making music of their own and others.

Even though the course description of "general music" is used within course catalogs or master schedules in secondary schools, it will not be used here due to the lack of specificity in the label. For clarity, teaching settings will be described in specific terms, such as a "songwriting class" or a "world percussion ensemble," so as to leave no doubt of the curricular intentions of the class. While teaching episodes or examples will be presented for specific course types, savvy music teachers can easily adapt any of the exemplar scenarios to their own secondary school music settings.

Growing numbers of secondary schools are offering classes that may be referred to as "multicultural music," of which there are two varieties. The first type of class in this category is a survey course, sometimes called "survey of world music traditions" or "global music." This type of class does not focus on one world music culture but affords ample opportunities for listening, performing, and connecting to diverse musical styles from around the world. The curriculum for this type of course covers the similarities and differences in global music cultures and their musicians, while celebrating the immense diversity of sounds to be found.

The second type of multicultural or global music class gives students the opportunity to learn the performance tradition of a specific music culture. Examples of this type of class may include mariachi, gospel choir, Indonesian gamelan, Zimbabwean marimba (sometimes called "Zimarimbas"), Caribbean steel band, bluegrass band, or West African drumming. At times, the facilitators of these classes are culture-bearers themselves, whether they are faculty members of a school or artist-musicians who are brought in for particular experiences. At other times, it is music teachers who are learning new instruments, repertoires, and ways in after-school, weekend, summer workshops, graduate study, and community work. In addition to the valuable skill-building that happens in these classes, secondary music students learn the important cultural meaning these musical traditions have for the musicians who maintain them. The celebrations, struggles, and traditions of the music cultures start to become clear to secondary students through lessons developed with WMP considerations in mind. Students can develop and grow in empathy for their school, local, and larger global community through these teaching and learning experiences.

Many middle and high schools offer courses that allow students to become skilled on a particular instrument in a setting outside of the conventional band or orchestra. In many cases, students will progress at their own pace through the prescribed musical material. Group guitar and piano are the most frequently offered classes of this type. In more recent years, rock band and popular music classes have been introduced during the school day. Emerging popular music studies are promoting musical learning through listening and imitation rather than reliance on music notation. Songwriting is occasionally offered in secondary school settings, which may or may not require guitar, piano, or theory as a prerequisite; this class allows students to refine their lyric writing and chord progression skills, while providing a forum to perform for peers. Popular music classes, songwriting, guitar, and piano are becoming more prevalent within secondary school music programs as an alternative or addition to traditional large performance ensembles. These alternatives are often viewed by secondary students as more relevant to their lives, as well as building contemporary skills that they believe they can continue to develop beyond graduation.

With technological advances, music classes are developing with a focus on composing, recording, and producing. These classes could be called Music Technology, Music Composition, or Music Production. In some music programs, these offerings have been specifically designed to attract music students who may be uninterested in participating in band, orchestra, or choir, or who are unable to do so due to lack of instrument instruction in their younger years. Most of these classes are held in computer labs and use software packages that aid in music notation or help students create the sonic output. Content within these classes can include multimedia development, learning electronic musical instruments, or live sound reinforcement. With the advent of these types of classes, secondary students are given the opportunity to learn musical skills that may have been previously off-limits to them; before the development of music software like Garageband, secondary students could not elect to take a composition course without fluent understanding of music notation. These technology courses, as well as many of the innovative secondary music classes already discussed, provide more access to music education for all secondary students, not only those who have had previous experiences with performing ensembles.

Many secondary school music programs offer music theory to develop musicianship keyed to notation and literacy concepts found in Western art music as well as to prepare students for collegiate music study. These courses often feature fundamentals and basic musicianship at the entry level while upper levels may introduce part-writing and aural skills. While these courses focus on reading notation and traditional aural skill acquisition, creative teachers can introduce activities that incorporate performing, composing, and improvising as well as the concept of music as culture, rather than solely a collection of sonic stimuli to be categorized and analyzed.

It should be noted that music theory, especially Advanced Placement or International Baccalaureate versions of music theory, may marginalize various forms of musical learning as well as music genres. Just as university courses in theory teach Western art music with little acknowledgment of the world's musical cultures, so, too, do secondary school theory courses exclude music beyond the Western art styles. Just as Western art music study requires notational literacy, so, too, should secondary school theory courses require practice of the oral-aural means of music learning. High school theory classes often examine music as a written form, to be analyzed and dissected, but not to be experienced in an embodied way. While theory courses may include aural skills, the emphasis is on aural skill drilling rather than on a more enjoyable (and productive) means of developing listening skills. The inclusion of WMP within these types of classes can signal not only experience with a greater selection of brilliant musical styles but also enhancement of playing-by-ear skills.

Secondary school music programs invite all students of varying abilities and interests to participate in the musical happenings of the classroom and can offer a diverse array of music-making experiences. Some students may enter secondary school having private piano lessons, or having sung in a church choir, but many have had no formal music instruction. One of the strengths of offering diverse music courses is that there are more entry points into learning a musical skill, whereas traditional ensemble membership may require students to have started in elementary school. Music classes outside the scope of traditional ensemble performance (Figure 1.1) welcome students with different aptitudes that may have been undervalued in the large ensemble format. Consider the high school girl who has learned to play guitar by ear, or the middle school boy who experiments with beats and loops on his home computer to make his own music, or the teenager who translates overpowering emotions into evocative lyrics. Secondary school music classes can provide a space for these young musicians to feel a sense of belonging and to grow their burgeoning musicianship.

Although there is great variety in music class offerings in middle and high schools, there is little extant research on the incidence of secondary school music outside of traditional ensembles. What is known is that most secondary schools offer band, orchestra, and choir, but far fewer programs feature other musical options. It is telling that a majority of schools are not yet responsive to the myriad of musical engagements that may appeal to student populations, nor to the diversity of musical expressions that are found locally or that are treasured here and there across the globe. Western art music continues to influence the content of the curriculum, and even as secondary school ensembles occasionally provide opportunities to play and sing music from elsewhere in the world, this music is typically learned through

Figure 1.1   High school students creating film soundtracks in a digital music production class

Photo courtesy of Karen Howard

Western art music methods (and may well be performed without the cultural nuances of the musical tradition). Campbell (2004) noted that "this is but one model, and a colonial one at that, which fixes European music (and its staff notation) and its pedagogical processes highest in a hierarchy atop the musical expressions and instructional approaches of so many other rich traditions" (p. xvi). This exclusive curricular content is startling, given the populations of secondary school students whose families trace their ancestries to places elsewhere than Europe or whose families constitute remarkable folk traditions such as blues, bluegrass, gospel music, mariachi, and conjunto that have been growing in communities for a century or more. Moving forward, music teachers should continue to investigate the access to and quality of theirs and other secondary music programs. Those in the field of music education need to embrace the vast majority of secondary school students who, left to their own devices, love music but reject school music experiences.

Some students dream of "doing music," and they may sing and play on their own outside of school, yet they may have no interest in secondary school music offerings that are limited to the conventional ensembles. For students who are drawn to musical study during middle and high school, the curricular content of secondary music classes need not be singular, but should include diverse opportunities for performing, creating, and responding. While the goals in previous generations of secondary (general) music classes may have been to prepare students for ensemble membership or to teach the rudiments of music notation, secondary school music teachers can emphasize the building of musical skills and knowledge that will pave the way toward their musical futures, be it within or outside of formal music institutions.

Secondary School Music Students

There are some over-arching developmental changes that occur in adolescence, and they do impact what is designed and delivered by teachers in the secondary music classroom. While every student is truly unique, thus necessitating the need to know each one individually, music teachers can benefit from understanding the common attributes of their students.

There is a widely held belief that musical development is only attainable for select people and that only the musically "talented" students should be educated and trained. Young people hearing these cultural messages may believe that music study is not "for them" if they have not excelled in traditional music-making activities earlier in their schooling, and they may be reluctant to participate in school music activities. Middle schools and high schools with traditional large choral and instrumental ensembles may exclude up to 90% of the school population, and they may further transmit messages to students that they are "unmusical."

Despite this notion of a musical elite, people of every nation and culture are musical, and all are capable of making and responding to music. In fact, music-making is a uniquely human experience, and schools should be providing ample opportunities for all students to explore their innate abilities for musical expression. Music teachers, especially those who encounter students in secondary music class-rooms, should proclaim that all humans are musical, in varying ways.

With the understanding that all students are music students, it is pertinent to explore the specific characteristics of secondary school music students. Students enrolled in middle and high school range in age from 12 to 18 years of age. During their adolescence, students grow from childhood to the threshold of adulthood. Their experience of puberty is highly idiosyncratic, even in terms of physical development. Even though girls typically enter puberty (around age 10 or 11) earlier than boys (around age 11 or 12), how individual children mature relies on many genetic and environmental factors.

Along with the physical development that occurs during adolescence, the arrival of hormones is the catalyst for neurological changes that influence emotional responses and executive functioning. This executive functioning includes decision-making, organization, impulse control, and planning for the future. Consequently, many adolescents have issues with self-control and decision making when presented with pleasure-seeking opportunities. Students are generally more motivated by rewards than punishments. As teenagers mature, they display stronger reasoning skills that are often logical or have moral considerations. In problem solving, older adolescents are more methodical and use step-by-step solutions rather than trial-by-error strate-gies. Later in adolescence, teenagers can think abstractly and make rational judgments. Older students can also understand other perspectives and are more interested in complex issues like social justice. Young people, especially those in late adolescence, yearn to address real-world problems, challenge the status quo, and communicate through artistic expression.

Secondary music teachers are wise to push their students to think critically about the world around them, as they are more than ready to explore the complexities of being human. Secondary students yearn to understand the cultural meanings of music, including how and why music is performed and what it means to the musicians who perform it. Understanding music as culture allows the music to become alive in the students' world and have meaning beyond the mere aesthetics of sound. Furthermore, critical examination of the world around them, including their schools, their neighborhoods, and their country may present issues of inequity and systematic challenges. Students of this age are ready to explore solutions to these matters of social justice, and many are eager to build a better world.

During the years of secondary school, students are creating their identities: defining who they are and what they value, committing to personal relationships, understanding their sexuality, exploring their gender or ethnic identities, and deciding future career possibilities. Within secondary music classrooms, teachers must offer many different roles, role models, and experiences to encourage students to incorporate their musical development into their processes of identity creation and understanding of cross-cultural matters. Music teachers are in a prime position to note and celebrate cultural distinctions as presented in selected musics and cultures. Students at this stage in life are often passionate advocates for social justice, including acknowledging and disengaging racism, homophobia, classism, and cultural appropriation. Furthermore, music teachers need to provide encouraging feedback that promotes musical development, in all its incarnations, as opposed to valuing only specific musical skills.

In adolescence, listening to music becomes an important part of a student's life. On average, adolescents listen to several hours of music per day, and listening to music is a favored activity. Teens listen to music for many reasons, including mood regulation, identity development, and the creation of peer relationships. Middle and high school students listen to a diverse and eclectic catalogue of music, at times with little awareness as to the cultural background or significance of the sounds or musicians. Students may listen to popular music that reflects their cultural heritage, or students may indulge in the exciting sounds coming from a myriad of geographic locales from as diverse a set of locations as Nigeria, South Korea, and Iceland.

Despite the active listening habits of young people, as students enter adolescence they are often less interested in the curricular music offerings at their schools. Students may feel their school music programs are not relevant to their musical world and experiences. For practitioners of secondary school music, there may be a tendency to believe students do not value "music" because they appear to have limited musical experience. In reality, music is an important facet of students' lives, meaning that music teachers need to raise their own awareness of this reality and adapt the content of their music classes to be relevant and engaging.

Many secondary music classes do not require auditions or prerequisites to participate, thus leaving the door open for all students to enroll in music studies regardless of the extent of their earlier education and training. This process ensures that no student is privileged over another, as school music offerings should fit the needs of every student. Music classes are typically elective classes in secondary settings, especially in high schools (many secondary schools require music or another arts course as a graduation requirement), and therefore enrollment in these courses is dependent upon the perceived value by students of the course. Music teachers do well to broaden the palette of secondary school music offerings in order to ensure student interest leading to their enrollment. While some students may lack initial motivation to study music, most students know music to be an important part of their lives and are musically intrigued when given hands-on experiential opportunities to make music, learn of the broader cultural traditions around them, and to listen to music for its meaning to them as compared to the musicians from the culture of origin.

It is important for a reflective teacher to discern between understanding how the typical student develops and connecting with students as unique individuals as they connect them to music cultures of the world. While most students will likely develop in a typical manner or pass through similar stages, it is important to remember that there is great diversity within each young person's journey to adulthood. It is even more important for the music teacher to learn about their students as people than to categorize students by their developmental progress.

What Students Learn in Secondary School Music

For many teachers in secondary school music classes, there is great flexibility in the scope and sequence of the music instruction and activities. Teachers own the content of their courses, and most secondary school music teachers accept the importance of providing a variety of learning experiences that develop the multiple musical competencies of their students. Secondary school music teachers do well to incorporate activities that allow students to listen, to respond, to perform, to improvise, to compose, and to connect with people, cultures, and ideas.

Most secondary school music classrooms, from guitar class to advanced music theory, include experiences where students encounter new musical styles and literature through listening activities. These kinds of experiences have been a staple of secondary music classrooms since the introduction of recorded music a hundred years ago. Listening should be a vital part of all secondary music classes, from music theory to guitar to world percussion to steel band. It is important to include sonic exemplars within the focus of study (e.g., examples of accomplished guitarists in a guitar class), but also to present musical diversity wherein students can experience new timbres, rhythms, and forms within their focus area of study.

Listening is the gateway to further musical development; guided listening allows secondary students to hear like a musician. The adept teacher must facilitate intentional and active listening experiences within music classes to avoid passive listening that is little more than perceiving music. Strategies such as creative or choreographed movement, listening maps, guides, aural challenges, and verbal descriptions of what the listener is experiencing can be utilized to promote a deeper engagement with the sonic happenings. These types of activities can be facilitated in all secondary school music classes, such as class piano, songwriting, or a survey of world music traditions.

WMP within the secondary school music classroom provides channels for deeper listening to any music, from any time and any place. Through the phases of WMP, the musical experiences of adolescent students can live within a concentrated and focused listening of which they are intellectually capable. Students can feel the music as they hear it, and be encouraged to move to it, or to find the personally and culturally meaningful messages that are communicated by it. Because of several years of musical experiences behind them, either in or out of school, secondary school students are capable of recognizing musical features and styles through multiple encounters with the music. With guidance from the teacher or a culture-bearer, secondary school students can be drawn into the details of the music. They grow musically from their Attentive Listening to a piece and to their greater involvement as participants in the music. Adolescent listeners can listen objectively and subjectively, analytically and with conceptual images in mind, and many enjoy the safety and even satisfaction in their search for personal and cultural meaning in the music. With careful listening, adolescents can make their way to other artistic processes like performing and creating, well-tooled and confident in the music they have come to know over repeated listening experiences.

Secondary school music teachers have the freedom to provide their students with many types of music experiences. In fact, some focus primarily on participatory and performance-oriented activities rather than on listening or creative experiences, especially in classes that emphasize performance skills, such as world percussion ensemble or class piano. Developing performance skills should be included in all types of secondary music classes, even advanced music theory or survey of world music traditions. Participatory experiences allow students to experience the music in an embodied way. Singing, playing instruments, and dancing are physical modalities of the music that can be utilized in most secondary settings, such as Zimbabwean marimba ensembles or music composition.

Music teachers can present new performance opportunities to their secondary students using instruments such as ukuleles, dulcimers, djembes, or other instruments (or suitable substitutes) of world music cultures. With new technologies such as digital applications on mobile electronic devices, students can play virtual instruments such as guitars, pianos, and percussion instruments with little technical training. In fact, students of this age are often the ones teaching their teachers how to use such technology. These types of digital "apps" can be a welcome addition in theory or survey classes. Software developers are creating apps that expand the possibilities within secondary school music classrooms, so that students can learn how to play Indian *tabla*, Japanese *koto*, or Peruvian *zampoña* (siku or pan flute) by tapping the screens of their personal devices.

Within the framework of WMP, performance becomes an outward expression of musical understanding that begins with Attentive Listening, leading to Engaged and Enactive listening, and Participatory Musicking. For the high school guitar student, performance displays the acquisition of technical skill and awareness of style, as informed through intentional listening. For the music theory student, performance demonstrates an understanding of the theoretical concepts that have been learned. For group piano students, performance can display the ability to create improvisatory passages using new scales learned as part of a unit on a particular music culture. As students learn to perform music of world cultures, the experiences become a means of knowing cultures, people, places, and their times. Additionally, secondary music teachers using WMP should strive for embodied performances that are integrated across disciplines, incorporating dance, drama, movement, poetry, and discussion of spiritual aspects as presented in the culture. Music teachers can choose to include music of cultures that have experienced oppression and marginalization, cultures that seem to exist on the periphery of mainstream awareness, and those traditions that seem at risk of disappearing.

There has been a continuing interest in the potential for school music to encompass composing and improvising. Many music teachers seek additional training for themselves in popular music, composition, improvisation, and song-writing and classic teaching approaches (e.g., Kodály, Orff-Schulwerk, Dalcroze) that encourage musical creativity through exploration. In middle and high schools, musical creativity is brought to the forefront by introducing classes (e.g., songwriting, music technology, music composition) that focus on generating new music. But outside of these courses, secondary music students may have few opportunities to develop their creativity within music class. Although there are efforts to encourage more creative work within music programs, many teachers report that composition and improvisation activities are not commonly used within their classrooms. This phenomenon may be a result of the cultural boundaries of music education, where musical creativity of the individual is undervalued; more likely, improvisation and composition may be overlooked in classrooms because music teachers have limited experience with these musical activities. Creative activities can easily be included in any secondary music class: creating grooves in world percussion ensemble, designing melodies in piano class, or improvising with the pitches of a particular scale in theory class.

When incorporating WMP within secondary school music, composing and improvising, when inspired by world music cultures, allows students the opportunity to express themselves within the context of learning about musical cultures, both familiar and new. Creative music activities may alleviate some of the challenges that are encountered in secondary school music classrooms. For instance, performance of the newly composed or improvised material could be the focus of such learning, leaving notation of the creative output as merely optional. Students in a songwriting class can share their creations that incorporated lyrics written with the 10-line *decima* format used in son jarocho music from Mexico. Global percussion students can take turns improvising eight-measure phrases on the goblet-shaped *darabouka* while a recording of Turkish *saz* music plays. Theory students can sing the simple melodies they created while playing a cadence on the piano typically used at the end of songs in the Republic of Georgia. These synergistic experiences allow students to experience world music cultures as uniquely theirs while respecting the cultural values alive in those musical worlds.

With WMP, secondary music students become informed about the universal phenomenon of music in the lives of people. Students at all levels develop tools that help them navigate their experiences of daily life, including interactions with new people, cultures, and ideas. Music allows students to make connections between their own cultures and global cultures through collaborative performances and compositions. Secondary school music students can learn how their musical experiences relate to other art forms, disciplines, contexts, cultures, and their daily lives. They can learn the ways that music has been used around the world to motivate social movements seeking equality and justice. As students make connections between their personal musical experiences and the greater world, their performances, creations, and responses to music will also be more richly informed.

Even though there is great diversity in course offerings in secondary school music programs, the objectives are the same: to grow musically in concepts and skills, to develop individual understanding of self, to express emotion, and to connect with other people and cultures. Music teachers who employ the dimensions of WMP within their secondary school music classes will engage students in meaningful teaching and learning experiences that require students to thoughtfully respond, perform, and create. In addition to experiencing a comprehensive music education, students will forge cultural understandings of their diverse worlds while also acknowledging the human factor of music's social power.

Encircled in West African Polyrhythms

Twenty-four ninth-grade students stand in a large circle in their high school Global Music Traditions class, laughing after reviewing the chant "Tsobue" (Figure 1.2) from the West African country of Ghana. They always crack up after the "Ooh! Aah!" response. It is time to add the axatses *(gourd shakers) into the mix, so Mr. Shepherd and his students set out to review the previously learned rhythms first. Two of the students, Audra and Vikas, remind the class where the claps fall in the ostinato pattern, while Mr. Shepherd retrieves a* gankogui *(double iron bell) and stick from the bin sitting outside*

Tsobue

learned from Kwasi Dunyo

Figure 1.2   Ghanaian chant, "Tsobue"

of the circle. As he starts to play the bell ostinato, Sammy moves her head to the beat, her brown ponytail bouncing in time as she watches his hands.

Gregory looks longingly over his shoulder at the pile of gankoguis, waiting for Mr. Shepherd to give the signal to get an instrument. Several students practice in the air as they count the pattern out loud, "low, high, high, high, high" or "1, 2, 3, 4, 5." Mr. Shepherd walks around the circle playing the gankogui, watching the in-air practicing and listening to how they count, stopping where needed to model and reinforce, moving on to the next section when ready.

Since Mr. Shepherd had already modeled the technique for playing the axatse the day before, the students are ready to get their hands on the gourd shakers. When enough of the students are ready to successfully split into groups, Mr. Shepherd counts the students into sections: one for the stepping-clapping ostinato, one for the gankoguis, and one for the axatses. Loud sounds, each within its individual pulse and speed, fill the next moments while students review their parts and the axatse players explore their instruments for the first time—feeling the seeds, shaking them this way and that, looking inside the hole, laughing at the different shapes of the gourds, and switching instruments with a neighbor to try different sounds. The melody of "Zaminamina" (Figure 1.2), a song from Ghana that was learned two classes previously, can be heard from different parts of the circle.

Mr. Shepherd brings the group's focus back to him where he is standing in the center of the circle. The gankogui group starts first, and the group works to smooth out some difficulties with the placement of the second note, the typically tricky spot for students, regardless of their age. Once the gankogui pattern is grooving steadily with Mr. Shepherd's support, the stepping-clapping ostinato group finds their way in. Although the students are learning all of the parts "by ear," there is a chart on the screen showing the rhythmic notation for the different parts and how they interlock. Charlotte, tall with long blond hair, has her usual solemn expression on her face, but moves beautifully as she claps and scoops her hands on the second and third beats. Lastly, the axatses are added until the three parts meld together.

When Mr. Shepherd signals for a stop, Shane smiles down at his axatse, as if to say, "How about that?" Mr. Shepherd explains the process for switching the instruments and waits while they give their instruments to someone else. Tiffany scurries

Zaminamina

Translation: You are all welcome, Yes, Welcome.

Figure 1.3   Ghanaian tune, "Zaminamina"

Transcribed by Karen Howard

---

back to her spot to practice once she has an axatse in her hand, and Sarah jumps across the circle after passing off her gankogui. They repeat the process one more time so that they perform all three parts. With this portion of the lesson at an end, Mr. Shepherd comments, "You guys showed me that you are ready for drumming tomorrow!" as he gestures to a row of hand-carved drums from Ghana lined up against the wall. Glenn, a tall, lanky teenager of few words, exclaims "Yeahhh!", blue eyes wide open, while several other students start to drum on their laps.

The students in Mr. Shepherd's class were experiencing a lesson that attended to traditional elements in school music programs: singing, rhythm work, playing instruments, movement, and note-reading. Throughout a series of lessons, Mr. Shepherd also shares stories with his students of how the instruments are made, video clips of the recreational genre Kpanlogo being performed in various settings, pictures of secondary schools in Ghana, and a visit from a Ghanaian culture-bearer who will lead a drumming workshop planned with Mr. Shepherd. A teacher like Mr. Shepherd thoughtfully facilitates discussions related to the history of the slave trade, particularly in West Africa, and students then learn of the people behind the music, the sociocultural history of the music, and that history's connection to contemporary society and struggles with continuing racism in the United States.

Philosophical Anchors in Secondary School Music

When considering the philosophical foundations behind curriculum design in secondary school music programs, sociocultural considerations must come forward alongside sonic attributes and structures, especially since music can be more fully comprehended in meaning and function by knowing its social and cultural context. Because a comprehensive understanding of a culture necessitates knowing its expressive and artistic components, so, too, does an understanding of music require some knowledge of its associated culture. In order to guide secondary students toward knowing the different musical systems present in their own communities and across the world, teachers should be proficient in addressing the sociocultural issues these systems entail. Cultures that have experienced marginalization often use music as a means of creating unity, awareness, and sparking hope amongst a community. Musical traditions that were at one time derided by a dominant culture group have, again and again throughout history, gone on to become an artistic darling of the group in power, often leading to a tangled of web of cultural appropriation. Limitations resulting from lower socioeconomic status have led to ingenious musical creations, and yet the disadvantaged status remains. Musical skill development has always been central to secondary school education programs, but the goal of developing WMP through musical experiences is a critical thrust. WMP embraces matters of a globally oriented musical canon attuned to a goal of equity and justice, and the use of culture-specific curricular materials and methods.

Culturally Responsive Teaching

Aligned with all teaching-learning plans that are sensitive to the needs of students, Culturally Responsive Teaching (CRT) is a pedagogical philosophy that focuses on the advantages and strengths of cultural diversity. There is no "one size fits all" approach to secondary school music teaching that works well for all students, so that approaching curricular design and instructional delivery in ways that relate to the cultural-familial perspectives of students can ensure learning. Culture influences expression, including student ways of speaking, writing, relating to others, learning styles, and beliefs surrounding teaching. It is influenced by wider factors such as home and community settings, economic trends, social situations, gender, age, class, education, and even immigration status (Gay, 2000). Students arrive to secondary school, and to music classes, via different social and belief systems from which they construct meaning. Likewise, the cultural backgrounds of music teachers and their previous teachers determine how they develop instructional plans, facilitate learning by their students, and form preconceived beliefs about their students. In CRT, pedagogical decisions are made that reflect a responsiveness and understanding by music teachers toward the lives and cultural experiences of their students.

There is a growing awareness by music teachers of the importance of social justice, cultural democracy, and the inclusion of diverse peoples and their perspectives. While this awareness is at times more academic than applied, some teachers are finding circumstances in which they can enact these values. There are those secondary music teachers who are providing their students with a broad view of the world's cultures in music and through music, and who are identifying local musicians as guests to classrooms so that they might tell their stories, sing their songs, play their instruments, and engage students in dialogue of the distinctive as well as common features of their musical lives. Creative teachers are opening students' ears through listening to music from various artists from across the world, challenging them to seek out musical components by ear, supporting them in their attempts to sing or play what they hear, questioning them about the possible meanings of the music, calling into question the role of music in their daily lives or at particular events such as weddings, holidays, and seasons. Teachers who are keen on developing music education programs through a social justice lens are preparing informed citizens of the world who approach musical study as compassionate and curious learners. By challenging the existing paradigms in music education, a sense of worth might be placed on all of their students and all of the music cultures brought to the learning experiences.

Ethnomusicology and World Music Pedagogy in Secondary School Music Programs

Ethnomusicology is a discipline that offers a framework for the exploration of musical diversity and its development into the curricular study of world music cultures, and which underscores the importance of sociocultural factors relevant to music and musicians. Rather than considering only the faraway people and places, ethnomusicologists frequently emphasize local musical practices and making connections between music and its place in a given culture. They attend to key educationally relevant constructs such as authenticity, context, transmission, and the importance of honoring the views of cultural insiders, each of which is described in the following sections. Campbell (2003) encouraged the use of an ethnomusicological approach in teaching music, which she defined as "a mode of inquiry with its blend of musical and cultural perspectives" (p. 17).

AUTHENTICITY

The construct of authenticity is an important topic for music teachers who are intent on providing quality engagement in the world's musical cultures for their students. Music teachers frequently worry over the unrealistic requirement of re-creating a musical experience as precisely as possible to the original sound and context. Should they fail to make the exact musical match of their student performers to the recording of musicians from the cultural origin of the music, they may fear that they have failed at authentically re-creating the piece. This pressure, and the resultant fear, can demobilize teachers to the point of removing themselves from further work in music beyond those styles with which they are familiar, particularly if the failure is a public one in which someone from the musical culture is present who may raise a question or even show a facial expression of disapproval. But it should be seen that the music teacher and students in secondary schools comprise a unique culture that is real and authentic in its own right. In order to feel a sense of success in working with musical selections from various places in the world, the original context is naturally considered, but then so are the realities of the particular teaching environment—the students, the classroom ambiance, the availability of (or lack of access to) instruments and other resources.

In a well-reasoned statement, ethnomusicologist Huib Schippers (2010) described "strategic inauthenticity" as the intentional connection between the original setting for a piece of music and its new reality within the music classrooms. This term is an apt descriptor of what may occur regularly in secondary school music programs, since the music is re-contextualized the moment it is taken out of its original culture. Music teachers can choose mindfully just which components will be less authentic than the original context, yet fully appropriate and authentic for a school music setting. Perhaps in time, a more diverse repertoire will be considered standard, and "multicultural music education" will stand as "music education" in any context, thus allowing music teachers to be less concerned with replicating a musical tradition in exactly the same manner as in its original context.

Music teachers do well to recognize that the music classroom is its own culture. Re-contextualization of music traditions is present in every song, dance, recording, and concert present in a school music setting. Accepting and respecting this reality can contribute to moving forward the ideals of multiculturalism and endeavors seeking social justice. Teachers are responsible for representing the complexity and nuance of a selected music culture as well as making space for it in an existing curriculum. This is a large undertaking for any music educator.

CULTURE-BEARERS

While music teachers can function as sorts of artists-in-residence in schools when presenting music from outside of their own personal musical training, it is not practical to expect musical and cultural expertise across multiple musical genres. To that end, it has become common practice in music education to seek out artist-musicians in the community who are bearers of specific cultural traditions. These guest facilitators can offer up-close-and-personal musical experiences and can add credibility to curricular programs in music. These culture-bearers add a human dimension to the study of a musical culture that can be powerful for students and their teachers. When culture-bearers are able to share their musical knowledge and skills, there is an easing of the pressure on music teachers to be "the expert" on endless varieties of music. A culture bearer can bring the musical context and culture from a place of marginal interest to central prominence in the music education setting.

Secondary music teachers recognize that culture-bearers have the expertise of their musical heritages to share. Even so, culture-bearers may require help in translating the material in a pedagogical manner that allows students to understand and perform the music. Not all culture-bearers are equally effective, and some of their teaching may benefit from the support of the music educator with class management or in strategizing teaching ideas that fit the learning modalities or developmental levels of students.

TRANSMISSION OF MUSIC

The standard practice of developing musical skills in schools is that teachers transmit new knowledge while students receive, acquire, and integrate it into their collection of existing skills. The transmission of music is at the core of interests in the practices of music teaching and learning, and integral to research relative to the processes of perception, reception, cognition, and creative musical expressions. Secondary school music teachers communicate their knowledge of music, as they also strategize instructional sequences to enable their students to learn musical skills as singers, players, and creators of valued repertoire.

The topic of music transmission is of interest to ethnomusicologists, and to a lesser extent to folklorists, anthropologists, and scholars in linguistics and speech communications. If secondary students are to gain a sense of a new musical culture, the ways of music transmission within the culture should be part of the process. An exploration of the processes of music transmission, teaching, and learning allows analysis of the different characteristics inherent in the music itself, and the interactions among the teacher, students, and culture-bearers. Attention may be given to the technical, oral, and aural techniques, and the social transactions in which music is transmitted between teachers and their students. Music teachers are still learners, who then transmit what they learn of a music culture within the culture of the school.

Music teachers do well to broaden their understandings of teaching and learning processes from cultures different from their own. Without impeding traditional notions of music literacy, students are allowed to experience how a traditional music is learned within its culture. To achieve this, lessons can incorporate a variety of teaching and learning models typically used in a music class and also found in the selected music cultures, including oral-aural practices or bodily-kinesthetic experiences. Transmission modes vary, and some teaching-learning techniques may be more fit for informal than formal learning circumstances. A certain cynicism is evident within circles of music teachers regarding whether certain modes of transmission, such as learning by ear through the oral tradition, can (or should) exist within school music programs. Music teachers are at times hesitant or unwilling to step outside of their own personal training and belief system in order to go full tilt into not only the music of another culture but also the system by which it is taught and learned.

Practical Matters in Diversifying Secondary School Music Programs

The work of designing courses, creating curricular programs, and crafting engaging lessons keeps music teachers on their toes. The practice of WMP adds no extra work on the part of the teacher, nor does it replace long-held traditions. It is inclusive of an array of familiar pedagogical techniques and tools, even as it is intended to be applied to music from outside the realm of Western art music to feature lesser-known traditions. The intention of the sequence is to create culturally relevant learning experiences that reflect a need to embrace local and global cultures across the curriculum, including the content and method of the secondary school music program. Following are several important considerations for music teachers in secondary schools that will forge a way forward to creating dynamic, globally inspired education in and through music.

Dimensions of Multicultural Music Education

James Banks (2004), a leading figure in the movement to multiculturalize the school curriculum across subjects, advanced "dimensions" in the typology of multicultural education: Content Integration, Prejudice Reduction, Equity Pedagogy, Knowledge Construction. Each dimension interrelates with the others even while also carrying distinctive characteristics, and all are relevant to the work of music teachers in secondary school music courses.

Content integration in secondary music consists of a teacher's use of examples from a variety of cultures to teach concepts, principles, generalizations, and theories in a music course. In some school music settings, content integration or repertoire is the only approach to multiculturalizing a course, such as a choir that sings an arrangement of a traditional song from another country, but misses the opportunity to learn of the culture and people who know and make the music. A second dimension, prejudice reduction, encompasses strategies that can be used to help students develop more democratic attitudes and values. Secondary music teachers need to provide students with examples of thoughtfully selected cultural material regarding minority groups in order to fill knowledge gaps and address existing biases (Gay, 2000), and opportunities to work and talk with culture-bearers therefore debunking the thinking that one cannot understand another culture. The dimension of equity pedagogy exists when music teachers employ pedagogical strategies that facilitate the achievement of students from diverse racial, ethnic, and social-class groups (as described by proponents of Culturally Responsive Teaching). Musical and sociocultural comprehension is deepened when students understand that musical cultures worthy of study exist throughout the world, each with its own unique path to constructing cultural knowledge. Equity pedagogy is also found when a secondary music teacher uses pedagogical techniques and strategies from the music culture and shares this understanding with the students, thereby honoring and legitimizing multiple ways of learning and knowing.

Banks (2004) used the label "knowledge construction" to refer to teachers helping "students to understand how knowledge is created and how it is influenced by the racial, ethnic, and social-class positions of individuals and groups" (p. 4). It can be complicated and confusing to try to develop knowledge from another's perspective. If music teachers themselves are involved in studying something new, regardless of how far along in the learning process they might be, they are experiencing exactly what their students undergo in puzzling through new experiences in order to develop a fresh perspective on music and its means of knowing it. A critical analysis of the nature of cultural knowledge, be it in a song, a story, or a poem, is valuable in that it draws secondary students to the perspectives of cultural insiders and acknowledges their particular modes of learning. As knowledge is made as well as discovered, the cultural and historical context of the music is critical. Music teachers have opportunities to engage their students in an examination of cultural knowledge behind the very music that is being studied, rehearsed, and performed.

Secondary school music teachers have been successful in teaching students to sing and play together. Much of the knowledge constructed from Western art music experiences (or Western "school music") continues as it was first conceived many decades ago. Secondary music teachers can participate in the crafting of curricular programs that encourage the musical development of their students while also offering innovative ways of knowing a broad spectrum of customs, folkways, and preferred practices of peoples. For secondary students and their teachers alike, this process of learning might foster curiosity about their own belief systems: how music is valued, used, learned, and taught. Students may come to understand the relative nature of music cultures—that one is not more valuable than another, but rather just different with its own unique means of expression. Through an examination of the manner in which particular musical knowledge is constructed in a given culture, more meaningful connections may be made with the people and the music.

Although many music teachers claim to believe in the importance of multicultural and social justice ideals and the value of teaching repertoire that reflects respect for diverse musical cultures, surprisingly few reflect this position in the repertoire they select for study. Some may feel ill-equipped to branch out into genres outside of the traditional and familiar Eurocentric canon. Globalized and multiculturalized secondary school music education requires innovative program offerings, differentiated learning modalities, and the cultural competence of teachers to be able to communicate the various musical and cultural backgrounds to their students.

Toward a Global Empathy

Musical skill and knowledge development are principal goals of a curriculum that reflects the practices in WMP. Global citizenship and cultural sensitivity are large-scale outcomes that emerge from educational encounters within secondary school curricula. Manifestations of a sensitivity to and understanding of diverse cultures encompass a spectrum that spans from a fundamental awareness of similarities and differences across cultures to a deep empathy for people of various circumstances. This cultural sensitivity, along with a sense of the self as a responsible global citizen, is developed by secondary music students through thoughtfully crafted music education experiences that are inclusive of musical, sociocultural, and pedagogical content.

There is concern that secondary music education may serve to support the status quo and to reinforce societal prejudices and stereotypes, rather than attend to the real lives of students, their interests, and their needs. They may be aware of the importance of equitable treatment of students, and they may react to blatant declarations prompted by bias or ignorance, but details of pedagogical design through a lens of global understanding are sometimes seemingly inaccessible. Yet when this sort of design is evident, as in the course and curricular designs suggested throughout the following chapters, music teachers are more successful in opening students up to what it means to be socially biased and how to avoid it.

Descriptions of secondary school music courses, and the students who enroll in such courses, provide a backdrop to the application of WMP for teachers who wish to put into practice a global consciousness, a multicultural awareness, and a belief in an inclusive curricular program that serves students of all experiences to know music and culture. Secondary music teachers have a responsibility to regularly reflect on their own cultural beliefs and values as well as to examine how those affect their ideas on pedagogy and instruction. Designing instruction in this thoughtful and fluid manner allows teachers and their students to grow their awareness of the larger global community.

A Way Forward

There is a path ahead for developing an understanding and respect for the world's musical cultures in secondary school music programs. WMP provides a set of considerations for knowing music and culture in secondary music courses. Secondary music courses entail a host of possibilities for musical experiences and studies within middle school and high school, including new paradigms for music-making that have yet to be codified or duplicated. There is fertile ground in secondary schools for the implementation of WMP in a grand variety of courses and classes, and the provision of diverse musical content and learning experiences will help to open up musical study to all students regardless of their earlier experience and training (or lack thereof). The promise of musical study in secondary schools needs to be inclusive of the expressive possibilities across many cultures, so that students can fill their ears with many musical styles, as they also grow a respect for the people who make the music across the world.

Secondary music students have the full capacity to grow exponentially in their musical understanding and cultural knowledge. As they continue to mature through their adolescence, their thought processes become more rational and abstract, which lends them the means for exploring, questioning, criticizing, and puzzling out the complexities of the world in which they live. As music is a significant part of their identities and experiences in the world, it is an important bridge from themselves, their family and friends, to others in the world whom they will do well to seek out, to understand, and to accept for the different but equally logical ways of being.

Secondary school music programs should offer students a diversity of learning experiences that develop a variety of musical skills and understandings. In secondary music classes, students need ample opportunities to immerse themselves in quality recordings together with classmates, friends, and on their own, because attentive and active listening leads the way to their further musical involvement and to cultural understanding. Students need opportunities to participate and to perform music of a wide spectrum of styles, to enjoy creative experiences such as improvisation and composition that are too often overlooked in music programs, and to study the ways in which music can lead to insights on a culture's history, religion and ritual, societal beliefs and values, and artistic practices of every kind. Through procedures advanced by WMP, these experiences can be known by secondary school students.

Mr. Shepherd and Ms. Harmon in the brief vignettes represent the work of secondary music teachers who are looking to create meaningful experiences for their secondary school students. At all age and grade levels of secondary school, students benefit from practices that are crafted with attention to the constructs embedded in WMP, and which emanate from the fields of ethnomusicology and music education. These constructs include Culturally Responsive Teaching, matters of authenticity and context, contributions by culture-bearers, and modes of transmission that are part-and-parcel of the music selected for study. Secondary school students are highly capable of embracing music as both a sonic and human experience. They can also be guided to develop empathy toward people who make music and who enjoy the music that is made, in various cultures both at home and abroad, which is surely a noble goal and an educational ideal with which to be reckoned.

The incorporation of new approaches alongside long-standing traditions is achievable. In the following chapters, depictions of familiar practices for musically educating secondary school students are presented alongside innovative pedagogical approaches from the world's expressive practices, including underrepresented yet dynamic world music cultures. The time is now for creating a globally conscious and socially responsible music curriculum. WMP has the capacity to bring students and their teachers together in understanding music in its cultural context and developing the sense of self as an important member of a broader global society.

References

Banks, J. A. (2004). *Handbook of multicultural education* (4th ed.). New York: Jossey-Bass.

Campbell, P. S. (2003). Ethnomusicology and music education: Crossroads for knowing music, education, and culture. *Research Studies in Music Education, 21*, 16–30.

Campbell, P. S. (2004). *Teaching music globally: Experiencing music, expressing culture.* New York: Oxford Music Press.

Gay, G. (2000). *Culturally responsive teaching: Theory, research and practice* (2nd ed.). New York: Teachers College Press.

Schippers, H. (2010). *Facing the music: Shaping music education from a global perspective.* New York: Oxford Music Press.

Listening Episodes

"Hot Cheetos and Takis," (Video, August 9, 2012) Y. N. Rich Kids. 13twentythree, retrieved from https://youtu.be/7YLy4j8EZIk

"Kodo," (2012). On *Yoshida brothers best, Vol. two.* Sony Music Corp. Available on iTunes.

2

Attentive Listening for Cultural Awakenings

The room is crowded with steel pan instruments. The higher-pitched pans are set up in the front of the room and the multi-pan bass instruments are placed near the door. The ninth graders are standing behind their designated pans with sticks in their hands. They are restless—itching to start playing. Mr. Lowell has been teaching steel pan ensembles in high schools for more than 20 years, and his students learn mostly through an oral-aural transmission process without need for sheet music, scores, or music stands. He begins his lessons with an exercise in Attentive Listening, introducing his students to many of the world's musical traditions, but he also uses Attentive Listening to present exemplars of steel pan ensembles he sees as top models to emulate.

"As we listen," Mr. Lowell begins, "try to catch the rhythm of the bass line. If you can, try to put the rhythm in your feet, stepping on the beat. If you are able to do that, add the maraca part in your hands." He mimes shaking maracas, motioning up and down with his hands. He starts a recording of a steel-pan version of the jazz standard "Begin the Beguine," performed by the Bamboushay Steel Band. The students instantly move, almost gyrating, to the music. As the recording continues, the movement becomes more focused and uniform, as students begin to put the bass line in their steps. Some students look at their classmates' feet to solidify the bass line in their steps. Smiles form as the group moves to the music; more than half of them are pantomiming the maracas while stepping to the bass rhythm. After about a minute of the recording, Mr. Lowell turns the volume down and asks the class to clap the bass rhythm, which the students perform strongly in unison.

"Let's listen to that section again, and this time, try to pat the rhythm of the melody on your legs," he instructs the students. The students have been listening to this selection for the past few lessons. The students pat the rhythm of the melody as they continue to sway to the beat. After a full minute of listening, Mr. Lowell decreases the volume again.

"Who can remind the class about where this music comes from? What was it used for in its original culture?" Mr. Lowell asks the class. "It makes you want to move, to

party, to celebrate," announces an energetic student with a wide grin across his face. His answer is met with snickering and impromptu dance moves by several of his peers.

"You're right, Demarcus," Mr. Lowell adds, a smile creeping over his own face in response to his students' enthusiasm. "Steel pan music has been used for festivals and celebrations from the very beginning. Who remembers where this music comes from and how it got started?"

He calls on Zooey, who explains that steel pan music began in Trinidad and Tobago, a twin island country in the Caribbean. "Great answer, Zooey," Mr. Lowell comments. He further questions the students about how the pans were created, and calls on Hyochan to describe the origins of steel pans. Hyochan explains that descendants of freed slaves created instruments that mimicked the sounds they were accustomed to, using discarded or everyday materials, including cooking pans, trash cans, or oil drums.

"Exactly right, Hyo. With these new instruments, they celebrated in their traditional way but also created a new musical genre. Steel pan music is infectiously festive and still used in celebrations in and around Trinidad and Tobago today. All right, let's work on a new groove."

The World in a Classroom

The classroom can be, and often is, a multicultural place where distinct understandings of the world by varied cultural groups coexist. This collision of cultural differences could be a result of immigration across borders, economic opportunity in urban centers rather than rural enclaves, or even changes in social norms within communities. In many classrooms, there can be cultural diversity in the composite of the student population, in which there exists a mix of racial, religious, political, economic, or ethnic identities of the students. As the communities in which students live will only become more diverse over time, it is necessary for teachers to help students in their interactions and collaborations with students of varied cultural backgrounds.

Through meaningful experiences with the world's musical cultures, music teachers provide interactions with diverse cultures that can allow students to develop a deeper empathy toward others while building their musical skills as well. This double-duty pedagogy can help to defuse harmful stereotypes based on race, religion, or nationality even while students are developing their musical skills as players, singers, dancers, listeners, and creators of original music. By opening their ears to new musical cultures, music teachers can also work to open the minds of their students and build their tolerance and respect toward the people of these cultures. Experiencing music from a global perspective allows students to identify the similarities as well as the differences among their classmates, their neighbors, and members of the greater community. It offers an opportunity for conversation about shared experiences, emotions, or attitudes, and even between people who may be quite distant from one another geographically.

Sonic Beginnings

Music is ubiquitous within the human experience. Music is pervasive in our daily lives—be it in religious rituals, in political rallies, in commercial spaces, in protest marches, in family celebrations, or in children's playing. Every studied culture and civilization has had some form of musical expression. It is clear: there is a human need to be musical. But like the rich variety of flora and fauna that inhabit different parts of the globe, human enterprise has developed evolving and divergent musical traditions, with the sonorities of music performed across the globe equally varied, not only in timbre, but in purpose and value. Some musical traditions are committed to preserving important relics of the past while others seek novel sounds for new expression.

While the origin of human music-making is unknown, several theories have been developed. Music may be a natural social bonding agent among people. In regard to evolution, it could be that music was a natural extension of how mothers communicate to their children and, as a result, music helps cement the bond between parent and child, especially at a time when a baby could not survive on her own (Dissanayake, 2006). Music may be a result of human collaboration, where rudimentary music was an innovative method for carrying out tasks together or unifying a clan together toward a common goal. Music may have been an important tool for developing human cultures as a mnemonic device, incorporating cultural history or wisdom into oral traditions that can be transferred from generation to generation. While it remains unclear why music has been intricately woven into the human experience, music remains a mystical and powerful force in the world today.

The ancient music of early humans is not preserved for our reflection, but it is likely that it was heavily influenced by the natural soundscape of where they lived. Earth is not a silent place; even the barest environs have the ambient song of gentle winds. The earliest humans would have attended to the subtle sounds of their environment, listening to the sounds of nature, animals, and other humans; their survival relied upon aural acuity. The earliest music-making was likely singing or body percussion; the earliest instruments were likely biodegradable, such as reeds, wood, or skins. Now, like those early humans, young people are constantly surrounded by sounds within their environment—with many of those sounds being musical. Before embarking on excursions to musical cultures in the music classroom, it would be prudent for the music teacher to spend time with the students in opening their ears to the sonic surrounds of their lived spaces. It is important for students to explore their own aural awareness and understanding of sound, including timbre, pitch, tone, rhythm, duration, and consonance. Exploring sounds that are familiar to students will provide a lexicon for discussing the curious sounds that they will experience in listening to the world of music beyond the West.

Sound Encounters

Listening is the foundation of musical understanding and is an imperative for musical development. Singers and players require listening in order to learn, even when notation is available, and for much of the world, listening is the key to becoming an articulate, expressive, and fluent musician. In the southern United States, a half-dozen teens sit crowded around a speaker in a garage to imitate a riff from a current hip-hop hit, trying to vocally mimic the performer's virtuosic run. In Vietnam, a small group of students of *ca trù*, a form of sung poetry, sip tea as they listen to the intricacies of the ornamentation and rhythms as their teacher performs. In India, a guru (teacher) sings a new song phrase-by-phrase as a sitar student listens intently and then imitates the sung phrases. In Ghana, an apprentice drummer listens and responds to a master teacher's use of complex polyrhythms by repeating what he has played. In Trinidad, a composer-arranger teaches the tenor part to a steel pan player by rote, playing the part over and over until the student can replicate it, and then moves on to teach another part. In France, a young piano student listens to her teacher model the expressive timing in a Chopin nocturne. Across the world, deep and thoughtful listening is undeniably important to the development of musical skills as well as the transmission of musical culture.

In most young people's lives, music is a natural part of the environment—in social gatherings, in religious practices, in school and community functions. The lives of middle and high school students are replete with music. On any given day, a student in Toronto, Tel Aviv, Tokyo, Trondheim (Norway), and Trenton, New Jersey (U.S.) may be musically involved in various ways: listening to top 40 on the radio on their way to school, performing mariachi in music class, tuning out the outside world to listen to Nigerian pop music on the commuter train, rehearsing Renaissance vocal music for a religious service, grooving to Scandinavian house music while running on the treadmill, shopping the aisles of the local grocery as cool jazz plays. Young people have many musical experiences, both intentional and haphazard, formal and casual.

From an early age, children are immersed into a cultural soundscape that informs them of the values of their community. Although students consume music of so many varieties and kinds, the music teacher is privileged to help shape the musical understanding of those musical experiences. Students enter a secondary school music class with varying degrees of musical knowledge and skill. Some students will have emotional connections to the music of their lives, whereas others may have technical awareness of chord progressions, harmony lines, or rhythmic syncopations. A few may know how a particular song came to be or how it fits within a tradition. Some may have an awareness of all of these elements, whereas others may have only a superficial understanding of the music they encounter. Campbell (2005) found that some music teachers are skeptical about emphasizing listening, "considering it a passive process, in which case they may move it to the sidelines, choosing instead to exert an enormous flurry of instructional energy around the active development of performance skills and compositional activities" (p. 30). The music teacher's task is to channel the diverse experiences of informal and formal music experiences into musical understanding.

Attentive Listening: First Steps Forward

Listening is fundamental to learning music, and it is foundational to World Music Pedagogy (WMP), at the base of performing and creating. Secondary school students likely have considerable experience listening to music, but a teacher's guidance is essential for introducing students to new and unfamiliar musical territories. Three distinct types of music listening are featured within the composite of WMP, and together they lead students from basic aural recognition of musical features of a recording to their emulation or approximation of the music vocally or on instruments. The three listening phases are Attentive Listening, Engaged Listening, and Enactive Listening, each one developing from the one before.

Attentive Listening is the fundamental first step into the music, the entry point into what the musical content and features may be. As an introduction to a musical work, this dimension is both a musical and a cultural awakening, and a guide to the discovery of the sonic matter of the music as well as initiation into the origin of the music in terms of its musical meaning. Attentive Listening is marked by many questions or challenges, each one preceding an opportunity to listen and seek out the answer or respond to the challenge. There is no expectation for performance, be it singing or playing, or dancing, as the teacher calls for students to listen to dimensions of rhythm, melody, timbre, texture, and formal aspects of the music and to wonder about the potential use and function of the music, the meaning of the lyrics, and such.

Abundant opportunities to listen need to be afforded to students during this dimension of WMP. For every facet of the music that the teacher wants the students to attend to, or for every question that the teacher asks, the students should be given at least one opportunity to listen. This may require additional listenings to establish that the students are absorbing or identifying the sonic attributes that are central to the learning. During Attentive Listening episodes in secondary classrooms, the teacher should keep music examples limited to around 60 seconds or less, so that students can hone in on the important musical material. Opportunities may arise where the teacher uses longer segments, especially with more advanced secondary students who are examining concepts like form, but longer listening segments expend valuable teaching time, certainly as the clips are played multiple times. For any given example, students should experience the musical example a minimum of five or six times, or as many as ten or more times. Attentive Listening episodes can be extended into multiple class meetings over several days, reviewing as well as listening anew to different aspects of the musical example.

For successful Attentive Listening episodes, a teacher must have a clear understanding of the listening goals for the class (e.g., "What kinds of instruments are being played?", "What is the meter for this section of music?", "What text do you hear repeated?"). The teacher is the guide in the soundscape and must know the answers to the questions that she asks, as well as what new directions to take her students next through deeper listening and understanding. As the recording is sounding within the class, the teacher must model a listening face to her students, where she is visibly absorbed in the musical happenings; this is not a time when the teacher can tune out or attend to other classroom duties. The skillful teacher may help off-task students attune to listening experience by simply using proximity or moving near students who have difficulties focusing, while maintaining a visage that is rapt in listening.

Attentive Listening is an initial aural exposure that leads to participating with the sound, through more and more intentional music-making behaviors. The students can proceed from Attentive Listening to Engaged Listening and Enactive Listening, as will be discussed in Chapter 3. This progression allows students to wade into the sonic material, building their skills bit by bit, leading to musical growth in performance and understanding.

It should be noted that while the listening dimensions are generally sequential, and are effective when presented in order, it is not necessary that they always be. For instance, a teacher may return to Attentive Listening after leading students to participate vocally or on instruments, perhaps having learned by listening to just one part of a more complex musical work. With a return, the teacher may start up again with Attentive Listening, asking questions of another musical part in order that students can then become involved in that aspect of the music. Teachers do not need to feel compelled to involve students equally with each type of listening for each musical selection, as in precisely nine listening experiences each of an Attentive, Engaged, and Enactive sort. The art of teaching and learning requires sensitivity and flexibility, and music teachers should feel empowered to design their lessons in a way that will encourage musical understanding while respecting the music that they explore.

The dimensions of WMP are approached in ways similar to education psychology scholar Jerome Bruner's (1960) idea of the spiral curriculum, where students with varying levels of experience can interact with the most complex ideas. This spiral curriculum invites students to revisit learning steps and stages, where new experiences shape their earlier understandings. Upon each visit with the material (i.e., the music), student learning is solidified and progresses from simple to more complex understanding.

The first step toward musical understanding requires opening the ear and becoming aware of the multifaceted nature of music as a sonic experience. One aspect of musical awareness is an examination of how the musical sound is made: which instruments are used, what materials are used to make the instruments, how the instruments are played, and what the timbral qualities of the sound may be. Another facet of opening the ear to musical understanding includes the structural features and forms of the music, the pitches, pitch groups, and even scales that comprise the melodies and harmonies. Knowledge of musical context offers further enlightenment and can be learned by imagining, discovering, asking, and responding to questions of who may be playing or singing the music, why the music is important, how the music fits a tradition, how it is learned and transmitted, and how it affects the performers and the listeners.

When planning lessons that employ Attentive Listening, it is important to recognize that any music, A to Z, is open for selection and use, from the art music of Afghanistan to the popular music of Zimbabwe. The music teacher can incorporate a rich and diverse repertoire for secondary students to experience, knowing that they will be guided through multiple listenings, questions, and challenges to music far from their musical and cultural experiences into the midst of the music's structures and meanings. A selection of recordings can be explored through Attentive Listening, to include diversity in texture (e.g., monophony, homophony, and polyphony) as well as instrumentation, including vocal music. A mix of musical genres can comprise a set of Attentive Listening experiences, including work songs, dance songs, and religious music. Important, however, is the realization that just one selected recording can be the aim of an experience in Attentive Listening, as many repeated listenings draw students ever more deeply into the recording and to questions about the music, musicians, and its cultural meanings. The involvement by students in fundamental listening opens the way to further dimensions of WMP in a secondary school music classroom.

Throughout the book, many examples of teaching and learning episodes will be presented that highlight the pedagogical strategies within WMP. Three specific examples will be presented in each of the five chapters on the phases of WMP (a marimba piece from Zimbabwe, a son jarocho from Mexico, and Roma wedding music) and will be labeled as "Learning Pathway" episodes. All of the Learning Pathway episodes have been collected in an Appendix so that the full experience of the five phases of WMP is illustrated through these three examples.

Learning Pathway #1: Attentive Listening in Action—Marimba Music of Zimbabwe

Although some musical traditions have histories that are centuries old, marimba music from Zimbabwe has only existed since the 1960s. This style of marimba music emerged in what is now the independent state of Zimbabwe; however, during the mid-20th century, the territory was controlled as a colony of the British Empire. Since its innovation, Zimbabwean-style marimba music has proliferated in neighboring countries such as Botswana and South Africa as well as in non-African countries such as Australia, Canada, Sweden, the United Kingdom, and the United States.

In 1961, Robert Sibson was the director of the Rhodesian Academy of Music, located in Bulawayo, the second largest city in the country. Sibson appreciated the local musical traditions of the Ndebele and the Shona people and respected how these musical cultures permeated the daily routines of the people. He was concerned that the musical heritage was going to be lost as people were moving from rural areas to the city; moreover, the segregated and colonial education system did not teach local traditional music in schools. In an effort to safeguard the cultural heritage, Sibson helped create a college that focused on African musical traditions, primarily through training teachers to incorporate traditional music within their schools. This academy for the study of traditional music was founded, and was called *Kwanongoma* (the place where drums are played or the place of singing).

After discussion with several stakeholders, including administrators of African music academics, ethnomusicologists, and local civil servants, it was decided that the marimba would be one of the instruments to be used as a teaching instrument at Kwanongoma. While the marimba was more prevalent in Zambia and Mozambique, it was an instrument deemed distinctly African, in that it had not been commandeered by the colonial influences. The leadership at Kwanongoma also liked the idea that the marimba could be made in different sizes, allowing for large ensembles to be created, from double bass marimbas to soprano marimbas. Marimbas were not the only instruments taught at the college; Kwanongoma also trained teachers in *mbira*, theory, voice, guitar, and piano. *Mbira* (thumb piano) is a traditional instrument of the Shona people, played by thumbs and index fingers on metal keys. These keys are fitted on a wooden board that the players can hold in their hands, and sometimes the board is placed inside a large round and hollowed out calabash to increase the resonance of the music.

Zimbabwean marimbas generally have wooden keys and resonators of various lengths and widths. These resonators can be made out of different materials depending on tradition and availability; resonators can be created from gourds, PVC tubing, fiberglass facsimiles of gourds, or aluminum. Marimba ensembles have instruments with different pitch ranges: soprano, alto, tenor, baritone, and bass. Instruments are designed on the diatonic C scale with added F sharps. The inclusion of F sharps allowed songs to be played in both C and G, which made the instruments more versatile, especially as accompaniment for singing.[1]

"Nyoka Musango," as featured here and throughout the book as a Learning Pathway that is experienced through the five dimensions of WMP, is performed by Lora Chiorah-Dye and the Suketai Marimba and Dance Ensemble. Chiorah-Dye was born and raised in Zimbabwe and later immigrated to the United States to be with her then-husband, Dumisani Maraire, in the 1970s. While living in the U.S., she taught her three children the traditional music she grew up with, including marimba and mbira (thumb piano) music from the Shona clan in Zimbabwe. Shona music incorporates many different simultaneous melodic voices, as many as eight to ten at the same time. However, the parts move more independently than in classical Western European traditions and are woven into the musical fabric intricately. With her family, Chiorah-Dye had the beginnings of a performing ensemble. In 1980, Chiorah-Dye formed the Suketai Marimba and Dance Ensemble as a way to showcase the heritage of the Shona people while introducing Zimbabwean music and dance to North America. In addition to providing dynamic performances for audiences, the ensemble maintained a mission to work with young people, teaching them traditional music and dance. Suketai quickly became a celebrated ensemble as one of the first ensembles of their kind in North America, and they have garnered worldwide acclaim.

The piece was originally written and performed by musician Thomas Mapfumo. He was given the nickname "The Lion of Zimbabwe" as well as *Mukanya*, a title of honor within the Shona clan. From the beginning of his musical career, Mapfumo's lyrics were overtly political, supporting the revolution that was developing in the rural areas. His musical style that incorporated protest became known as a musical genre: Chimurenga. *Chimurenga* means "struggle" in Shona. During the colonial occupation of the 1970s, Mapfumo's music called for the overthrow of the government, with lyrics like "Mothers, send your sons to war." In 1979, the government disapproved of the critical music that Mapfumo was writing and banned his record "Hokoyo!" from the state-run radio station. He was also thrown into a prison camp without being formally charged with committing any crime. Despite the government's efforts, his music was still played in popular night clubs and on other radio stations. Large protests called for Mapfumo's release, which was eventually granted three months after he was detained. Even after Zimbabwe gained independence from British control in 1980, Mapfumo continued to be an outspoken critic against the government. His criticisms shifted from a need for freedom from colonial powers to corruption within the nascent Zimbabwean government and the unjust treatment of poor people. Mapfumo continues to perform internationally while promoting justice and peace for his homeland.

Chiorah-Dye arranged Mapfumo's song to be performed by a marimba ensemble. The translation of "Nyoka Musango" means "Snake in the Grass," which is a common saying of the Shona people. The text of the song suggests that the listener should be wary and watch out for snakes. It is understood that the song warns against many things other than literal snakes, but also anything that may harm when you are not paying attention. Many Shona songs are based on proverbs that can have multiple meanings, which gives the listener the freedom to decide the true meaning of the text. Episode 2.1 offers students the opportunity to listen attentively to Chiorah-Dye's ensemble.

Episode 2.1: Zimarimba: Marimba Music of Zimbabwe (Learning Pathway #1)

Specific Use: World Percussion Ensemble

Materials:

- "Nyoka Musango," Lora Chiorah-Dye and the Suketai Marimba and Dance Ensemble, Smithsonian Folkways Records

  Marimbas, hosho, body percussion, vocals

Procedure:

(Attentive)

1. "What instruments do you hear?"
2. Play track (00:01–01:05).
3. Review answer: *hosho* (gourd shaker), handclaps, vocal lines, marimbas.
4. If students did not hear all instruments, allow another listen.
5. Play track (00:01–01:05).
6. Review instruments in the piece.
7. "The entrance of the marimbas are staggered. Listen to the first, second, and third marimbas enter. As they enter, is each line higher or lower than the one that precedes it?"
8. Play track (00:01–00:20).
9. Review answers. The second marimba is higher than the first. The third marimba is higher than the preceding two.
10. Have students listen for the bass line: "Listen for the lowest note in the bass line. Find a word that describes the tone of that low note."
11. Play track (00:01–01:05).
12. Review words that students use to describe the low bass note. Words like "buzzy" or "vibrant" may be used to describe the tone of the bass note.
13. Have students track the bass line pattern and tap when the low bass note is sounded at the beginning of each pattern. This may take multiple listenings to the track to accomplish successfully.
14. Play track (00:01–01:20).
15. Have students continue to tap on the low bass note with one hand. With the other hand, they should tap the handclaps (or the teacher could divide the class into two groups, one tapping on the bass note and one on the handclaps).
16. Play entire track (00:01–05:50).
17. Assess students' ability to synchronize with the bass line, the handclaps, or both.

Checking for Musical Understanding

One of the challenges of Attentive Listening is checking for students' understanding. It is impossible for a teacher to peer inside the heads of her students to know if they did indeed hear the focal point and principle objective(s) of the episode. The creative music teacher can employ different informal techniques to check for understanding. For instance, the class could be sitting in a circle facing out and away from the center, and students may be asked to raise their hands when a particular sonic phenomenon is occurring (e.g., a change of instrument, a rhythmic motif, a high-pitched melodic phrases). For some secondary students, social or visual cues may help identify what musical components are important. For example, in Learning Pathway #2 (Episode 2.2), students are guided to listen to the *leona* part in the son jarocho piece titled "Siquisirí," and the teacher can check for student understanding by asking students to perform the bass rhythms along with the recording.

Learning Pathway #2: Attentive Listening in Action—Son de Jarocho from Veracruz, Mexico

Many musical traditions developed in Latin America are syntheses of Indigenous, African, and European rhythmic and melodic structures. There are more than a dozen distinctive Mexican musical traditions from particular regions. One of these musical traditions is *son jarocho*, an Afro-Mexican musical tradition from Veracruz, an area of the Caribbean with prominent African diasporic cultural elements in its music, arts, and cuisine. The African influence in son jarocho is directly tied to Veracruz's history as one of the largest ports of entry for enslaved Africans in the Americas. Almost half of all slaves brought to the Americas between 1595–1622 went to Mexico. Son jarocho ensembles are made up of various guitar-like stringed instruments, including the *jarana jarocho*, *requinto jarocho*, and *leona*. Siquisirí is a popular and oft-performed song in son jarocho groups. More context is provided in Chapter 3, along with discussion of the instruments of the son jarocho tradition.

Episode 2.2: Son de Jarocho from Veracruz, Mexico (Learning Pathway #2)

Specific Use: Guitar Class

Materials:

* "Siquisirí," Son de Madera, Smithsonian Folkways Recordings

  Son jarocho featuring leona, guitarra de son, jarana tercera, contrabass, and vocals

Procedure:

(Attentive)

1 "What instruments do you hear?"
2 Play track (00:01–01:10).
3 Review answers (guitars, vocals).

4 "The ensemble in the recording is made up of stringed instruments of various sizes—they are all similar to the familiar guitar. Does the first instrument play a melody line or chords? What about the second and third instruments to join in?"

5 Play track (00:01–01:10).

6 Discuss that the first instrument is a solo melody line, the second instrument joins with chords, and the third with a melodic bass line.

7 Show pictures or videos of son jarocho instruments, playing by themselves.

8 "What is the relationship between the vocal part and the guitarra de son (the higher melodic instrument)?"

9 Play track (00:01–01:10).

10 Discuss how the vocal line and the guitarra de son interact back and forth throughout the song.

11 "What is the meter of this music? Can you tap it quietly?"

12 Play track (00:01–01:10).

13 The meter is 3/4, although the introduction uses a variety of meters.

14 Have students listen to the *leona* part (the lowest part) and listen for rhythmic motives (Figure 2.1).

15 Play track (00:01–01:10).

16 Discuss what students heard in the *leona* part (e.g., quarter note bass line).

17 Have students listen to the *leona* part for the entire track to identify recurring rhythmic motives in the bass line.

18 Play track (00:01–4:02).

19 Discuss the recurring rhythmic motives; students can chant or clap the motives if they are unable to notate them. The teacher can then present examples (see Figure 2.2) on the board and have students perform.

Figure 2.1 Examples of *leona* rhythmic patterns in bass line

Learning Pathway #3: Attentive Listening in Action—Roma Wedding Music

The following episode is Learning Pathway #3, an exuberant piece of music performed by members of the Roma community who emigrated to New York City. The Roma originated in India, migrated westward during the 11th century, and settled throughout Europe by the 15th century, including in Macedonia and Bulgaria. It is not clear why the Roma migrated from India, thereby creating a diasporic culture spread throughout the world, but it is known that persecution has followed their trail wherever Roma have settled, including the many Roma that were killed during World War II. The largest concentrations of Roma communities are in Central, Eastern, and Southern Europe and East into Turkey. Roma have also migrated to North and South America. In English-speaking cultures, it is common to hear Roma referred to as "Gypsies," which is considered derogatory by some (but not all) both inside and outside of the culture due to its implications of deceit and trickery.

Episode 2.3: Roma Wedding Music
(Learning Pathway #3)

Specific Use: Advanced Placement Music Theory

Materials:

- "Čoček Manhattan," Yuri Yunakov Ensemble, Smithsonian Folkways Recordings

  Saxophone, clarinet, keyboard, electric bass, and drum kit

Procedure:

(Attentive)

1 "What instruments do you hear in this piece? Specifically, listen for what instrument plays the solo."
2 Play track (00:25–1:55).
3 Discuss answers (saxophone, clarinet, accordion, drum set, guitar, bass guitar). Allow an additional listen to identify all instruments.
4 Play track (00:25–1:55).
5 Review instruments.
6 "What instruments are featured in the first section? What instruments are featured in the solo section?"
7 Play track (00:25–1:55).

8   Review answers. Beginning section: saxophone, clarinet, and accordion are playing melody in unison. Solo section: saxophone while guitar and accordion accompany. Bass and drum set play throughout the clip.

9   "What is the meter of the piece?" Guide students to tap silently with music.

10   Play track (00:25–1:55).

11   Discuss answers. The piece is in 9/8 time.

12   "Is the meter divided evenly into three beats or is there some other subdivision?

13   Play track (00:25–1:55).

14   Review answers. The overriding metrical pattern is $2 + 2 + 2 + 3$. There are some moments where it varies, but it maintains the overall 9/8 meter.

15   "We will listen to the recording once more, and please put the beat somewhere on your body or tap quietly on your desk."

16   Play track (00:25–1:55).

17   Assess students' ability to tap on the proper beats.

Providing Context in Attentive Listening

During initial Attentive Listening episodes, many music teachers begin by contextualizing the sound recording. Schippers (2010) reminds us that the primary reason for providing context is to further musical and cultural understanding, not to provide geographic trivia. When providing the context of a musical source, the teacher can do more than point to a country on a map in order to describe social, historical, and cultural importance of the musical events that the students are going to experience. A successful approach to providing context to musical examples centers on learning about the music, by providing information about the performers, how the music is used within the culture, the development and techniques used to play the instruments, cultural norms about who can perform, how music is learned and performed, and what meaning it has to the people who hear it.

This does not mean that the sociocultural context must all be front-loaded prior to any listening. In fact, an incremental elaboration about the musical context may be helpful for secondary students to process the information as they become more immersed in the musical sounds. The details of the context can be sprinkled among multiple listenings or even among the different listening phases. The context allows students to develop a deeper understanding of the meaning of the music and to attend to musical elements more closely.

Attentive Listening in Action: African American Singing in the United States

Sweet Honey in the Rock, an a cappella singing group that explores the African American experience, was formed in 1973 by founder and artistic director Bernice

Johnson Reagon. This all-female group was named after a gospel tune that was popular in Protestant and Pentecostal churches in the southeastern U.S. in the early 20th century. The work of this ensemble carries on the long-standing tradition of gospel-style a cappella singing, following the lead of gospel quartet groups such as the Blue Jay Singers, the Birmingham Jubilee Singers, and the Southern Harps. The ensemble is still active today, more than 40 years after its creation, although the personnel has changed over the years. The group incorporates many types of repertoire in their performances, including traditional African American spirituals, work songs, gospel tunes, freedom songs, folk melodies, as well as newly composed pieces.

Before her work with Sweet Honey in the Rock, Bernice Johnson Reagon was a civil rights activist and organizer in her home state of Georgia. As a university student, her early activism included organizing students to demand equal employment rights and integration in transportation. Early on, Reagon realized the power of using music to unify and encourage demonstrators for civil rights. In 1960, after being dismissed from her university for her activism on campus, Reagon became one of the co-founders of the Freedom Singers, a music ensemble from within the Student Nonviolent Coordinating Committee (SNCC) that travelled around the U.S. promoting civil rights and performing at demonstrations, most notably at the March On Washington in 1963, a watershed moment in the fight for civil rights where more than 200,000 Americans descended upon the U.S. capital to rally for equal rights.

From the ensemble's beginnings under the direction of Reagon, Sweet Honey in the Rock has continued to focus on important social and political issues of the African American community and have advocated for activism. The group's dedication to presenting issues of social justice is a hallmark of their legacy. For instance, on the ensemble's recent album, *#loveinevolution*, the group addresses police brutality and gun proliferation in the single "Second Line Blues," where the singers intone the names of African American victims such as Trayvon Martin, Michael Brown, and Sandra Bland among others over the stark accompaniment of a snare drum. The ensemble wants to illuminate with frank honesty how different groups are treated within the U.S. and to provide hope that community can be developed through mutual understanding.

The following episode includes a version of the African American spiritual "The Sun Will Never Go Down" and was arranged by Reagon. The African American spiritual is one of the largest and most-significant bodies of American folksong tradition and is closely associated with the enslavement of African people in the southern United States. Spirituals, sometimes called "sorrow songs," are deeply religious in nature and often contain coded messages as slaves were restricted in their ability to communicate with each other. There is great musical variety within the form of the spirituals, but many are centered on the oppressive burden of slavery. Reagon reported hearing her mother singing "This Sun Will Never Go Down" to her brothers as they fell asleep. She mentioned that this song, like many African American spirituals, is about transitions. This musical example can be used in a popular music ensemble; students, through Attentive Listening, can explore the value of lyrics and ornamentation in conveying emotional intent.

Episode 2.4: "The Sun Will Never Go Down" by Sweet Honey in the Rock

Specific Use: Popular Music Ensemble

Materials:

- "The Sun Will Never Go Down," Sweet Honey in the Rock, Flying Fish Records African-American spiritual

  A cappella singing

Procedure:

(Attentive)

1. "What kind of singers are in this recording? How many singers?
2. Play track (00:01–01:15).
3. Discuss answers. There are four women singing independent parts.
4. "What are the words the singers are singing? What words are repeated?"
5. Play track (00:01–01:15).
6. Review identifiable phrases such as "the sun will never go down" and "the flowers are blooming."
7. "Listen to how the words are being sung. What do you think this song is about?"
8. Play track (00:01–02:23).
9. Discuss that the song is about things getting better, possibly in a different time or place.
10. Present melodic fragment to students (Figure 2.2 is an example) and direct students to listen to how the singers add ornaments to the vocal lines.
11. Play track (00:01–01:15).
12. Discuss how the singers use ornamentation to add interest to the vocal parts, specifically how the ornamentation reflects the text. Ask students to identify other words that are ornamented in the other verses.

Figure 2.2   Melodic fragment of "The Sun Will Never Go Down"

13 Play entire track (00:01–02:23).

14 Discuss experiences where students may have felt similar to the text that is presented in the piece. Have students comment on the music that they listen to when they have similar feelings.

Attentive Listening in Action: China

The role of music within Chinese culture has changed considerably along with the political, economic, and religious developments that have occurred over the past 3,000 years. In the earliest days of Chinese civilization, music was viewed as a stabilizing force within communities and was central to social harmony and longevity of the state. Under the influence of Confucianism, the development of musical skill was viewed as a way of self-improvement or a source for making a person a better, more perfect self. The organization of the music was a metaphor for the way society should be organized.

Traditional music emphasized order and balance and incorporated only traditional instruments. Traditional Chinese instruments are categorized by one of the eight types of materials of which they were made; these eight groups or *bayin* are silk, bamboo, stone, wood, metal, clay, gourd, and animal skin. Like other musical traditions, Chinese scales are constructed around 12 discrete pitch areas. Melodies generally incorporate a seven-tone scale but predominately use only five core pitches (*wu sheng*) with two accommodating pitches (*bian*) that are used for transposing or modulating to different key areas. The five essential tones are often compared to the five elements: earth, wood, fire, metal, and water. Additionally, traditional Chinese music often has instruments playing in unison or in highly similar fashion, rather than distinct or accompanying functions heard in other musical traditions. Melodies convey mood, sonic contrast, or forward motion through the use of rhythmic devices or the pitch organization of the melody rather than harmonic structures or progress.

The following episode focuses on a World Music Traditions course. The musical focus in this episode is on Chinese art music as performed by Wong Kuen, a *ti-tzu* musician who offers musical representation of pigeons in flight. The *ti-tzu* is a traditional bamboo transverse flute with six holes. The ti-tzu may have decorative tassels, strands of silk, or adornments made of bone. One of the holes is covered by a membrane, usually made from part of a bamboo play, which allows the player to create a buzzing quality to the sound. In addition to having a reedy and airy tone, the ti-tzu can sound both rich and penetrating. This type of instrument is quite ancient, as several ti-tzu pieces, believed to be 5,000 years old or older, have been excavated by archaeologists. It is a widely popular instrument that is used in many genres of music, including Chinese folk music, Chinese opera, and modern Chinese orchestras. Expert players learn to use advanced techniques such as circular breathing, flutter-tonguing, use of harmonics to play extreme ranges, and grace notes to display their virtuosity. Wong Kuen composed this piece, borrowing an eight-bar melody from another ti-tzu composition called "Peaceful Pigeons" written by Liu Kuan-Yueh.

Episode 2.5: Pigeons Flying—Programmatic Music of Traditional Chinese Music

Specific Use: World Music Traditions

Materials:

• "Ko tzu fei," Wong Kuen, Smithsonian Folkways Recordings

   Classical Chinese piece played on the ti-tzu (flute)

Procedure:

(Attentive)

1   "What instruments do you hear?"

2   Play track (00:01–00:42).

3   Discuss answers. The sole instrument is the ti-tzu (transverse flute).

4   "This piece is called Pigeons Flying. How does the music depict the image of pigeons flying.

5   Play track (00:01–00:42).

6   Discuss answers. Guide students to specific musical sounds that may represent flight (e.g., flutter-tonguing, glissandos, airy tone, octave leaps, staccato articulation).

7   Have students identify different articulation techniques within the clip.

8   Play track (00:01–00:42).

9   Review with students where different articulation techniques are used (e.g., trills (00:01–00:08), glissandi (00:22–00:28), grace notes (00:38–00:42)).

10   Review that expert players use flutter-tonguing as a technique. Have students listen to identify this technique in the clip.

11   Play track (03:00–03:25).

12   "Is this piece metrical or free meter? If it has a meter, what is it?"

13   Play track (00:01–00:42).

14   Discuss that the piece is mostly free meter, with short sections that feel metrical. Play clips where there is a metrical pulse in the piece (e.g., 00:38–00:42).

Attentive Listening: Considerations for Teachers

It is important during this first phase of Attentive Listening for the music teacher to facilitate multiple listenings, and it may require five or six (or more) times before discoveries by ear can be made. The repeated exposure to the musical sources will allow students to isolate specific elements of the music (and for the teacher-as-guide to ask specific questions prior to each listening experience). During the subsequent listenings, the teacher should shift the focus of the listening to other musical elements of the sound. For instance, the initial listenings can focus on instrumentation while subsequent listenings orient the students toward meter or rhythmic motives.

Attentive Listening episodes can be incorporated into all sorts of secondary school music classrooms and for multiple purposes. First, Attentive Listening can encourage a depth of listening in the musical focus of the particular class. In a guitar classroom or a percussion ensemble, world music examples of that repertoire from multiple cultures can provide students with worthy models of musical style and nuance. Second, Attentive Listening in music classrooms can also be used to promote aware-ness of how the musical tradition that they are learning about happens all over the world. Examples from the world's musical cultures that use instruments that are similar in technique and construction can be presented to students to show how diverse cultures make music similarly. In a guitar class, for example, a music educa-tor can present aural examples of various stringed instruments: the *oud* from the Middle East, the *dongbula* from Kazakhstan, the *sitar* from India, the *charango* from Peru, and the *balalaika* from Russia. Lastly, Attentive Listening allows the transfer of musical understanding of concepts to a vast repertoire of world music expressions that could be quite different in sound from the students' experiences, but will be connected by a common understanding of how the music is conceived and constructed.

During listening activities within the classroom, the ear is naturally drawn to those elements that pique the listener's interest. Listeners might notice a melodic hook or hocket (notes in one part coinciding with rests in another part) between instruments. When designing Attentive Listening episodes within classrooms, flexibil-ity should be allowed within the discussion so students can inquire and discuss how the musical selection is personally interesting to them. As students get practice with the features of Attentive Listening, they will be able to detect increasingly intricate musical ideas or nuances.

Attentive Listening in Action: Moroccan Oud

Morocco, a country at the northwestern corner of the African continent, has been influ-enced by many musical traditions: Berber folk music, Andalusian classical music, and sub-Saharan African expressions. The piece used in the next episode is an example of the *aita* style, which is performed in most of the populated areas of Morocco, espe-cially in the central part of the country. Meters are mostly 6/8 or 12/8, which allows the duple and triple rhythms to be played successively or concurrently. The musical interest of the *aita* is largely created by the interplay between the free vocal line and the rigid rhythmic accompaniment. This piece was composed and performed by Abdeslam Cherkaoui, a prominent performer of classical Moroccan music. In addition to studying classical Arab song forms, Abdeslam spent 10 years traveling throughout north Africa as a migrant musician. This experience allowed for the incorporation of folk-style ele-ments into his compositions. The following episode features the recording in which Abdeslam uses an *oud* to accompany himself; the oud is a fretless stringed instrument with a pear-shaped body, similar to the European lute. The oud has been and is cur-rently used in many Middle Eastern and Muslim musical traditions.

Episode 2.6: Arabian Nights: A Love Song from Northern Africa

Specific Use: Songwriting

Materials:

- "Ya Hbibi Malek Sahi," Abdeskan Cherkaoui, Smithsonian Folkways Recordings

  Middle eastern oud with vocals

Procedure:

(Attentive)

1 "What part of the world do you think this musician is from? Why?"
2 Play track (01:06–02:02).
3 Review answers: Middle East/North Africa (clues within the music could be the vocal tone, language, instrumentation).
4 "What kind of instrument is accompanying the singer?"
5 Play track (01:06–02:02).
6 Discuss answers. The students should readily identify that there is only one stringed instrument in the recording. Give a brief description of the oud.
7 "What is the relationship between the oud and the singer?"
8 Play track (01:06–02:02).
9 Discuss that the voice is often doubled by the oud accompaniment.
10 "The word *hbibi* (pronounced ha-bee-bee) means lover or beloved in Arabic. How many times do you hear the singer sing the word *hbibi*?"
11 Play track (01:06–02:02).
12 Review answers. "Hbibi" is sung five times in the clip.
13 Have students listen to the piece in its entirety. Ask students to identify the mood of the song and what they think the song may be about.
14 Play track (00:01–05:11).
15 Review with the students that the song is a love song, but one of sadness. Full translation of the lyrics can be found on the Smithsonian website or liner notes.
16 "Listen to the recording one more time, and listen for examples of how the musician expresses the meaning of the text through the music."
17 Play track (00:01–05:11).

Sound Before Sight

One of the benefits of approaching musical learning through Attentive Listening, even for older students, is that musical understanding can happen without the necessity to teach notation. For many musical traditions, notation is not used in the transmission of the musical knowledge. In musical cultures where notation is used, it is generally a form of shorthand for future performances of the piece. In musical traditions where notation has been long established, the musical realization is still incomplete by the notation alone. Published scores do not notate every nuance, and certainly expressive elements of timing and articulation are given limited visual representation in Western staff notation. Bypassing notation altogether (especially in oral-tradition pieces) allows the music teacher to involve secondary school music students who have had little formal experience in music notation. Attentive Listening is a technique, then, that emphasizes listening before literacy, thus allowing students to develop musically in ways that are similar to how many musicians learn to become musical within their own traditions.

Although written notation can help preserve musical traditions, it is not always necessary for the transmission of important musical cultural ideas. Musical traditions that incorporate written notation are similar to written histories (McLucas, 2010). Until quite recently, histories have been written from the majority perspective, often from a place of elitism, leaving the stories of those in the minority left untold. Similarly, completely oral-aural music traditions may not garner the same attention in schools and institutions as music from the Western art tradition, as the existing power structures have devalued them and pushed them out of current curricular designs. Today, with the fortunate development of technology and archival recordings, music from oral-aural traditions that had been outside the scope of most music classrooms can now be experienced with authenticity and ease.

Secondary school music classes vary greatly in focus and design, from the broad goals of a general music class to domain-specific classes such as Advanced Placement Theory, guitar class, or songwriting. Even within this great diversity, Attentive Listening has many benefits for students of all levels, as they can build their aural skills within the framework of curricular goals of the class. As an example, the following vignette describes ways that Attentive Listening can be used effectively within a music technology course.

World Music Pedagogy in a Music Technology Class

Ms. Davenport's sixth period of ninth-graders (ages 14–15) is a Music Technology class with a focus in composing and arranging (Figure 2.3). *With strident fluorescent lighting overhead, the small classroom contains 20 computer work stations with piano keyboards set up around the perimeter. Ms. Davenport starts the class, mentioning that the objective for the period is to explore how texture and instrumentation give variety and interest to a piece of music—a skill that her students are expected to develop in their own electronic compositions. Specifically, she adds that this objective will be met through investigating folk dance music from the British Isles. She introduces the class to the context of the piece that the students will be studying, a dance medley featuring the tunes "The Smokey Lum," "Maggie's Pancakes," "Dancing Feet," and "The Mason's Apron" performed by the Scottish folk band, Tannahill Weavers.*

"On this first listen, try to identify all of the different instruments that you hear," Ms. *Davenport instructs. "Some instruments may be unfamiliar, so it's okay to make*

Figure 2.3   Student working on project in Music Technology lab

Photo courtesy of Candice Davenport

an educated guess." Ms. Davenport has the recording cued up on Spotify and begins to play the recording. It is apparent that many students begin to feel the groove of the music, and some students immediately begin jotting down their ideas about the sources of the musical sounds.

After the full first hearing, the class brainstorms what instruments they heard. They quickly identify the instruments that are familiar to them: guitar, fiddle, and flute. Fred excitedly explains that the bagpipes were used in the second half of the piece. Kris tentatively speaks up, "I heard a percussion instrument, but I don't know exactly what it was."

"What did it sound like?" Ms. Davenport replies.

"They couldn't be castanets, could they?" Sonja interjects.

"Yes, they do have a bright, clear sound like castanets, but these instruments are actually called bones. They're called that because they used to be made out of animal bones, like goats' ribs. Today, they are normally made out of wood and are used in a lot of different folk music, including music from the British Isles. Nice catch! Now we're going to the recording again and, as we listen, please identify which of these instruments is playing the melody. Sometimes, there are instruments doubling the melody, so listen closely."

After the second listen, Ms. Davenport charts out which instruments have the melody, starting with the fiddle at the beginning. The class cooperatively sketches out major sections of the piece. Ms. Davenport gives an additional task; in small groups, students must chart the instrumentation for the entire piece. She encourages them to use measure numbers or time stamps to show when instrumentation changes and to draw a graphic organizer. Ms. Davenport is excited to see how her students will transfer their understanding of form and texture from this listening activity by including variety of texture and instrumentation within their own creations that they make using compositional technology.

Attentive Listening in Action: Scottish Reels

The reel is a specific type of music that is used to accompany folk dances and is one of the four traditional types of dances from Scotland, including the jig, the strathspey, and the waltz. Reels have been performed in Scotland for hundreds of years, possibly as far back as the Middle Ages, and have since become popular in Ireland and North America as folk dance music. These folk dances include prescribed choreography with dancers grouped into sets, possibly coupled pairs forming a square or lines. During the music, there is often a caller who will announce the upcoming dance gesture. This form of dance and music was used primarily as social entertainment in rural parts of Scotland, but they are now enjoyed in many urban centers in parts of the United Kingdom and other parts of the world.

Most reels are in 2/2 or 4/4, with a cut-time feel emphasizing each beat (or beat one and three in common time). Reels also normally have two melodic sections with an AABB form. In dance sessions, tunes are generally combined in a set to provide variety throughout the dance. The recording featured in Episode 2.7 incorporates four reel tunes, and the instrumentation changes when each new tune begins.

Episode 2.7: Reel to Reel: Scottish Dance Music

Specific Use: Music Technology

Materials:

- "Smoky Lum/Maggie's Pancakes/Dancing Feet/The Mason's Apron," The Tannahill Weavers, Green Linnet Records

  Scottish Reel featuring fiddle, whistle, bones, guitar, and highland bagpipes

Procedure:

(Attentive)

1 "Try to identify all of the instruments that are being played."
2 Play track (00:01–04:21).
3 Discuss answers. Instruments that are used in the track include fiddle, flute, guitar, bones, and Scottish bagpipes.
4 If students are unable to identify all instruments, play smaller clips (e.g., 01:15–01:46 for fiddle, flute, and guitar, 02:16–2:45 for bagpipes and bones).
5 Have students chart out the piece by instrumentation. This could be done with the entire class or in small groups. Students can use time-stamps to indicate when instruments enter or exit the texture. Encourage students to use graphic notation, creating their own listening map.
6 Play track (00:01–04:21) or allow students to listen to tracks independently.

7   Discuss how students organized the instrumentation. Have students exchange listening maps or chart out the structure of the piece on the board.

8   Play track (00:01–04:21), allowing students to follow the chart and check their work.

9   Briefly review the concept of syncopation. Direct students to listen for when the guitar (accompaniment) is playing syncopated rhythms in the piece. Students can raise their hands or notate on their listening maps when the syncopations occur.

10   Play track.

11   Discuss where the syncopation occurs in the guitar part (01:01–01:03, 3:53–3:59), using the listening maps as a reference; the teacher can isolate the syncopated parts to reinforce student understanding.

Avoiding Teacher Bias

When designing Attentive Listening episodes, music teachers should avoid the privileging of Western art music ways of understanding music, and instead strive to explore how people in various cultures understand their respective musical expressions. This can be a difficult challenge because biases and past experiences can influence how to conceptualize musical learning, especially by those who have experience in only one musical culture, such as Western popular music or Western art music. Although it may be impossible to have a complete understanding of the musical values of every culture a music educator may introduce within her classroom, the attempt should be made to understand how the concept or skill is taught within the original context. For instance, it is inappropriate to identify the pitch sets of Indian *ragas* as "major" or "minor," without an understanding of the ways in which Indian musicians (and listeners) associate ragas with times of day, moods, and particular sentiments. In Episode 2.8, there is an example of how the music of Western Samoa can be viewed as related to, yet distinct from, Western music traditions.

Attentive Listening in Action: Western Samoa

The Samoan islands are located just below the equator in the Polynesian region of the Pacific Ocean, approximately halfway between Hawaii and New Zealand. The islands are made up of two distinct principalities: American Samoa and the independent state of Western Samoa or Samoa I Sisifo. Most Polynesians live in coastal villages in oval-shaped houses without walls called *fale*. Each Samoan belongs to a certain extended family but lives within a smaller household that is headed by an elected chief.

Traditional Samoan music is primarily vocal. There are many types of traditional Samoan songs, such as lullabies, juggling chants, marriage songs, songs of sorrow, paddling songs, dance songs, historical songs, and songs of praise. More contemporary Samoan music has been strongly influenced by the harmonies that Western missionaries brought with them. Traditional songs were discouraged or outright banned, with religious music being offered in its place. The Samoans accepted the new music of hymns and psalms because it appeared to have some characteristics that they were already familiar with: chordal part-singing and call-and-response forms. European musical idioms and styles were adopted and adapted at the expense of traditional music. After European arrival on the islands, Samoan songs became a mélange of Indigenous and Western sonorities.

In Western Samoa, there are many small vocal groups comprising three to five young people, most often boys, accompanying themselves on acoustic guitars. They play the popular music of Samoa: old popular songs arranged in a modern style, but also newly composed contemporary songs. Their three- or four-part singing in Samoan sounds relaxed and happy, or even sentimental. Many times, the boys sing in falsetto voice. Of the performers, one plays the lead guitar, another plays the "bass" (on an acoustic six-string guitar), and a third one plays the rhythm guitar. In the following episode, Le Patiloa is the vocal group that performs in the recording. In this group, three boys and one girl play and sing together.

Episode 2.8: Strumming in Samoa

Specific Use: Advanced Placement Music Theory

Materials:

- "Ua lata mai le aso fa'amasino," Le Patiloa, Smithsonian Folkways Recordings

  Guitar, bass, vocals

Procedure:

(Attentive)

1 "From what part of the world do you think this music comes?"
2 Play track (00:01–01:06).
3 Discuss answers. Brief describe the context of the piece and show on a map where the Samoan islands are located.
4 "What instruments do you hear?"
5 Play track (00:01–01:06).
6 Review answers (guitars, bass, voices).
7 "How many voice parts do you hear?"
8 Play track (00:01–01:06).
9 Discuss that there are three different voice parts, two boys and one girl singing.
10 Have students explore the relationship between the voice parts. (Are they singing in unison, in harmony? Do the voice parts move in parallel,

contrary, or oblique movement?) The music educator may need to review with students the definition of these vocabulary words.

11 Play track (00:01–01:06).

12 Discuss that voice parts mostly move in parallel movement.

13 Have students follow the contour of the voice parts. Pick one part and decide if it is going up or down in pitch. Students can draw a sketch of the contour as a line on paper or follow it with their index finger.

14 Play track (00:01–01:06).

15 Allow students to share with each other their own contour.

16 Play track (00:01–01:06) to review their contour.

Teacher Feature: Kathy Armstrong

Kathy Armstrong Performing With Her Students

Photo courtesy of Ian Holland

Kathy Armstrong is an educator, performer, and founder of the Baobab Community, a non-profit arts education organization located in Ottawa, Canada. This organization provides music experiences for young people to collaborate and perform West African drumming and dance. This organization has provided multicultural exchanges since 1995. While Kathy has received conservatory training in music at the university level, she has also received significant training over the last 25 years in Ghanaian drumming both in Ghana and in Canada. Additionally, she continues to work with culture-bearers to inform her practice and to work with her students. In the following interview, Kathy discusses her thoughts about studying music from Ghana and the merits of a diverse music repertoire.

Q: Why is it important for young people to have experiences like Ghanaian drumming and dance?

A: Learning about music from different cultures can enhance connections between people and provide students different opportunities to make those connections. Anytime that we learn something that is unfamiliar to us, or new in whatever way, no matter what the subject, it actually informs us about ourselves and about the world around us. That's very valuable information. In the field of education, we want our students to be learning about themselves, who they are, as well as the larger picture, what role we play in the world. I think that music that is presented from a variety of different cultural backgrounds is helpful. It lets students try something that might be new, so they don't have any preconceived idea about it. This is a great equalizer in the classroom where students already might be playing certain roles. By providing an experience that is new, they get a better sense of everyone trying together.

Q: How do you facilitate experiences with students to open their ears to new musical cultures?

A: When introducing students to Ghanaian music, I start with basic drumming parts, but I'm already thinking about how they are going to be interacting with each other. I want to get them connecting as much as possible. One of the things I love about Ghanaian drumming is that it promotes such active listening because it's an aural tradition. From the onset, it's already getting the class cohering as a unit. We work on layers of drumming and connect the rhythmic patterns through speech. This is a very typical way of teaching in Ghana. I use this idea of speech and have rhythms or phrases that go with them. Immediately students are engaged, cognitively and physically.

Some of the musical features of Ghanaian drumming fall into the category of participatory music that Thomas Turino[2] talks about. Those characteristics have a lot to do with active listening. When students are engaged with the musical activity through the body, they have to be listening. A lot of people think that drumming is just about hitting stuff, but it is really about listening and having a conversation with your fellow players. It really does open up awareness and connections between students.

Q: How do these experiences of Ghanaian drumming lead to shared understanding across geographical distances?

A: When we have immersion experiences such as when we take our group to Ghana or bring Ghanaian guest artists to our classes here in Canada, the students experience an engagement. They feel that personal connection, and I feel it makes the world a little bit smaller. We can see what the similarities are between us, and we get excited about it. When things are approached with integrity, or as Debbie Bradley called "respectful engagement,"[3] there is an opportunity for a lot of free will in the sense that we are exploring together. When the Ghanaians who collaborate with us share their art form, they are very generous with us. The students understand that, and there is a spark that happens. It connects us all.

Attending to Sonic Features: A Passage to New Musical Cultures

Attentive Listening is a gateway to musical understanding. In many musical traditions, this focused kind of listening provides access to musical activities in ways that utilize the ear more than the eye, and gets straight at the heart of music as an aural art form. Attentive Listening allows students to develop the same type of listening skills that musicians the world over use while performing, in many folk, traditional, popular, and (many) art music genres. This type of intensive and concentrated listening provides students with multiple exposures to new and specific musical cultures, and guides them to hearing specific sonic phenomena. Musical understanding is further developed as the music educator moves the point of focus with additional listening, exploring timbre, rhythm, harmony, form, and tone. Learning through Attentive Listening allows the student to transfer musical knowledge and understanding to other listening experiences that happen outside of the music classroom, within the soundtrack of the student's life.

It may be that some students who enter secondary school music classrooms have limited musical literacy or technical skills; yet, most, if not all, have an extensive history of listening to cherished and diverse musical styles. The savvy and reflective music educator will capitalize on this and will lead students to further understanding of musical processes and forms. By opening up students to the world's musical expressions through the pedagogical techniques employed within Attentive Listening, sonorities and cultural practices are introduced and beckon the students to learn more about the people behind these musics. This first phase is a departure from the familiar to the unfamiliar, and sometimes the slate must be swept clean so that students can know music that is new to them with fresh ears and minds. As they awaken to the music through repeated listenings, they can also awaken to the people and cultures whose music it is. Students then learn of the rich diversity of humankind, and can form connections to the shared experiences of people across the globe.

Notes

1 For more information about Zimbabwean marimbas and their history, see Minnaar-Bailey (n.d.).
2 Participatory music-making is a concept that Thomas Turino offers in his book *Music as Social Life*.
3 Bradley, D. (2015). Bradley suggests that music educators should approach multicultural music with a "respectful engagement" (p. 200), in contrast to "authenticity," which is a barrier to diversifying the canon.

References

Bradley, D. (2015). Hidden in plain sight. In C. Benedict, P. Schmidt, G. Spruce, & P. Woodford (Eds.), *The Oxford handbook of social justice in music education* (pp. 190–203). New York: Oxford University Press.

Bruner, J. (1960). *The process of education.* Cambridge, MA: The President and Fellows of Harvard College.

Campbell, P. S. (2005). Deep listening to the musical world. *Music Educators Journal, 92*(1), 30–36.

Dissanayake, E. (2006). Ritual and ritualization: Musical means of conveying and shaping emotion in humans and other animals. In E. Brown & U. Voglsten (Eds.), *Music in manipulation: On the social uses and social control of music* (pp. 31–56). New York: Berghahn Books.

McLucas, A. D. (2010). *The music ear: Oral tradition in the USA.* Burlington, VT: Ashgate Publishing Company.

Minnaar-Bailey, M. (n.d.). *The history of Zimbabwean marimbas*. Chaia Marimba Book 2. Retrieved from http://chaiamarimba.com/uploads/History_of_Zimbabwean_Marimbas.pdf

Schippers, H. (2010). *Facing the music: Shaping music education from a global perspective*. New York: Oxford University Press.

Listening Episodes

"Čoček Manhattan," Yuri Yunakov Ensemble, Smithsonian Folkways Recordings. Saxophone, clarinet, keyboard, electric bass, and drum kit. www.folkways.si.edu/yuri-yunakov-ensemble/cocek-manhattan/world/music/track/Smithsonian.

"Ko tzu fei," Wong Kuen, Smithsonian Folkways Recordings. Classical Chinese piece played on the ti-tzu (flute). www.folkways.si.edu/wong-kuen/ko-tzu-fei-pigeons-flying/music/track/smithsonian.

"Nyoka Musango," Lora Chiorah-Dye and the Suketai Marimba and Dance Ensemble, Smithsonian Folkways Records. Marimbas, hosho, body percussion, vocals. www.folkways.si.edu/lora-chiorah-dye-and-sukutai/nyoka-musango/world/music/track/smithsonian.

"Siquisirí," Son de Madera, Smithsonian Folkways Recordings. Son jarocho featuring leona, guitarra de son, jarana tercera, contrabass, and vocals. www.folkways.si.edu/son-de-madera/siquisiri-siquisiri/latin-world/music/track/smithsonian.

"Smoky Lum/Maggie's Pancakes/Dancing Feet/The Mason's Apron," The Tannahill Weavers, Green Linnet Records. Scottish Reel featuring fiddle, whistle, bones, guitar, and highland bagpipes. Available on iTunes and Spotify.

"The Sun Will Never Go Down," Sweet Honey in the Rock, Flying Fish Records. African American spiritual, a cappella singing. Available on iTunes.

"Ua lata mai le aso fa'amasino," Le Patiloa, Smithsonian Folkways Recordings. Guitar, bass, vocals. www.folkways.si.edu/le-patiloa/ua-lata-mai-le-aso-faamasino/world/music/track/smithsonian.

"Ya Hbibi Malek Sahi," Abdeskan Cherkaoui, Smithsonian Folkways Recordings. Middle eastern oud with vocals. www.folkways.si.edu/abdeslam-cherkaoui/ya-hbibi-malek-sahi-lover-why-are-you-forgetful/music/track/smithsonian.

3

Participatory Musicking

At her suburban high school in the Midwest, Ms. Ellsmore prepares for her Advanced Placement (AP) Theory course made up of a small group of juniors and seniors who are excited about music and want to learn more. These students are mostly from the school's performing ensembles and include several who are looking to make music their career path. During a recent class, the students listened to a tune from Macedonia. They were listening to identify the instruments played, timbre and number of vocalists, and to map out the form. The students then sang the tonic note of the different chords as they listened to the piece again with cuing for when to change their pitch from Ms. Ellsmore. On a repeated listening, the students figured out the underlying rhythm as emphasized by the rhythm section of the band and transcribed it using notation software. They finished this lesson with some of the class playing the rhythm on drums, while others played the basic chords on keyboards, and the remaining students sang the melody on a neutral syllable.

The students frequently connect the concepts they are learning to the music they listen to or play. This happened when some of the band students who enrolled in the AP class instantly recognized the mixed meter (7/8) from a piece they are playing. Mitch, a guitarist who has come as a senior to the class as his very first school music course, often offers musical examples of concepts (such as 5/8 meter, or natural minor, or Mixolydian mode) that are off the beaten path, because he does not listen to music of the Western classical canon. Usually, he offers songs from alternative or indie groups. Recently, he asked about a term he came across that was unfamiliar to him, "gypsy scale." He described it as sounding like the harmonic minor scale except that it had the "half step–augmented second–half step" pattern at the beginning of the scale instead of only at the end.

Ms. Ellsmore immediately appreciated several things about the moment: that this student could show that there are other types and styles of music outside of the limited scope of the AP Music Theory curriculum, that everyone is able to observe Mitch's curiosity about music and that he explores music on his own time for fun, and that she is given the chance as their teacher to connect what he heard and read to what they *already know about scales. He opened a door to talk about the term "gypsy," and Roma people, and music for which the scale is so prevalent. She gave them a quick overview about Roma and the hijaz scale that day, but returned the next day with modern musical examples of Roma music. Another student mentioned that he came across the double harmonic scale, and it felt like a cross between the hijaz scale they were studying and harmonic minor scales because it had the minor second–augmented second–minor second pattern in both tetrachords. Her students have fallen in love with concepts that are outside of the standard AP theory curriculum.*

In her seventh year of teaching high school music, Ms. Ellsmore is also a graduate student in choral conducting and is nearing completion of her coursework. One of the last courses that she enrolled in featured singing traditions from outside Western art music. As part of her study, she was introduced to key features of Bulgarian and Macedonian folk singing. Several of the melodies that she learned were in the very scale that her student, Mitch, was probing, this mode commonly known as "Hijaz." Ms. Ellsmore was delighted to hear Mitch's question and comment. Her efforts to expand her own knowledge and experience with a broad range of global repertoire gives her the confidence to take advantage of this teachable moment.

With the first dimension of World Music Pedagogy (WMP) under way, secondary school music students are paying keen attention to specific musical features, even as they are opening their minds to the cultural origin and ownership of individual works. Developing Sound Awareness and Attentive Listening skills (Chapter 2) are integral steps in growing the capacity of secondary school students to understand what makes music cultures "tick." Within the second WMP dimension, Engaged Listening, students listen-and-do, perhaps a single part leading to layering in other parts while listening to the recording. As they graduate to the third dimension, Enactive Listening, students experience full-on performance of selected parts, eventually moving away from the recording. The emphasis is on the oral-aural channels of knowing music more fully with every opportunity to listen, so that students progress through identifying features of music to entering into partial participation by singing and playing (Engaged Listening) to a comprehensive embrace of the music in full-out performance (Enactive Listening). Students learn to understand and value the music on a deeper level when they are involved in partial and preliminary ways (Engaged Listening) and in the re-enactment of the music by performing it close to its recorded model (Enactive Listening). The embodiment of the music in the second and third dimensions of WMP brings participants closer together through the shared experience of musicking.

Musicologist Christopher Small (1998) coined the term "musicking" based on the concept that "music is not a thing at all but an activity, something that people do" (p. 2). Small posited that the very existence of musical works is so that performers have something to perform. A musical performance is a much richer and more complex experience than the musical work or its impact on a listener. Small sought to understand what people do as they take part in a musical performance of any kind in order to better understand its purpose in life. Keeping in mind the importance of this concept of musicking—something that students do—can guide educators as they select repertoire and plan lessons. By incorporating performance, the act of "doing" music, into all music classes students can engage with the music, the culture, and each other on a deeper level. This system of participatory musicking via deep listening and performative experiences lies at the very heart of the dimensions of WMP.

Listening develops from the initial question-answer emphases, as teachers develop it into "something that people do." By inviting students into the musicking experience, they can become actively involved in the making of music with the recording. They can listen as they contribute a musical part alongside the recording: singing a melody, tapping out a rhythm, playing a repeating few pitches or a durational pattern that is there in the music, dancing or eurhythmically moving to aspects of the music. Through a carefully constructed plan, students can be invited by the teacher to play the rhythm of a Roma *Čoček* on a *darabouka* (drum), or to play a Zimbabwean *mbira* (thumb piano) melody on the piano or keyboard, or to strum the chords of a Mexican *son jarocho* on a guitar to emulate the sound of the *jarana*. These participatory experiences overlay the recorded works and support the further listening by students of selected works. Through repeated listening, they become increasingly familiar with the music, so that they are finding their way as active musicians, musicking as the recording plays on.

This chapter provides pedagogical examples that draw students through the second and third dimensions of WMP: Engaged Listening and Enactive Listening. The three Learning Pathways—Zimbabwean marimba, Mexican son jarocho, and Roma wedding music—are included as well as several other rich listening suggestions. Engaged Listening is the active participation in some form of musicking behavior as the recorded music is playing or guest musicians perform live, so that they are joining in and contributing as singers, players, or dancers on part of the music. Students are "engaged" musically as they listen to the recording. Through repeated listenings (from as few as four or five times to as many as twenty), they may contribute multiple parts, becoming so familiar with the recorded work as to enable them to make the music as the recording plays—and eventually without the recording. This is Enactive Listening, when the musicking by students shifts from participation to full-on performance. This dimension requires secondary music students to develop their deep listening skills, alternating between performing and listening, in order to be more stylistically representative of the musical culture that they are exploring and to let the music live within the students' bodies and ears.

Music in a Participatory Mode

Ethnomusicologist Thomas Turino (2008) concluded in his work *Music as Social Life: The Politics of Participation* that music is at the core of society's most important occasions. It is helpful for music educators to examine how the music-making in their classroom aligns with these characteristics. Turino distinguishes between different types of performances within musical cultures, referring to them as either presentational or participatory. In presentational performances, there are distinct and prescribed roles for and between the audience and the performers, where the responsibility of music-making lies primarily with the performers. Generally, audience expectations include attending to the music prowess and technical abilities of the performers or the intricacies of the composition or improvisation. The musical experience is viewed as a product for the audience to experience. The music of presentational performances has specific characteristics that lead to these distinctions between audience members and performers.

In pedagogical practice, both participatory and presentational performance are noble goals, the likes of which color the daily teaching-learning exchanges of teachers with students. The aim of participatory musical performance is to include as many people into the music-making as much as possible, viewing all audience members as potential participants. In participatory performance, the feature is the distinct music-making process rather than a final end product. Like presentational forms of performance, certain musical attributes encourage inclusion in music-making events. Participatory music typically features repetitive forms, recurring melodic and rhythmic components, which allow participants the opportunity to learn or master a musical behavior within the sound. The texture is thick and dense to allow for a variety of competency levels to participate together. Music has layered beginnings and endings, and the course of the music is often led by a facilitator rather than following a prescribed course as dictated by a score. Compared to presentational types of performances, there is minimal contrast in participatory music. Constancy in meter and rhythms allows participants to settle into the groove. There can be highly technical or virtuosic performance within participatory performances, but it is not typically the central focus of the musical event.

The categorization of music performances as presentational or participatory is not dichotomous, as Turino argues, but rather plays out along a continuum. Some music may invite both presentation by the performers as well as participation by the audience. For instance, a classical aria and a rock song are both likely to be viewed as presentational in nature, and yet an audience is more likely to participate in the musical happening of the rock band's performance of a song, singing and dancing, than they are to be involved in a classical aria. Musical events in many cultures can emerge as a hybrid combination of presentational and participatory characteristics, as musicians begin to perform and then invite the involvement of their listening audience.

Through the dimensions of WMP, and in particular through the first three dimensions, the student experiences both presentational and participatory types of music-making. Attentive Listening is primarily a presentational experience that aims for student concentration on elemental features of the listening selection, and the task of music teachers is to challenge students to seek and find particular musical features as they listen to selected recordings (even as they awaken to facets of the music's origin culture). In the process of Engaged Listening, the emphasis goes to a participatory experience within the frame of the recording, so that the same listening example that was only just beginning to be understood in the initial stage is now available, through the greater familiarity of students, for a fuller involvement through participation that offers the potential for development of new musical skills.

Experiencing music through participation is important for the formation of personal and social identities, spiritual and emotional communication, and in allowing people to feel part of a community through participating together in musical performance (Turino, 2008). This concept is one of *communitas*, or what anthropologist Edith Turner (2012) described as inspired fellowship, as it reflects a collective state achieved through performance where all personal differences are removed, allowing people to unite through their basic humanity. While aiming for this sense of *communitas*, a parallel goal in music education could be to provide learning experiences that allow students to become fully involved in the moment, the sound, and the feel of the music. Psychologist Mihály Czíkszentmihályi (1991) identified this highly focused mental state as "flow." He designated dimensions of the flow experience that include: full and focused attention, the merging of action and awareness, freedom from worry about failure, the disappearance of self-consciousness, the distortion of the sense of time, and the experience becoming its own reward.

By designing satisfying musical experiences that have just the right level of challenge for the participants, secondary school students will build a connection with the music as well as to one another. To bring students to this level of intense concentration, a teacher needs thoughtfully crafted lessons that are designed with a range of activities and challenges to meet a spectrum of abilities. By including clear goals throughout the process, providing and receiving meaningful feedback, and creating a balance between challenge and skills, students may be brought into a state of flow and a sense of *communitas*.

Learning Through Engaged Listening

Engaged Listening is the second dimension of WMP, following on first listenings and inviting active participation in the recorded music. This second dimension emphasizes the embodiment of key features in the music through singing, playing, and moving. These experiences require a deeper listening than is typical of students when they are streaming music through headphones or working through initial Attentive Listening experiences, as they are now expected to synchronize themselves with the music. Music-making activities highlight elements within the music and provide opportunities for a deeper consideration and analysis of musical constructs in the process. Engaged Listening facilitates examination of the use of music within a culture and to the communities that participate in the music. By engaging with music at this level, it is possible to activate in students a sense of wonder and a broader understanding of the wider music of the world.

There are three curated selections as illustrations of the Engaged Listening experiences of students in secondary school music settings. When given meaningful and frequent opportunities to listen, students can increase their fluency with the core elements of a musical work. Music in this chapter's episodes sample practices from Eastern European Roma musicians in Macedonia and Bulgaria, from Mexico in the folkloric genre of *son jarocho* in both traditional and contemporary forms, from African American rap that combines with the melodic hook of a song from the 1960s, and from Zimbabwe in the way of marimba music. There are start-ups of model lessons in these illustrations, each of which incorporates a myriad of repertoire, genres, and cultures. Teachers can follow these suggestions as guideposts, apply the pedagogical ideas to other repertoire of their liking and experience, and be inspired by recordings and pedagogical suggestions to create unique and motivating learning experiences using music of their own choosing.

There are pedagogical suggestions for the selections and their activities that can be geared toward various secondary school music classes, including but not limited to guitar, percussion ensemble, group piano class, and theory. The intention is that any of these episodes can be adapted into a variety of secondary school music settings. Of course, the music teacher's preparation and commitment are critical to successful learning experiences. Although much learning of global traditions can take place at home through reading, discussions, culture-bearers, and the Internet, examples are included here of music educators utilizing ethnomusicological techniques by traveling directly to a location to collect materials and learn the ways of the music culture. The learning continues upon arrival back in the home setting by figuring out how to embed the new music cultures into existing and just-created curricula. The following excursion into Macedonian history and culture is meant as a model of the type of important information that secondary music teachers should incorporate into their music lessons.

Macedonia and the Balkan Peninsula

Formerly under Ottoman Turkish rule, Macedonia shares borders with Greece, Serbia, Bulgaria, Albania, and Kosovo as part of the Balkan Peninsula and is home to a rich variety of musical traditions among its many linguistic, ethnic, and religious communities. Macedonians, Albanians, Roma, Turks, Greeks, Jews, Christians, and Muslims have all contributed to distinct and interconnected musical traditions. Routes connecting Europe with the Near and Middle East brought travelers to the Balkan Peninsula, bringing their native cultures, which eventually were changed and blended. For centuries, a variety of foreign invaders sought control of the peninsula and, in the 15th century, the Ottoman Turks succeeded. For almost 500 years, people lived under the Ottoman Empire. By the end of the 19th century, Serbia, Bulgaria, Greece, Montenegro, and Romania had gained their independence from the Ottomans. By 1918, the Socialist Federal Republic of Yugoslavia was formed. Throughout the 1990s, Yugoslavia fell apart as a result of catastrophic civil wars. Consequently, each of the former republics, including Macedonia, set up its own independent nation-state.

Throughout these turbulent decades, isolated rural mountain regions enabled villagers to preserve their ancient ways of life, including musical traditions, undisturbed. Musical traditions in Macedonia are typically divided into rural and urban genres, and they span a variety of vocal and instrumental performance styles. Each of these communities maintained distinct vocal repertoires in their languages and cultivated solo traditions on instruments such as the *gajda* (bagpipe), *kaval* (end-blown flute), and *tambura* (plucked lute) (Figure 3.1). Folkloric singing in Macedonia is usually a vibrant, loud sound suitable for outdoor performance. Villagers often sing to accompany work outdoors or indoor women's working bees known as *sedenki.*

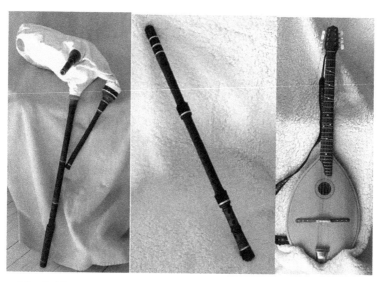

Figure 3.1   Gajda (bagpipe), kaval (end-blown flute), and tambura

Photo courtesy of Karen Howard

Communities also sing *na trapeza* (at table) songs at social events and during ritual celebrations while seated around the table.

Government-sponsored institutions determined, shaped, and preserved the folkloric repertoires of Macedonia. Since the founding of the state radio and folklore ensembles in the late 1940s, songs collected from rural areas have been arranged with instrumental ensemble accompaniment. Rural vocal traditions have been largely overlooked due to the increasing dominance of the formally trained and highly orchestrated performances by state folkloric ensembles and the spread of mass media.

Gypsy Caravan: Music from Macedonian Roma Culture

Roma musicians in Macedonia typically learn from older musicians by watching, listening, and extensive practice. In Macedonia, Roma musicians are simultaneously desired for their virtuosic musicality and rejected for their ethnic and cultural identities. The very culture that birthed these cultural practices no longer exists as it once did. Not surprisingly, globalization and emigration have depleted the Roma population who practiced these cultural forms to sustain community identity.

Music Educators in the Field

Two music teachers journey to Macedonia in Eastern Europe in search of a summer music festival near Lake Ohrid in the central region of the country. The festival attracts musicians and dancers from throughout the Balkans. Traditional folk ensembles from Macedonia, Serbia, Albania, Bulgaria, Montenegro, and Croatia gather for a full week to perform in an outdoor athenaeum for the public. Reveling continues into the wee hours of the morning as the performers gather at local establishments to eat, drink, sing, and dance long after the public shows are over. These teachers have heard the music for many years, from afar on recordings, and a visit to the origin place of Macedonian music is an opportunity to reinforce what they know and add new insights (and possibly pedagogical material).

There is a Macedonian friend on this journey of the two music teachers, and he is acting as driver and translator throughout their adventure. They explain to him their hope to hear and see as much traditional music as possible. He takes them around to various music venues in the capital city of Skopje, and to watch buskers on street corners. One of the teachers has a particularly strong interest in Roma music, and hopes to hear it live, but the Macedonian friend claims that there is none (because many Slavic people do not socialize or otherwise integrate with the Roma). They walk by Roma buskers, and see through the windows of a restaurant that a Roma band is performing at a wedding reception. Yet their friend continues to assert that there is no Roma music to hear. It becomes clear that their friend knows very well where Roma musicians may be found, but after several days he does finally admit the strong bias that many Slavic people hold. He expresses ambiguity as to his own feelings toward Roma, and yet he participates in the not-seeing.

The teachers join the friend on a visit to the state-sponsored National Folkloric Music and Dance Troupe, Tanec.[1] While the group does not perform the Roma music the teachers hoped to hear, they enjoy the professional musicians and dancers in rehearsal of Slavic-flavored Macedonian music. It is a highlight on their journey, and some of the music seems influenced by the Roma sound, perhaps given the proximity of the two cultures for centuries. The visit solidifies their interest, inspires them further to teach the music (and dance), and provides them with recordings to share with their students.

Episode 3.1: Engaged Listening in Action—Macedonian Roma

The following episode features music from internationally beloved Macedonian Roma singer Esma Redzepova. Ethnomusicologist Carol Silverman (2003) has written extensively of Redzepova's contributions to Macedonian Roma music culture. In her work on Roma women in the Balkans, she interviewed Redzepova, the self-proclaimed "Queen of the Gypsies." Esma expressed that singing in Romani was a statement of pride in her heritage. When Esma was first making a living as a singer, it was considered shameful to sing in Romani. Many Roma hid their ethnic identity for fear of oppression and bigotry. Esma performed regularly until her death in 2016.

Episode 3.1: Esma Redzepova: Macedonian Queen of the Gypsies

Specific Use: Advanced Placement Music Theory

Materials:

- Esma Redzepova, "Ušti Ušti Baba," Smithsonian Folkways Recordings

  Kaval (flute), clarinet, accordion, tambourine, darabouka, vocals

Procedure:

(Engaged)

1 Students have previously listened multiple times to the recording of "Ušti Ušti Baba" earlier via the process of Attentive Listening.

2 Play entire track with students, using the score for the song to follow along (Figure 3.2).

3 Have the students identify all of the pitches used in the song. This scale is known as *Hijaz* (Figure 3.3).

4 Play track (0.11–0.30) to listen to what is presented in the score. Check the pitches used in the song and compare to the Hijaz scale.

5 Using solfège syllables, numbers, pitch names, or a neutral syllable, have the students sing through melodic exercises using a visual representation of the scale on a screen/board. Try steps, skips, neighboring tones, and singing in thirds. Be sure to emphasize the first three tones of the scale (in

the case of C Hijaz—the C, Db, and E natural). These are important to the characteristic flavor of Hijaz-based melodies.

6　Learn a basic *darabouka* (drum) rhythm (Figure 3.5).

(Enactive)

7　Play entire track and accompany on darabouka.

Return to this piece in future lessons to include the following steps toward Creating World Music (Chapter 5).

(Creating)

8　Create rhythmic variations for the basic *darabouka* pattern.

9　Have students create short *taksim* (improvisations) using the pitches of the Hijaz scale. The principal chords of the scale (Figure 3.4) can guide improvisations.

10　Sing or play the main melody followed by individual student *taksim*.

Figure 3.2 Ušti Ušti Baba

HIJAZ SCALE

Hijaz is one of the most commonly used scales throughout the Balkans, Turkey, and parts of the Middle East. Familiarity with the scale is beneficial to assist in creating *taksim* (improvisation). Hijaz, like other modes and scales, can be played from any starting pitch. An example of C Hijaz is given in Figure 3.3.

Not all of the chords are important in Hijaz. There are only four principal chords: I, II, iv, and vii (Figure 3.4).

DARABOUKA RHYTHM

A basic rhythm for the *darabouka* (goblet drum) may read as in Figure 3.5. There is a myriad of quality online tutorials for learning other rhythms and techniques for this type of drumming.

The suggestions in Episode 3.1 can take several lessons to accomplish. A music theory teacher might select particular steps to include in a lesson, or to incorporate multiple steps over several lessons. Learning activities such as suggested for Ušti Ušti Baba requires consideration of the overall course objectives. In an advanced theory course, typical student learning objectives may include: reading melodies in all clefs, notating rhythms using standard notation practices, singing and playing on keyboard intervals and chords in all inversions, transposing keys, sight-singing, harmonizing melodies, and expressing ideas through composition.

Music theory students can transcribe their darabouka rhythms and perhaps even their rhythmic improvisations if taken in short sections. Even for advanced theory students, transcribing sounds into written notation takes time and requires both aural and notational skills. For instance, a particular student may have amazing skill at hearing and replicating the music but little facility with Western notation. Theory teachers who employ this idea need to plan accordingly as well as to float among working students to help those who may be stuck in the transcription process. They

Figure 3.3 Hijaz scale

Figure 3.4 Principal hijaz chords

Figure 3.5 Basic darabouka rhythm

can also transfer their short melodies created in the Hijaz scale onto a different instrument as it is not uncommon for theory students to also participate in music ensembles or private lessons. The music teacher might select several tunes featuring different scales such as natural minor or mixolydian. The students can work to identify known scales reflected in the melodies, including Hijaz. An interesting twist could be including a scale not yet learned to compare with Hijaz and other known scales.

Episode 3.2: Engaged Listening in Action—Romani Band Reimagined

The following pedagogical episode centers around a video of Romani musicians playing the *zurla* (double-reed woodwind) (Figure 3.6) and *tupan* (drum). Throughout Macedonia, the tradition of *zurla* and *tupan* music has been maintained by Roma musicians who train within their families, and each family tends to specialize in either *tupan* or *zurla*. It is common for family members to play together, connecting across

Figure 3.6   Zurli

Photo courtesy of Karen Howard

generations, with a player from separate generations—a father and son, for example, forming a duo.

Folklorist Martin Koenig traveled to Gevgelija, Macedonia, on the Greek–Macedonian border to record a local Romani band. In the video featured in Episode 3.2, Koenig filmed the group improvising on *zurli* and *tupan*. This video represents repertoire and performance styles not heard from the state-sponsored radio programs or in folkloric productions, but captures local musicians instead. They are Romani musicians, many of whom are in great demand for urban weddings. They know the repertoire of local communities and are able to perform songs in Ladino, Macedonian, Albanian, Turkish, and Romani languages, so that they are marketable for the weddings of families from these cultures. As mentioned in the opening moments of the video, there was no audio until 2015, when Koenig asked a local Roma musician to figure out what the music would have been by watching the movement of the musicians' hands.

Episode 3.2: Romani Band Reimagined

Specific Use: World Music Traditions

Materials:

- Rare video footage of Romani band in Macedonia, 1968

Procedure:

(Engaged)

1 Explain the setting of the video. The audio has been added after the fact. There is explanatory text during the opening credits of the video to help set the scene.

2 Play video (0.20–2.55).

3 Ask "What would you need to understand and see in order to figure out the music as was done in this video?"

4 Play video (0.20–0.30).

5 Students figure out the pitches the lead *zurla* player is using by listening to short melodic phrases, stopping and starting the video as needed. If relevant to the particular class, notate the pitches.

(Enactive)

6 Play video (0.20–0.41).

7 Using this short section (0.20–0.41), students start to sing along with the short melodic phrases on a neutral syllable.

8 Split the group in half: one half plays or sings the root pitch as a drone (on piano, guitar, voice, or woodwind), and the other half sings these short melodic phrases over the drone on a neutral syllable as modeled by the teacher.

9 Play track while half of group plays or sings the drone and the other half sings the short phrases. Switch so that they try each part.

Extended experience: Can the students identify a music video that they might be able to do the same based on the visuals? What would the students need to know about the genre and instruments in order to come close to an accurate replication? What kind of video footage would they need in order to see, imagine, and then try to replicate the musical sounds? Simply turning the sound off on a video is an easy way to try this.

Students in classes like World Music Traditions want to make music, even if the course is not strictly performance-based. Secondary students want to interact with the instruments, the sounds, and each other. Not only is this what they crave, but they learn much more through this process. A challenge is that the students in these classes have musical abilities across a wide range, but they can do so much more than typically credited by music teachers. When teaching a course or even single class such as this for the first time, it may seem akin to a simple music appreciation design using various music cultures. Quite the contrary—instruction designed through WMP is a vehicle for developing musical skills and knowledge, and to explore musical cultures that are unfamiliar, or close to home and pertinent to the lives of the students, or part of current events.

African American Hip-Hop Culture

While hip-hop music has reached global standing, it is still common to hear music teachers express strong disagreement about the genre's place in school music settings. When they hold this conception to be fact, students from all backgrounds are disempowered by a loss of opportunity and respect for a particular music culture and genre. Much of what music educators in secondary schools know of hip-hop music has come via media representations, which often reflect negative stereotypes. In fact, meaningful interactions with hip-hop can serve to lessen cultural divisions between students and teachers. Music teachers do well to avoid the idea that hip-hop music is only for youth culture, or for those who identify with the culture. A more accepting stance is needed on the part of music educators who employ their own hierarchies' value in judging and critiquing hip-hop music. As Tricia Rose (2008), scholar of black culture in the U.S., stated, "We must fight for a progressive, social justice-inspired, culturally nuanced take on hip-hop—a vison that rejects the morally hyper-conservative agenda" (p. 29.) By including hip-hop music in meaningful learning experiences, educators can challenge themselves to develop a fluency with this important contemporary genre and culture.

Episode 3.3: Engaged Listening in Action—Hip-Hop's Arrival in School Music

The hip-hop group Arrested Development was an alternative to so-called gangsta rap music in the early 1990s. The musicians in the group worked to combine influences from across African American music genres, including hip-hop, blues, gospel, and R&B. The lyrics of *People Everyday* address violence and sexism. With clear inspiration in the refrain pulled directly from Sly and the Family Stone's hit of the late 1960s, *Everyday People*, the new message in the lyrics urged African American youth to be socially and politically aware and to work to empower others in their communities. This song is included here as an example of rap lyrics that have a thoroughly positive and empowering message and an opportunity to address the challenge of the use of the "n" word by the musicians. In the following Episode 3.3, students in a Popular Music class that includes performative experiences examine the message in a hip-hop tune.

Episode 3.3: Everyday People, People Everyday

Specific Use: Popular Music Ensemble

Materials:

- "People Everyday," Arrested Development, Smithsonian Folkways Recordings
- "Everyday People," Sly and the Family Stone, Epic Records
- "People Everyday (In the Style of Arrested Development)," Sunfly Karaoke Ltd.

Procedure:

(Attentive)

1 Students will listen to the entire Arrested Development recording with lyrics printed to follow along.
2 Play track.
3 Create a list of the instruments (including digital and vocal).
4 Play track again and create a listening map that shows the entrance and order of voice and instruments (e.g., 00.00–00.15: electric guitar, claps, drums, vocals—call and response). The track will need to be paused to allow time for the students to discuss and note. It is likely that the teacher will need to move back and forth within the track to facilitate this.

5 Students will listen to the Sly and the Family Stone version and discover just what was sampled. Again, have the lyrics available to follow. Discuss the difference in the time periods of the two songs (late 1960s, early 1990s) and compare to race and racism in contemporary society.

6 Play short sections of track again in order to discuss the different musical genres that are heard.

7 Offer students the opportunities to either discuss or journal if they have personally experienced or witnessed anything like the struggles described in the lyrics.

(Engaged)

8 Perform a verse of the Arrested Development tune either without accompaniment, along with the original recording, or with the karaoke version.

Return to these pieces in future lessons to incorporate the following steps toward Creating World Music (Chapter 5).

(Creating)

9 Select a current event related to civil rights or racism and have the students create a rap using call and response (as in the Arrested Development version) to describe the event.

10 Use other rap songs with inspirational messages as exemplars for student journal responses, lyric writing, digital beat-making, and possible performance.

Selected artists and recordings to consider include:

*Macklemore & Ryan Lewis. (2016). "White privilege." On *This unruly mess I've made*. Macklemore, LLC. Available on iTunes and Spotify.

*Tupac Shakur. (1998). "Keep ya head up." On *2Pac greatest hits*. Death Row Records. (In a manner similar to Arrested Development's use of Sly Stone's earlier song, Tupac used the hook from "Ooh Child" by the Five Stairsteps from 1970.) Available on iTunes and Spotify.

*Queen Latifah. (1993). "U.N.I.T.Y." On *Black reign*. UMG Recordings, Inc. Available on iTunes and Spotify.

*Eric B. & Rakim. (1988). "Follow the leader." On *Follow the leader*. Geffen Records.

*Lecrae. (2014). "Welcome to America." On *Anomaly*. Reach Records.

"Popular Music" is a large genre including a wide variety of sub-genres. Certainly, one of the most popular genres of the last 30 years is hip-hop, and more specifically, rap. While hip-hop is a popular music genre with many secondary school students, it is not a given that students will be familiar with the genre, similar to their music teachers. Students can approach the genre from different points of familiarity. One student might have experience rapping along with lyrics, whereas another might have heard the older Sly and the Family Stone inspiration for the newer tune. Yet another student might have experience creating digital loops with beat-making software and can be an assistant instructor for others who are less familiar with such technology. Others still might hold preconceived biases toward the genre and can be made aware of the integrity and contributions that hip-hop music and culture offers.

Teacher Feature: Striving Toward Cultural Relevance—Sarah Minette

Music educator Sarah Minette teaches jazz band, guitar, and beginning band at a large high school in Minneapolis, Minnesota. The student population self-identifies as 36% African American, 33% White, 19% Hispanic American, 7% Native American, and 5%

High School Music Educator Sarah Minette Working With Guitar Student Arturo Ulloa
Arturo is from the birthplace of Son Jarocho in Veracruz, Mexico. He taught himself the Richie Valens pop version of "La Bamba," but he also knew that it was a much older folk song.

Asian American. Teaching in this diverse community inspired Sarah to develop a new course "Hip-Hop, Rock, and Beyond." Her hope for this new course is to engage with her students in meaningful performing, listening, and discourse around the musical expressions that her students want to hear.

Q: What are your students' listening habits?
A: A lot of our students listen to hip-hop, but at the same time they are listening to Justin Vernon,[2] or older music from the 1980s, or folk music. There is such an interesting diversity of music that goes along with our students.

Q: How are you planning and preparing for the course?
A: I am planning the course so that it ties into what other academic classes are focusing on: racism, homophobia, transphobia, and ableism.

Q: What led you to create this new course?
A: I have been concerned with how I am incorporating the cultures of my students who are not from the U.S. into my classroom, my concerns about my inability to connect with students from other cultures. My colleague told me that we worry so much about bringing students' cultures into our rooms, but that this is a gateway into *our* culture. The students are experiencing American teen culture. If we were to go abroad, if I went to Somalia, I would experience Somalian music. I'm just trying to do it all, and it doesn't always work. I also wanted to create a course that invited students to discuss music, but weren't necessarily interested in learning how to play an instrument.

Q: What would you say to music teachers who want to teach courses about hip-hop, or creating scores for film, or guitar class, but feel ill-equipped to do so based on their conservatory-styled Western art music training?
A: I think some of the best learning occurs when we step away and allow ourselves to embrace the chaos that is learning. I think when we get out of the way, then natural learning occurs. Allowing students to struggle a little bit and get frustrated on their own is also part of the learning process. I also think that it's important to let them know that it's okay to struggle and that it is a part of the learning process. Too often we strive for perfection. That's not what music should be about. That's why, to me, this job is so liberating because it's not about perfection. It's about the experience and the progress. It's not about the final performance for these kids. It's about everything else. I also feel this way about jazz band. This past month, the students embarked on a transcription project. I wanted them to struggle a little bit with learning music by ear and not offering them a whole lot of guidance. That is what has helped me learn. The students reflected on the process and all agreed it was worth the struggle. They got over that hump, and in the end, were better listeners, and had a better understanding of the jazz language.

Q: Your parents are both classically trained musicians. Did that have an impact your teaching?
A: Actually, my Dad was what he called a "faker"—a great ear and terrible reading skills. But he was my fifth and sixth grade band teacher. Both of my parents are music educators. I started piano lessons when I was five years old. I am sure that is part of why it took me so long to realize what I now know today. I kick myself for not considering

what the possibilities of music education could be five or ten years ago. But, that was my experience, and that background has certainly informed me as a teacher. I just think, what would I tell myself ten years ago if I knew then what I know now. But I guess that is why we are on this journey and perhaps in the big picture this is why I am doing what I am doing right now.

Q: When I watched your class, they were playing Nirvana's "Smells Like Teen Spirit."
How do you prepare yourself for teaching a lesson such as that?
A: Well, I really had to think back to the basics—how can I simplify this in a way that my students who are non-English speakers might feel successful? At the same time, advanced students need to not be bored out of their minds. We had just finished a unit on "The Seattle Sound," and I wanted to give them an opportunity to play one of the most important songs from that genre, as well as experience an instrument that is really important to American music (back to that comment that my colleague made about bringing students into our culture). I allow them time to experiment, having an instrument in their hands, which is brand new for some of them. I grouped the students by experience. I took the students who had never played an instrument before and showed them the very basic pattern. Then student leaders formed two other groups and showed variations of the power chords. It's about the experience of making music, not being perfect. I don't even necessarily have proper guitar technique myself!

It is clear to Sarah that in this contemporary racially charged climate, this course will need to cover the controversial topic of cultural appropriation as it relates to Whites making money from Black music. She wants to lead the students to explore how social constructs intersect with hip-hop and other popular music genres. Also evident to Sarah is the need to have the uncomfortable conversation regarding the "n" word, as well as words that represent women or the LBGT community that are sometimes present in lyrics, notably often without a negative connotation. Sarah is white and realizes that she needs to be upfront about her understanding of the power—both negative and perhaps positive—behind the "n" word and her unwillingness to say it aloud herself due to being white, but yet recognizing the need to have it present in the learning space.

Learning Through Enactive Listening

Enactive Listening is a continuation of ever-deeper listening, over many repeated listenings, that draws students into the full embrace of the music in its every component and nuance so that it can be replicated and re-created in live performance. From a focus on listening to music with specific questions and challenges in mind, and through an invitation to participate in partial ways while listening to the full complex of the music, Enactive Listening is the point in the WMP process at which the music is sung and/or played as it is sounding on the recording. It is the oral tradition in action, in which secondary school music students are learning by ear the performance of the musical work. Notation may not be necessary, as it is the course of their continued listening, their partial attempts to participate in the music-making, that brings them to the threshold of learning it by ear. In fact, some notation cues may assist and support what is largely learned by ear, for example, a sketch of the melody, the words of the song, the chord progressions, a partial transcription, but the goal of Enactive Listening is to bring students to a performance level largely through their continued listening, matching the sound, hearing their teacher's feedback, working through a shaping of the sound with the recording, then without the recording, then again with the recording, and so on.

While the use of music notation may be a quick route into the music at times, it is beneficial for both educators and their students to pursue continued strengthening of aural skills. It is common to find students in secondary classes with a wide range of experiences regarding music notation literacy. As many of the music cultures presented in this volume do not use music notation, trying an aural approach can bring interesting variation in teaching approaches to the music class. Stylistic features, ornaments, and other culturally idiomatic nuances are often most effectively learned through aural study and analysis rather than a complicated visual representation. By deemphasizing notation's place in various music education settings, the learning opportunities open up to a wider student body. Not all students enter secondary school with the ability to read music notation. This sense that "I can't read music" certainly prevents some students from electing to participate in school music. The songs and instrumental pieces provided here challenge students to transfer stylistic features they hear in the recordings into their performance. This process of taking musical understanding and generalizing the musical and social constructs out across performances is music-making at a high level.

The following episodes offer suggestions for the teacher's consideration and inspiration, and it is a teacher's choice as to how the music is incorporated into lessons and to what degree. Even in this stage of striving to learn the music to performance level, students can be encouraged to consider elemental features of the music, the music's meaning, its role and importance within the culture of origin. The three Learning Pathways are featured throughout the next section of the chapter.

Learning Pathway #1: Enactive Listening in Action— Zimbabwean Marimbas

The marimbas of Zimbabwe are not far removed from marimbas in bordering areas such as Zambia to the north, Mozambique to the east, Botswana to the southwest, and South Africa to the south. There are marimbas across the region, while they were developed later in Zimbabwe, and became the instruments on which music was taught to the Shona- and Ndebele-speaking schoolchildren. Zimbabwe is yet another country that suffered under the oppression of legalized discrimination and racial segregation by white, colored, and black.

Ngoma is not only the Shona word for drum but is a central principle of traditional music across ethnic-cultural groups in Eastern and Southern Africa, in that performances typically involve performers in singing, dancing, and playing instruments (and often engaged in drama and poetry as well)—sometimes simultaneously, or with performers changing roles within a musical piece or across a program. In traditions marked by *ngoma*, performers are engaged in multiple artistic expressions, and there is no separation of these arts but rather an integration of all in the act of performance. A sampling of genres of music in Zimbabwe includes: folkloric traditions *mbakumba, shangara,* and *amabhiza,* a cappella music such as *imbube,* lullabies, children's songs, rites of passage songs, and contemporary Zim Dancehall.

In offering thoughtful lessons that lead to learning to perform *Nyoka Musango,* the teacher advances students from initial listening, to participatory listening, to the

Figure 3.7   A marimba in Zimbabwe

Photo courtesy of Jocelyn Moon

involved learning by ear that evolves from continued listening and attempts to play it as it sounds. Hear the real message in the proverb about the snake in the bush. It is a call to boys, girls, parents, and grandparents to take up arms against the dissidents and rogue elements and "kill the snake" before it comes into the home. Modern interpretation has been extended to describe a struggle for human rights, political dignity, and social justice.

Three distinct styles of Zimbabwean marimbas evolved between the 1960s and 1980s. The first was at *Kwanongoma* (note the word *ngoma* in the name of the school) in the 1960s and was brought to the Pacific Northwest in the U.S. by the late Abraham "Dumi" Maraire. Modifications made by instrument builders to marimbas made later in the U.S. included moving the placement of the iconic buzzer hole at the bottom instead of on the side and a much larger and louder bass instrument. The second type of marimba design emerged in the 1970s. Players desired a more traditional sound and appearance, so the PVC pipes were replaced with gourd-shaped resonators made out of fiberglass. The third design came during the 1980s based on a design from Mozambique. This version was more lightweight and lower to the ground with aluminum resonators with buzzers. Figure 3.8 shows a style of marimba that has become popular with music educators throughout the U.S. Some of the models have legs that fold underneath, and the wheels allow for easy storage, as space is often at a premium in school classrooms and rehearsal spaces. Episode 3.4 involves students in playing marimbas in an ensemble that features Zimbabwean music.

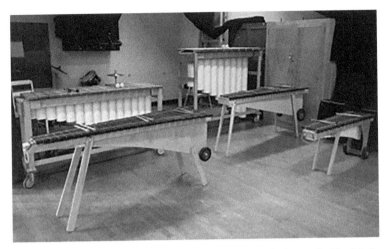

Figure 3.8   U.S.-made marimbas inspired by Zimbabwean design crafted by Mark Burdon

Photo courtesy of Karen Howard

Episode 3.4: Zimarimba—Marimba Music of Zimbabwe (Learning Pathway #1)

Specific Use: World Percussion Ensemble

Materials:

- "Nyoka Musango (Snake in the Grass)," Lora Chiorah Dye, Smithsonian Folkways Recordings
  Marimbas, vocals, hosho, claps

Procedure:

(Engaged)

1 Play track to determine what is heard (marimbas, vocals, claps, hosho).
2 Figure out where each marimba part enters by playing the beginning of the track repeatedly (e.g., marimba 1: 00.00–00.05, marimba 2: 00.06–00.10, etc.).
3 Play the entrance of each part.
4 Figure out the outline of each part without all of the repeating notes through repeated listening.

(Enactive)

5   Transfer the melody with repeating notes to marimba or xylophones using the recording to check for style and musical accuracy.

6   Discover where and how many repeating notes are present, or present notation of one part at a time.

7   Listen to the recording again to determine how the parts line up in the cycle with each other.

8   Present notation for all four parts when the students seem ready.

9   Play opening (on marimbas or guitars) with all four parts in the same order that they appear in the recording.

The steps in this episode can be spread across several lessons in order to provide sufficient time for practice and discussion.

Nyoka Musango

Thomas Mapfumo

Figure 3.9   Opening of "Nyoka Musango"

Shona music arrangements typically use many musical voices, as many as nine or ten, instead of a more Western standard of four-part harmony. The musical lines weave in and out instead of a layered or stacked fashion as found in Western European music. In a secondary school world percussion class, perhaps working toward three, four, or five parts to start is a practical choice. Depending on the length and frequency of the class, and the abilities of the individual students and class as a whole, more melodic lines can be added as the students seem ready for them. An effective use of time can be to have all students learn all of the parts together, and then switch to try each part. This allows for a thorough understanding of the interlocking nature of the melodic lines and a deeper connection to the piece through playing so many different parts.

Learning Pathway #2: Enactive Listening in Action— Son de Jarocho From Veracruz, Mexico

People from the Veracruz region came to be known as *jarochos*. Written accounts from the 1800s described unique *jarocho* traditions of socializing, music-making, and dress. Son Jarocho was first documented in the 1800s. The *sones* (songs) of Son Jarocho were popular on radio stations popping up throughout Mexico in the 1930s and 1940s. The verses of *sones* (songs) are improvised by the singers. The songs functioned as a historical text. Those who sang, played, or danced banned sones were punished and jailed during this time because the lyrics were considered to be a threat of revolt against the colonial government. A decline in interest turned around as a result of a social movement in the 1970s that celebrated folk traditions such as Son Jarocho. *Jaraneros*, as the members of this movement called themselves, found an audience for their music that led to a full-fledged revival in the 1980s. This revival movement has continued into contemporary times and is

Figure 3.10 Instruments for a fandango from L to R: cajon, jaranas, marimbolo, quijada

Photo courtesy of Scott Macklin

considered to be thriving. The focus of the revival has turned back to the social justice roots of the genre through the messages and stories told in the lyrics. The music is created, performed, and celebrated in Veracruz and Chicano populations in large cities in North America at community parties with music and dance known as *fandangos*.

During slavery, hand drums were taken away from people of African heritage. In Veracruz, all rhythms once played by hand were transferred to the *tarima*, a rectangular wooden platform that doubles as both a stage for dancing and a percussion instrument during a *Son Jarocho fandango*. Son Jarocho dancers wear hard-soled shoes in order to make percussive sounds on the *tarima* when they dance. The legs and feet replaced the percussive movement of the hands, and the *tarima* became a percussion instrument. This led to the *zapateado* (percussive dance) of the son jarocho. Son jarocho playing and dancing is explored in Episode 3.5.

Episode 3.5: The Real History of La Bamba

Specific Use: Guitar Class

Materials:

- "La Bamba," José Gutiérrez and Los Hermanos Ochoa, Smithsonian Folkways Recordings
- "La Bamba," Son de Madera, Smithsonian Folkways Recordings

Procedure:

(Attentive)

1   Listen to identify the instruments.
2   Play track (00:00–00:45).

(Engaged)

3   Through multiple listenings, compare and contrast the Gutíerrez and Ochoa Brothers recording with the Son de Madera version.
4   Listen again to check the list of similarities and differences.

(Enactive)

5   Listen to the Gutíerrez and Ochoa recording to discover the rhythm of the guitar strum pattern.
6   Play track (00:00–00:24).

7 Play guitar or ukulele chords (I, V) with the discovered rhythm pattern along with these two traditional versions.

8 Figure out a rhythm to strum or use a composite of the audible strum rhythms such as:

(Attentive) Listen to the well-known Richie Valens version and explore what elements of the traditional son jarocho sound and style were kept intact and what elements were changed by Valens (a native of Veracruz).

The lesson suggestions included in this Episode up to this point are meant as preparatory strategies to move into Learning Pathways #2, "Siquisirí," to allow deeper Enactive Listening and participatory musicking.

Materials:

- "Siquisiri," (2009), Son de Madera, *Son de Mi Tierra*, Smithsonian Folkways Recordings. (Learning Pathway #2)

Procedure:

(Enactive)

1 Listen to the recording to identify the rhythm of the strum pattern. This rhythm is referred to as *sesquialtera*, meaning a ratio of 3:2.

2 Play track.
3 Using guitars or ukuleles, practice playing the chords (A major, D major) using the *sesquialtera* rhythm.
4 Play along with the recording.

Secondary students in guitar class are likely coming from a wide range of playing experience from novice to advanced, with the possibility of students who are far more skilled than the music teacher. These students are valuable resources for teachers. If it is not possible to offer a beginner and advanced level guitar class, then the music teacher must create differentiated learning experiences that meet the individual students wherever their skill sets land. One student might be challenged to play the sesquialtera rhythm with two basic chords, whereas another student might be able to catch the main melody by ear and start to pick it out. Yet another student might have the skill set to improvise a sophisticated melody, or create a new rhythmic variation for the strumming. During Enactive Listening, the students are often playing with a recording. This can allow space for beginner and advanced players to participate together while playing at their own levels, some working on the strumming pattern, others picking the main melody out by ear. Students in guitar class are often singer-songwriters and may welcome the opportunity to add some of the original verses from Son de Madera, or even use their creative writing skills to create their own *decimas* (10-line verses).

Learning Pathway #3: Enactive Listening in Action— Roma Wedding Music

The first recording in Episode 3.6 is by the previously referenced Esma Redzepova. It has a traditional sound, including accordion and virtuosic playing on the clarinet. The second suggested recording from the Roma cultural diaspora is the previously featured example of Bulgarian Roma wedding music by Yuri Yunakov and his ensemble. Yunakov is part of New York City's East European communities. Since the 1960s, many Balkan Roma have immigrated to New York City. This particular style of wedding music has come to refer to a Balkan popular music, characterized by rapid playing filled with virtuosic improvisations. With roots in traditional Balkan village music, this genre also shows influences of Turkish, Indian, and American popular music styles. Despite the Bulgarian government's efforts to restrict wedding music, including discriminatory laws that are aimed at Roma musicians, the genre continues to grow in popularity. Episode 3.6 further explores Learning Pathway #3 featuring a Čoček by Bulgarian Roma musicians from the Yuri Yunakov Ensemble for use in Advanced Placement Music Theory.

Episode 3.6: Roma Wedding Music (Learning Pathway #3)

Specific Use: Advanced Placement Music Theory

Materials:

Two different versions of a dance known as "Čoček" are suggested:

- "Gypsy Dance," Esma Redzepova, Smithsonian Folkways Recordings "Gypsy Dance" features the self-proclaimed Queen of the Gypsies, Esma Redzepova from Macedonia.

- "Cocek Manhattan," Yuri Yunakov Ensemble, Smithsonian Folkways Records
  Yuri Yunakov is a Turkish-Bulgarian Roma and puts a contemporary spin
  on his version of a Čoček.

Procedure:

(Engaged)

1   After working through the steps of Attentive Listening with both selections,
    compare and contrast the orchestration and general feeling of the groove.
2   Play track.
3   Have students tap the underlying rhythm (2+2+2+3) while listening.
4   Play track.

(Enactive)

5   Play track again. The teacher models the basic dance step while listening.
6   Teach a basic version of the dance. Add a variation once the students have
    mastered the steps. (See Čoček Dance Steps)
7   Use both suggested recordings of different čočeks for dancing using the
    same steps.
8   Transcribe a Čoček melody to play on instruments or have the students
    learn to play a section of the melody by ear.

Čoček (Choh-chek) describes a family of Roma dances from the Southern Balkans.
It is a prominent musical feature of Romani brass bands. Čoček's origins are from
Ottoman military bands. The dance has been handed down through generations mostly
by Roma at village weddings and celebrations. Čočeks are typically in 9/8 (2+2+2+3),
although Roma have broadened the form to include variations in 4/4 and 7/8. The
following choreography works with any recorded or live Čoček in 9/8. Other dance
variations can be found for čočeks with a meter in 4 or 7 if there is a desire to
explore the musical and dance genre further.

Čoček Dance Steps

Formation: Open circle, hands held (or not) down low

Meter: 9/8

Introduction: Let an even number of phrases pass, or until vocals enter.

The rhythmic phrase is 2+2+2+3. In folk dance terms, this phrase can be
referred to as "quick quick quick slow." Beats 1, 2, and 3 subdivide into groups
of "2" while beat 4 subdivides into a group of "3":

Measure	Beats	Steps
1	1	Lift Right foot
	2	Step straight back on Right
	3	Lift Left foot
	4	Step straight back on Left
2	1	Lift Right foot
	2	Step back with the Right
	3 & 4	Step twice in place with the Left and Right, changing the weight
3	1	Lift Left foot
	2	Step across in front with the Left—turning to face Right of center
	3	Step forward with the Right foot
	4	Step forward with the Left foot, turning to face the center to start the sequence again.

Styling tip: lifting of the foot is subtle. Imagine a puppet string lifting your knee to raise your foot. As the foot is lifted, bring the standing heel off the ground and then lower it again to touch the ground on the beat.

Including dance in a theory class is an innovative approach to helping students to embody musical concepts such as 9/8 meter, especially when it is not subdivided into three equal beats, or a dance phrase that does not always match with the musical phrase. Students may develop an understanding of the rhythmic groove of a čoček in a way that is not accessible solely through notation, or aural work, or even a combination of notation and learning by ear. If a music theory teacher does not feel comfortable or confident in teaching a basic set of dance steps, it is only a click away online to view video tutorials. The students can be of great help to a music teacher by viewing videos together to see how the footwork matches with the rhythms. If there is a local folk dance organization that includes traditions from a given area, in this case Bulgaria, one of the instructors could be invited to come work with the theory class students. There is much to be gained from the embodiment aural concepts from selected music.

From Deep Listening to Thoughtful Performance

Three dimensions of WMP have now been introduced and explored: Attentive Listening (Chapter 2), Engaged Listening, and Enactive Listening. They are linked, one developing on the heels of the one before it. Over days, weeks, and even months of study and experience, secondary school music students can grow into an understanding of diverse music cultures through this aural process by which they continuously use their ears in sorting through the components of the music, in order to be able to participate in it, and to learn to perform it. With each ensuing level of listening, they become more familiar with the recorded music, more confident to try out a part of the music as they join in with the recording, and readied to learn the music as much of the world's music is learned, by listening. They are musicking, growing more deeply involved in the music through active engagement such as singing, playing instruments, moving, and dancing. By supporting their secondary school music students in thoughtful encounters, music teachers can develop the musicianship of their students. As the music is learned, so too can students learn something of music's role and function in the origin culture, and develop cultural empathy, a respect for the musicians and those others in the culture who embrace the music.

When the sonic personality of a music culture is unfamiliar to students, notation alone will not suffice in bringing them to an understanding of the music. Students can develop their ear for music of many cultures, and they can do so through the teacher's invitation to an ever-greater involvement, a progressive development of immersion within the music to the point of "becoming the music," claiming it, learning it to the point of making it with the recording and eventually without the need for the recording. These experiences within WMP must be mindfully planned and clearly articulated, and teachers require their own careful listening, experience, and study prior to bringing into the music and music learning process. Such preparation is time intensive, but the results are notable. Students will develop a broader understanding of musical particularities, diversify their own aural acuity, hone their musical literacy and performance skills, and deepen their awareness of people, musics, and cultures in the world.

The illustrations are meant to exemplify the dimensions of WMP, but there is no single catalog of music to which the pedagogy is fixed. Teachers can come to know their own musical strengths and preferences, as well as what is best for their students. They can select a music culture that suits the place and time, their students' interests, the expertise of local musicians, and their own interest and expertise. Several advisories further are useful to the teacher: to try out the illustrations; to transfer the procedures to other musical selections; to listen repeatedly, analytically, thoughtfully; to seek out ethnomusicological interpretations as to what inspires the particular musical traditions, what contemporary sounds and styles are present within the musical culture, whether hybrid musical forms exist. Teachers can break from their notation base to aurally learned music as readily as they can shift from a school standard piece to music that is unfamiliar but that is deserving of a place in the curriculum. New music and innovative pedagogical twists and turns are ready for testing out and can be evaluated for their impact, discussed with colleagues or students, and modified or extended.

Notes

1 The official website for Tanec is www.tanec.com.mk.
2 Justin Vernon is the leader of the indie-folk group Bon Iver.

References

Czíkszentmihalyi, M. (1991). *Flow: The psychology of optimal experience*. New York: Harper Perennial.

Rose, T. (2008). *The hip hop wars: What we talk about when we talk about hip hop and why it matters*. New York: Perseus Books.

Silverman, C. (2003). The gender of the profession: Music, dance, and reputation among Balkan Muslim Rom Women. In T. Magrini (Ed.), *Music and gender: Perspectives from the Mediterranean* (pp. 127–144). Chicago: University of Chicago Press.

Small, C. (1998). *Musicking: The meanings of performing and listening.* Middletown, CT: Wesleyan University Press.

Turino, T. (2008). *Music as social life: The politics of participation.* Chicago: The University of Chicago Press.

Turner, E. (2012). *Communitas: The anthropology of collective joy.* New York: Palgrave Macmillan.

Listening Episodes

"Cocek Manhattan," Yuri Yunakov Ensemble, Smithsonian Folkways Recordings. www.folkways.si.edu/yuri-yunakov-ensemble/cocek-manhattan/world/music/track/smithsonian.

"Everyday People," Sly and the Family Stone, Epic Records.

"Gypsy Dance," Esma Redzepova, Smithsonian Folkways Recordings. www.folkways.si.edu/esma-redzepova-and-usnija-jasarova/gypsy-dance-cocek/world/music/track/smithsonian.

"La Bamba," José Gutiérrez & Los Hermanos Ochoa, Smithsonian Folkways Recordings. José Gutiérrez, Felipe Ochoa, and Marcos Ochoa, raised on farms in Veracruz, are considered to be three of the most accomplished modern-day son jarocho performers featuring the traditional regional Vercruz arpa (harp) and guitars called jarana and requinto. www.folkways.si.edu/jose-gutierrez-los-hermanos-ochoa/la-bamba/latin-world/music/track/smithsonian.

"La Bamba," Son de Madera, Smithsonian Folkways Recordings. The members of the group Son de Madera are key figures in the current revival of son jarocho. www.folkways.si.edu/son-de-madera/la-bamba-the-bamba/latin-world/music/track/smithsonian.

"La Bamba," Richie Valens, Classic Records.

"Nyoka Musango" (Snake in the Grass), Lora Chiorah Dye, Smithsonian Folkways Recordings. www.folkways.si.edu/lora-chiroah-dye-and-sukutai/nyoka-musango/world/music/track/smithsonian.

"People Everyday," Arrested Development, Smithsonian Folkways Recordings. Early 1990s hip-hop tune featuring positive messages in the lyrics. www.folkways.si.edu/arrested-development/people-everyday/african-american-spoken-american-history-poetry-prose/track/smithsonian.

"People Everyday" (In the Style of Arrested Development), Sunfly Karaoke Ltd. Available on iTunes.

Rare footage of Romani band in Macedonia, 1968. www.folkways.si.edu/rare-footage-of-romani-band-in-macedonia-1968/music/video/smithsonian.

"Ušti Ušti Baba," Esme Redzepova, Smithsonian Folkways Recordings. A classic čoček by the self-proclaimed Queen of the Gypsies. www.folkways.si.edu/esma-redzepova-and-usnija-jasarova/get-up-father-ustli-ustli-baba/world/music/track/smithsonian.

4

Performing World Music

At a private school in a large urban setting, the music room has a retractable wall that opens up to the auditorium. This set-up reflects the expectation for and celebration of sharing student musical work. The students at this school refer to teachers by their first names. Matt is their music teacher, going on ten years in the school, and an active performer outside of school, and as such is connected with a large number of local musicians. He makes good use of these relationships by inviting his friends into class for meaningful collaborations with his students.

Matt's eighth-grade general music students have been working on small group compositions featuring Latin grooves from the Caribbean, in particular Cuba and Puerto Rico. The students moved with ease through the first three listening stages of World Music Pedagogy—Attentive, Engaged, and Enactive—in previous lessons. They are now well-prepared to move into the phase of Creating World Music influenced by the Cuban and Puerto Rican music they have studied so closely.

Matt uses workstations to guide the students through various tasks that help scaffold the separate elements involved in creating music. There is a station filled with books of poetry, magazine articles, newspapers, and books to inspire lyrics for those writing songs. There is a percussion area with multiple instruments for creating rhythmic grooves. Melodies are dictated by a "roll of the die" to determine which pitches to include, or in what meter to create. Working in groups of three to five students, the compositions arrive at the final stages and are ready for sharing at a monthly assembly that features student work from multiple disciplines. One of the student groups created a four-part piece for three xylophones and guitar. As part of the learning process, Matt invites some of his friends into the class who are professional musicians and comprise a quartet including trumpet, piano, string bass, and congas. This group regularly performs Latin American traditions from the Caribbean, including the very Puerto Rican and Cuban styles the eighth-grade students have been practicing.

Families and the school community are invited to watch the open rehearsals involving the students and the quartet. A final sharing session is planned for the end of the project. The week before the audience gets to hear the compositions, the jazz quartet comprising Matt's friends comes to school for a two-day residency. Each small group gets one hour with the quartet to share their work and to create an arrangement that includes the adult musicians. The students are exhilarated to hear what adding professional players brings to their pieces. Excited conversation is heard between the students and the adults as they discuss, modify, and polish the new versions of their pieces. The final performance for the student body and family members is recorded and available for the community through the school's website.

The previous chapters explored three dimensions of World Music Pedagogy (WMP), each with a focus on the key experience of music as an aural art and of progressive levels of listening, from Attentive, to Engaged, to Enactive. There is a flow from one listening experience to the next, buoyed by the logical manner in which initial listening opens the gate to further listening all the way to participation and performance, and yet one must also acknowledge that even when learning to perform by ear (Enactive), it may be necessary to return to listening in order to participate in a more limited way while listening (Engaged) or to just sit quietly and still with listening with attention to particular components, to overarching frameworks, to the expressive content of a work (Attentive). These phases are not necessarily meant to be sequential, as an educator might move back and forth between the phases depending on the design of the learning and listening experiences.

Yet in music, many roads lead to the all-out performance of music. In secondary school music programs, learning music is typically assessed by the capacity of students to perform the music. School music programs may be open to the public whether in the evenings or on weekends. These concerts feature students singing, playing, moving, or dancing to the music they have learned by ear as well as through notation. Increasingly, there is an expectation from communities and school administrators that the school music program offers diverse musical perspectives, featuring music of the world's cultures. This chapter discusses the nature and extent, method and means for performing world music. Informal and formal performance suggestions are offered, for in-class and all-school programs, for a variety of the world's musical expressions. Secondary school music students enrolled in a grand variety of classes can perform on any number of instruments (or voices, or by way of their dancing bodies) any music from anywhere in the world, growing out of their Attentive-Engaged-Enactive listening experiences.

Performance in Secondary School

Secondary school music students move through the Enactive Listening phase that brings them to the brink of a full performance. What is considered "performance ready" is something more polished and refined. In courses that are outside of the typical performing structure of band, choir, and orchestra, there are numerous options for offering performance opportunities. Part of the appeal of these courses is the very fact that they are not intended to be driven by the high-stakes of public performance. Even so, regular opportunities to prepare music to share with an audience is an important part of the performative art that is music. Secondary music teachers can be creative when planning performance opportunities. If a formal setting is desired, combinations of groups are an option. Including the guitar class students in a spring concert, the Jamaican steel band welcoming the audience with a rousing number on the pans, or featuring a solo singer-songwriter between large ensembles are all fine options for formal performance. These transitions and features are made easier by having a larger group assemble behind the curtain or backstage while a smaller ensemble performs on the apron of the stage in front of the curtain.

There are occasions when having the whole school perform together may be feasible if the facility has a large enough space to fit the entire student body for an all-school music gathering. Another option is a festival-type performance featuring the Zimarimba ensemble playing a traditional tune followed by an arrangement of a contemporary pop song, theory students improvising in the hijaz scale while the dance team performs a Roma čoček, or a coffee-house style open mic that features students from the songwriting class.

Informal Performances

Music classes are typically aimed toward the polished public performance. This is often the highlight of a music program, and certainly the most visible (and audible) product. For some settings, however, a less formal style of performance known as an *informance* has gained in popularity. An informance can emphasize and even celebrate the learning process, with public demonstration of the ways in which the teacher and students interact in the act of learning, rehearsing, and growing more musical. An informance can take place in a variety of settings, from the music classroom, to the cafeteria, a hallway, a gym, a playground, or a genuine performing arts theatre. This less formal approach to performance provides opportunities to focus on learning experiences that do not necessarily translate easily to a traditional school performance context, such as composing or theoretical analysis.

There is no limit to the form an informance might take. It could involve collaboration with other music classes or interdisciplinary projects, or could invite members of the community into a participatory venture. It is possible for an informance to be streamed live on social media platforms, thus allowing for invited people to comment in the moment even if they live too far to attend in person. Another option is to treat an informance as a preliminary performance that can be followed up by a formal performance at a later date.

An informance can function as a tool of advocacy for the school and community. The process of arranging an informance gives students, administrators, and families an opportunity to connect with the richness of world music cultures being taught and learned in the classroom settings. These presentations can deliver information about the music culture, including sociohistorical and sociocultural context, compositional devices, and other salient musical features. The students can explain to the audience technical, musical, and culturally specific challenges that they encountered in learning the music. Students in the class might prepare a multimedia presentation, or share what would be considered not-yet-concert-ready world music traditions. The informance can be part of a formal concert or stand on its own.

Through an informance, audience members and participants can understand the various steps involved in the learning process and just how student decision-making is important to the music-making experience. Advance invitations can go to students in other classes, their teachers, school administrators, parents and families, culture-bearers, and community members. Students can be involved in determining the repertoire and order, creating performance notes, and crafting opportunities for audience participation.

Collaborations With Culture-Bearers

While one school features local artist-musicians of popular, jazz, and rock genres, other schools design (and budget for) residencies with culture-bearers that take performance even further toward cultural understanding. A culture-bearer is a person who identifies with his or her birth culture and has the interest and ability to transmit and share traditions and practices of that culture. The culture-bearer embodies cultural values and practices. Teachers who work with culture-bearers in music expend their own energy and expertise to prepare their students for insider perspectives on music to sing, play, and dance, and up-front-and-personal experiences with larger cultural topics. Culture-bearers are likely to model teaching and learning styles that are commonly found in their respective communities, which adds a depth of cultural understanding that could not be known through a more superficial integration of a music culture.

Ideally, culture-bearers who come to school for collaborative experiences should be expert in specific musical traditions and capable of performing for and teaching music to students. Being of a culture does not equal being equipped to successfully teach and transmit cultural knowledge. If a student has a relative from a culture, it does not automatically equal that person having the ability to share music or teach effectively. Even professional musicians might not have the necessary pedagogical skills to captivate a class of secondary school students. Culture-bearers are typically coming from far outside classroom culture and might have the right intention but not necessarily have the necessary experience and know-how to construct meaningful music-making with students. Preliminary planning sessions between a music teacher and culture-bearer are vital to creating meaningful learning experiences. These sessions can include suggestions for repertoire that the students can learn prior to the culture-bearer's arrival. In the planning stages, the music teacher should share with the culture-bearer what the students know and are able to do. The culture-bearer may share possible material that can allow for a collaborative brainstorming event to best plan the limited time together, whether it is one hour, one week, or even a longer residency.

When working with culture-bearers, a consideration is to plan for a variety of performative experiences ranging from long-held cultural traditions to more contemporary musical expressions in the given music culture. This is meant to avoid freezing a culture in an older and historic time, and to demonstrate that some music traditions—anywhere in the world—can change, while others may stay constant. This approach explores a culture from multiple vantage points. By presenting a broad range of music from a culture, a fuller representation of the people and culture emerges as opposed to stereotypical representations of people and their musical practices.

Culture-bearers can also participate in performances from those in the classroom to school-wide or larger community events. A steel-pan culture-bearer raised in Trinidad working with a secondary steel band can be featured on a solo break during a piece, or introduce the different pieces to provide cultural context, or stay after for a public question-and-answer forum. A master drummer from Ghana can take the spotlight as the lead player with the percussion ensemble performing a recreational social dance. A flamenco guitar player can play a featured piece during a guitar class performance in the school or at a local community event. A clarinetist from Bulgaria can be invited in to improvise a solo during an in-class performance by the piano class students. In the spirit of moving forward from entrenched performance practices, the remainder of this chapter follows the three Learning Pathways through to performance (Zimbabwean marimba, Mexican son jarocho, and Roma wedding music), as well as suggested programs from Ghana, Indonesia, Puerto Rico, Tahiti, and Brazil.

Performing Zimarimba in Global Percussion: Learning Pathway #1

An example of a secondary school music option that combines new and old practices is in the following vignette about an intensive study unit on Zimbabwean music with its culmination in a marimba ensemble performance. Such a curricular experience could well be developed as a semester-long course of its own in a secondary school, or as a six-week or two-month unit within a course in world music, or music history, or even a break away from the routine studies in a guitar, piano, or world music drumming course.

Pinehurst High School has an active Parent-Teacher Organization that raises funds each year to support programs in the school that are no longer funded by the school district budget. The music program includes general music class, half of the instrumental music program, a visual arts artist-in-residence, half of the library program, and reading tutors. As Pinehurst is in an area of the U.S. that has a 40-year history of Zimbabwean musicians teaching marimba and mbira music, it was the desire of the Pinehurst music staff and Parent-Teacher Organization to start a Zimarimba (Zimbabwean marimba) Ensemble at the school.

Funds were raised over a two-year period to commission a full set of Zimbabwean-style marimbas by a local instrument maker. It took close to 10 months for the builder to complete the marimba set for Pinehurst. The students, staff, and school community were excited for the arrival of the instruments. To celebrate the inauguration of the marimba program, a local Zimarimba group performed for the school and family community, providing a rollicking event that had everyone on their feet dancing joyously to the music. This new addition to the secondary school set a tone for change within the music department by changing the long-standing paradigm of a curricula focused on Western art music practices and large ensemble performance.

Whether featured prominently, such as in the Pinehurst High School Zimarimba Ensemble, or in a smaller fashion within lessons or a focused unit, the rich musical traditions of the Shona people of Zimbabwe bring much to a secondary school music class. Marimba and *mbira* (thumb piano) (Figure 4.1) music from Zimbabwe has spread in popularity in the U.S., the UK, and other European countries, with Zimbabwean Music Festivals (Zimfests) growing in number. Many groups have been created that perform and celebrate Zimbabwean music traditions. Zimbabwean musician Dumisani Maraire is credited with bringing these traditions to the U.S. during a residency at the University of Washington in 1968.

Mbiras are common in a wide spread of music cultures, and the name changes depending on the geographic region, including *ilimba*, *kalimba*, *matepe*, and *sansu*. Known as mbira in Zimbabwe, they have a long history documented back to the 16th century, unlike the recent addition of marimbas in the 1960s. Mbira music is a tradition of the Shona people. The traditional music conservatory known as *Kwanongoma* specialized in the performance study of the mbira. The main function of playing

Figure 4.1   "Mbira Nhare" or "Mbira Dzavadzimu" made by Jacob Mafuleni

Photo courtesy of Jocelyn Moon

the mbira is to connect to spirituality, to give thanks, and to celebrate life. The mbira is played as part of a personal meditation practice, religious rites, and recreation. It is not uncommon to see Zimbabwean youths playing mbira as they walk alone or with friends while repeating simple melodic phrases over and over. Mbira melodies are either transcriptions of songs normally heard in other contexts, songs specially created for the mbira, or individual compositions of the performer.

Marimba and mbira lessons in a global percussion class can stimulate student interest in Zimbabwean and other African cultures at large, and may lead to an energized and entertaining informance or performance for players and audience alike. "Nyoka Musango" is featured as one of the Learning Pathways throughout the chapters. The suggested mbira melodies can be learned aurally and played in short phrases. The mbira melodies could also be transferred to the marimbas. Secondary students can put together two or three marimba pieces, feature a small group of students playing each of the three mbira melodies, and then finish the performance with a rousing reprise of "Nyoka Musango."

Suggested Resources for Performing Zimarimba Music

*   "Nyoka Musango," Lora Chiorah Dye and Sukutai, Smithsonian Folkways Recordings (Learning Pathway #1). Marimba, hosho, call-and-response vocals.
*   "Zimbabwe Mbira—Three Melodies Played on a 14-note kalimba," Ethnic Folkways Library & Folkways Records and Service Corp.

- This 1990 documentary explores mbira traditions, its connection to the Chimurenga revolutionary struggle, and Zimbabwe's transition to independence. With extensive footage from the era, featured are interviews and performances by Thomas Mapfumo and Oliver Mtukudzi.

  https://youtu.be/5hF2Hstvrfc?list=PLyMF9s8PivLWucTmVS9hmc8jtTD-pvQir

Performing Son Jarocho in Guitar Class: Learning Pathway #2

In recent decades, guitar class has become a common curricular option in secondary school music programs. Guitar studies grew in popularity, even as guitars rose to prominence in popular music and for singing songs at informal gatherings, and appealed to students who were uninterested in the more traditional offerings of band, orchestra, and choir. For students without previous musical experience in large school ensembles, guitar studies found a welcome learning environment.

The structure of a guitar class is typically informed by the experiences of the music educator, who may have fundamental knowledge of guitar from playing at camp, in church, in a garage band, or through a single university course. Yet another music teacher may have no guitar experience so that, asked to add a guitar class to the course options, may find himself just a few steps ahead of their students in learning the instrument. Guitar class activity may involve the students playing simple chord progressions and strumming patterns for accompanying folk and popular songs, or on the other hand may involve students reading notes so to play multi-part classical and contemporary art music. Some guitar classes are modeled after pop bands that focus on chords, strums, simple motifs, and brief improvisations on just two or three pitches. Guitar courses typically cover a combination of topics that include history of the guitar, sonic exploration of pitches, positions and uses of the hands and fingers, rhythmic potentials for strumming, a repertoire of folk, popular, and possibly art music pieces, theoretical concepts such as keys, scales, cadences, and various techniques such as the performance of bass tones and pinch chords.

For guitar students, the string-centric genre of son jarocho is a perfect inroad to a particular music culture. For Chicanos (Mexican-Americans) and Veracruzanos (from the Veracruz region of Mexico), the son jarocho musical gathering known as a *fandango* is an example of a renewal and celebration of cultural heritage meant to honor and remember rural traditions in a broad reference to Mexican nationalism. A fandango is intended to build a sense of community and belonging. Strongly interwoven into contemporary fandangos is the struggle for dignity, respect, justice, and civil rights. Fandangos frequently occur at centers, projects, and events relevant to social justice, such as at El Centro de la Raza in Seattle, a community center that advocates for empowerment of the Latino community through a commitment to civil rights activism. The community musical expression of fandangos is consistent with its origins in being the voice for marginalized *jarochos* (people from Veracruz). The genre of son jarocho is deeply rooted in tradition while embracing innovation to remain relevant with new generations.

Son de Madera's version of "Siquisirí," explored in Chapters 2 and 3, is one of the three musical selections following all through the five dimensions of WMP to produce a complete WMP Learning Pathway. Certainly, the song could stand on its own for an in-class performance. If the intention is to infuse "Siquisirí" into a guitar class informance or performance, teachers can plan events within class that incorporate elements of a fandango. As the chords and strums are learned, students can be invited to learn to sing one or more son jarocho songs (in Spanish, of course) and to step rhythms—each of which is essential to the musical practice. Students may expend efforts together to build a *tarima* (Figure 4.3) (a small wooden platform, raised about four inches from the floor) for stamping out percussive rhythms with hard-soled shoes to accompany the guitar-playing and singing components. They can learn a basic son jarocho stepping pattern in the standard rhythm known as *café con pan* (coffee with bread) that features the rhythm (Figure 4.4) as a continuing ostinato. Guitar class students can alternate between playing guitar, singing the songs, and dancing the rhythms. A more advanced example of Son Jarocho footwork on the tarima is featured on video, as noted in the following section containing suggested resources. To top off the performance, a culture-bearer from a local Mexican son jarocho community may visit to play, sing, dance, and even introduce another standard instrument of the genre, a small stringed instrument known as *jarana* (Figure 4.2). This plucked lute can be acquired to enhance the performance of son jarocho music, although acoustic guitars or ukuleles make reasonable substitutes.

Figure 4.2   Various sizes of *jaranas*

Photos courtesy of Scott Macklin

Suggested Resources for Performing Son Jarocho

The following list includes teaching videos, recordings, and a basic footwork pattern that might be incorporated into a guitar class fandango to facilitate a son jarocho experience:

- "Siquisirí," Son de Madera, Smithsonian Folkways Recordings (Learning Pathway #2). Vocals, jaranas, guitar.

Figure 4.3   Rhythmic footwork on the tarima

Photos courtesy of Scott Macklin

Figure 4.4   *Tarima* footwork rhythm

- Son de Madera at the Smithsonian Folklife Festival. This video clip shows a performance from 2009 and clearly features the footwork on the tarima.
- Son de Madera performs Son Jarocho. This short video shows the songwriting process for creating lyrics in son jarocho selections.

While this performance was suggested for guitar classes, the ideas could certainly transfer to a piano or keyboard class, as these are offered in many secondary schools. In a typical setting, there may be a small number of student keyboards, due to limited classroom space, but with keyboards of four or five octaves that can accommodate two students per instrument. These keyboards may have a divider that allows each student two or three octaves, and outlets for plugging individual student headphones so that work can be done in silence and without interruption. Students can practice, compose and improvise, and figure out music theory exercises, and can submit recordings to the teacher of their work in class by pressing the "enter" button. An icon for the recording then appears on the music teacher's screen, and she can click, listen, and speak into a microphone to send individual feedback to the student. At times, students may be asked to remove their headphones and play through speakers, thus allowing them to all practice together or to play in parts as an ensemble. The lessons are crafted using music notation and learning to play by ear. Rather than strumming the chords on guitars, the piano class students can learn the chords on the keyboards, sing the verses, improvise short melodic phrases, and join in on the tarima with percussive footwork. There is no limit to the performance possibilities for son jarocho in secondary music classes.

Performing Roma Wedding Music in Theory Class

Bringing in music of the world's cultures belongs in all settings, including a theory class. Secondary students can learn of the composer (if known), the people who are of the culture, cultural context, historical meaning, and even try other instruments within the theory class setting. The following vignette describes an informance taking place in theory class.

In-class Informance

As the theory students have been working on the hijaz scale as it appears in Macedonian and Bulgarian Roma music, the time approaches to invite an audience into the class. The music teacher decides to invite the guitar ensemble to visit because they have class at the same time with a different member of the music department faculty. The theory students sit at keyboards to perform the main melody of Čoček Manhattan (Figure 4.5) *in unison, followed by each student taking a turn playing a* taksim *(improvisation) for eight bars using the hijaz scale as a guide. After every four students play their taksims, the group plays the main melody again.*

After the piece is over, each theory student moves over to receive one of the guitar ensemble students. The theory students teach the basics of the Čoček rhythm (9/8) and then the basics of the hijaz scale. It is a noisy and collaborative scene full of much teaching and learning. The guitar students take their leave and return to their classroom, where they spend the rest of the period working on the hijaz scale.

Secondary students in music theory class may reap the benefits of multimodal learning when they engage kinesthetically through dance and playing an instrument, and when they engage aurally and orally through improvisation and song-making. Combining theory students with other secondary music classes provides opportunities for meaningful teaching, learning, and performance experiences involving world music cultures.

Suggested Resources for Performing Roma Music

- "Čoček Manhattan", Yuri Yunakov Ensemble, Smithsonian Folkways Recordings (Learning Pathway #3). Saxophone, clarinet, keyboard, bass, drum set.

Figure 4.5 Opening melody in "Čoček Manhattan"

- Master of Traditional Arts—an ongoing interdisciplinary project produced by Documentary Arts. It focuses on the recipients of the National Heritage Fellowship, which is awarded annually by the recipients of the National Endowment of the Arts in the U.S. This website features selected traditional musicians in each state in the U.S. There is a full feature on Yuri Yunakov, including several high-energy performance videos. The performance venues include weddings, music festivals, and television shows. Retrieved from www.mastersoftraditionalarts.org/artists/367

Performing Ghanaian Recreational Music in Global Percussion

Global or World Percussion classes have grown in popularity, along with easier access to the instruments needed to create these international grooves. The following vignette explores a middle school global percussion class as they work with a recreational piece from Ghana, West Africa.

The students in Ms. Haywood's middle school global percussion class are in the last stretch of a three-month study of a recreational piece from Ghana known as "Kpanlogo." As is typical with this style of music from the Ga ethnic group in Ghana, it contains multilayered drum rhythms, bell patterns, shakers, dancers, and singing, all led by a master drummer "calling" out signals on a main drum or set of drums.

Ms. Haywood worked the parts in one at a time, adding to the mix each class session. She has enough instruments that each student always has something to play. Each student learns all of the parts so that they can move with ease between the instruments as they hear the interlocking of the rhythms. The students have also worked on a selected few of the myriad choices for kpanlogo moves, and they are deciding on an order for the steps that they like.

Although it is titled a "world drumming class," it is well-known at Ms. Haywood's school that singing is included in the class, just as it is found in the music cultures under examination. Dance, drum, and song are not considered separate concepts in many parts of the world, so Ms. Haywood brings this concept into her class as often as possible.

Ghana, West Africa: A Favorite of Drummers

Looking more deeply into traditional Ghanaian music practices, it is necessary to contextualize its place within the greater community. Ghana was the first colonized sub-Saharan African nation to gain independence from Britain in 1957. Ghana's music remains integral to the everyday lives of Ghanaians. Intensely rhythmic and suffused with layers of meaning, music in Ghana marks cycles of life, religious rituals, and teaches social values. Music from southeast Ghana, particularly from the Ewe and Ga ethnic groups, have fascinated ethnomusicologists, percussionists, and dancers from around the world for decades.

KPANLOGO: RECREATIONAL MUSIC FROM THE GA PEOPLE

Kpanlogo is a recreational dance and music form originating in the 1960s among urban youth in the Ghanaian capital city of Accra. It originated among the Ga ethnic group, most of whom live near Accra in the Bukom area, but is now popular throughout the country. Otoo Lincoln is credited as the creator of the underlying rhythm known as "Kpanlogo." A youthful recreation originally scorned by community elders, Kpanlogo became an expression of youthful identity and protest. Because of the exaggerated hip movements that the kpanlogo dance borrowed from popular musicians of the time like Elvis Presley and Chubby Checker, the older generation and executives of the National Arts Council initially opposed this new traditional genre, claiming that it was too sexually suggestive. This led to instances of dancers being beaten by the police, drums taken away, and even musicians spending a few days in jail. This intergenerational dispute was resolved in 1965 when President Kwame Nkrumah's government organized a display of 50 such youth music groups, and the Kpanlogo drumming and accompanying dance was officially endorsed.

Kpanlogo remains an important part of urban culture in Ghana, and it is performed at both informal and formal events throughout the year. Kpanlogo also draws influence from the highly popular genre known as Highlife, which is a combination of European instrumentation and dance steps with traditional Ghanaian rhythms, and was initially performed exclusively for the wealthy and elite colonial rulers during the British occupation of Ghana. Both of these styles of music are not specifically for ceremonies, events, or communication, but are treated more like pop music in other parts of the world in that it is good for getting together with friends, singing, dancing, and general merriment.

MUSIC AND DANCE CHARACTERISTICS OF KPANLOGO

Kpanlogo music is drawn from older Ga traditions. Three types of instruments are used: (1) kpanlogo drums, (2) *axatse* (gourd shakers), and (3) *gankogui, atokee,* and *firikiwa* (bells) (Figure 4.6). It is common to have three kpanlogo drums in an ensemble serving the roles of supporting drums and master drum. The main bell part (Figure 4.8) is one of the most common and oldest rhythm patterns found in sub-Saharan Africa. It is the very same as the *son* clave pattern heard in Cuban music and salsa.

Some dance moves of Kpanlogo represent the pulling in of fishing nets, a traditional occupation of the Ga people who live near water. Some Kpanlogo

Figure 4.6   Kpanlogo drums, axatses, firikiwa (L) and atokee (R), and gankogui

Photo courtesy of Karen Howard

movements are considered quite flirtatious, which may have contributed to its popularity among Ghanaian youth. It was common for youth to set up councils in their respective neighborhoods and create their own dance forms with new creative drum rhythms and songs. Sometimes older generations joined in and adopted the new moves.

Kpanlogo drums are similar to other Ghanaian drums in that a wooden shell is covered by an animal skin that is held taut with wooden pegs driven into the shell. The Kpanlogo shape is similar to the well-known conga drum. The main drumming rhythm that supports Kpanlogo is also called Kpanlogo, and this is one of the most common rhythms heard throughout Ghana. This rhythm was adapted from traditional rhythms that are frequently performed by Ga musicians, despite originating in other African regions. Kpanlogo rhythms form the basis of many different popular songs that are widely known throughout Ghana. The songs are most often call-and-response in nature and are considered to be an expression of Ghanaian national identity and a source of cultural pride.

A master drummer will perform on up to six Kpanlogo drums at a time with each tuned to slightly different pitches to give the rhythms a melodic effect. Included in the rhythmic texture are the claps of dancers and singers who are not playing instruments. These claps always fall on beats one and four of the rhythmic cycle. Another layer is comprised of two or three interlocking drum parts. Other important layers include the axatse filling out the sound with continuous shaking, with a final layer that includes the group vocals. The master drummer can initiate call-and-response phrases between the lead and supporting drums by playing specific musical cues to the ensemble.

Learning Kpanlogo can happen in multiple iterations of secondary school music. Sharing during performance can happen by inviting another class in, presenting as part of a school assembly, opening a school meeting, entertainment at half-time of a sporting event, a parent-teacher organization meeting, or at the school district administration meetings. The performance can be filmed and shared on the school's blog, or the class can go on a tour and teach the dance to local elementary school children. The performance possibilities are endless. The following includes suggested recordings for Kpanlogo, a Kpanlogo song transcription (Figure 4.7), and basic rhythms (Figure 4.8).

Suggested Resources for Kpanlogo Performance

- "Kpanlogo," Kofi Quarshie, Acewonder Ltd. (Available on iTunes). See Figure 4.7 for a transcription of one of the kpanlogo tunes included on this recording.
- "Kpanlogo," Nyanyo Addo, Weltwunder (Available on iTunes). Drums, gankogui, axatse, vocals.
- "Kpanlogo," Smithsonian Folkways Recordings. Drums, gankogui, axatse, vocals.

Students in global percussion might focus on one region of the world, such as West Africa. There is a vast array of material to partake in, to play, to perform, and to teach in this one geographic area. Other global percussion curricular designs may include multiple percussion traditions from a range of world music cultures. Students

Dzen a Myeh

1st time - top line only

Dzen - a - myeh ____ a - ta dzen - a - myeh ____ a - wo

dzen - a - myoh ____ e - sha ma - ma ko - me - to, (A - wo)*

The lyrics are in Ga, a dialect from the capitol region of Ghana.

Awo,   dzen a myeh. Ata,   dzen a myeh.
Ah-woh, jen-ah-myeh, Ah-tah   jen-ah-myeh

Ata,   dzen a myoh esha mama kometo.
Ah-tah jen-ah-myoh ehsha mama koh-meh-toh.

Translation:
Mother, night is coming.
Father, night is coming.
I have only one cloth.

*This "Awo" is called by a soloist in order to get the song to repeat again.
When the song is over, this call should not be repeated.

Figure 4.7   Transcription of a variation of "Dzen a Myeh" heard on Kofi Quarshie's version of Kpanlogo

Figure 4.8   Basic kpanlogo rhythms: (1) gankogui, (2) axatse, (3) first drum, (4) second drum. p="pa" on knee; t="ti" up in to hand; o=open; s=slap; b=bass; m=mute.

can explore commonalities and differences across the traditions to enhance their understanding of the music traditions brought forth. Ghanaian percussion traditions usually feature a master drummer who holds the ensemble together with virtuosic improvisation and specific musical cues or "calls." This is a perfect opportunity to feature a culture-bearer who has worked with the music teacher beforehand to plan the lessons, to practice with the students to help prepare them for performance, and to perform with the students in a full performance.

Continuing a Paradigm Shift for Secondary School Performance

Teachers of a world music class in secondary school might find a textbook to guide the course, or follow an independent path that allows them to teach to their strengths or the cultures represented in the particular school population. The phases of WMP encourage teachers to design teaching and learning experiences that allow a full spectrum of experience, from introductory attentive listening to partial performance engagement, to the thorough-going learning of a recording piece by ear so that it can be readied for performance. There is more, too, as listening leads also to composition and improvisation of music in the style of the recorded piece (see Chapter 5), and a study of the music for its cultural function and meaning is supported by the integration of understandings from other subjects and disciplines (see Chapter 6). A world music class in a middle school or senior high school is a most suitable location for any and all experiences in a grand variety of cultures and practices, and can far surpass a survey course wherein students read about a music culture and passively listen to sound clips.

Contemporary versions of the world music class can involve hands-on experiences with traditional instruments ranging from penny whistles to drums such as djembes, in-person or online collaborations with culture-bearers who live locally or across the globe, and explorations of ensembles such as steel band (of Trinidad and the greater Caribbean), Brazilian samba, and Indonesian gamelan. These ensembles may be available and active in the school or present and available in the local community for field visits by students. Consider the Indonesian gamelan, for example, and a master musician such as Joko Sutrisno, and the possibility of secondary school music students learning dynamic music from Bali known as "Kecak."

Indonesian Gamelan

Music is part of everyday life in Indonesia. The largest and most important musical ensembles are the gamelans of Java and Bali, which include from seven to seventy-five instruments. All gamelan traditions, even in Islamic communities of Indonesia, reflect a worldview rooted in Hindu-Buddhism, and gamelan is deeply connected with rituals. In fact, gamelan instruments, considered to be charged with charismatic power, are so important to the success of rituals that special rituals are done for the ensembles themselves.

Gamelan ensembles have become popular outside of Indonesia, typically representing the music of Bali or Java. Usually the instructor is a culture-bearer from Java or Bali, or is a student of a culture-bearer, and that determines whether the group performs Javanese or Balinese music. A gamelan ensemble consists of xylophones with metal bars, gongs of several sizes, drums, bamboo flutes, and singing. Melodies are played on metal xylophones while changes in form and tempo are guided by drummers. Gamelan music consists of layers of related melodies that coincide at specific phrase points punctuated by the sound of the huge gongs. Gamelan instruments are made in pairs, with drums and gongs designated male or female. In each pair of instruments, one is tuned slightly higher than the other and is associated with male, while the lower is associated with female. The three stages of life—childhood, adulthood, and elderhood—are mirrored in gamelan by the three sizes of melody instruments. The structure of the gamelan music is a cyclical mandala, a symbol that represents the universe, with musical phrases beginning and ending with the stroke of the gong.

The more layers of meaning a piece has, the more powerful it is considered to be. Gamelan music is performed for rituals such as weddings, to placate the spirits of the under-world, and for temple ceremonies to invite the gods to and from the upper-world. Gamelan music is a mandala in sound and is viewed as a musical re-creation of the cosmos.

Culture-Bearer Feature—Joko Sutrisno: From Java, Indonesia, to the Midwest, U.S.

Joko Sutrisno is a master gamelan musician from Java, Indonesia. He has been teaching in the state of Minnesota for more than 20 years. He is unique among gamelan instructors in the U.S. in that he works with students of all ages—from kindergarten to college to the community.

In Indonesia, Joko's father was a gamelan musician and master teacher of the school gamelan ensemble. His mother was a village dancer. Joko grew up in a home

Joko Sutrisno, Gamelan Musician

Photo courtesy of Karen Howard

that was next door to where the village gamelan was kept. The sounds of gamelan music filled his early years. The doors to the gamelan room were never locked, and some nights Joko was found sleeping near the instruments. Young Joko found the sounds of the gamelan to be magical and mysterious. His earliest playing experiences on the drum were all imitative. He heard a phrase and tried to replicate what he heard. Joko's father, an important gamelan musician, started to formally teach him when he was about eight years old. This meant a sort of "starting over" as Joko had taught himself to that point, including hand positioning and rhythmic patterns.

While Joko's father led the school gamelan ensemble, he did not teach Joko privately. The learning process for the ensemble members was mostly aural through basic imitation. Joko decided to continue his formal education for five additional years so that he could receive formal gamelan education at what is now known as the Indonesian Institute of Art in Surakarta on the island of Java.

After teaching and performing in Java, Joko was invited to teach in New Zealand. This led to an invitation eight years later to move to the U.S. and start the first gamelan program in Minnesota. Joko was excited to do so, as he had been developing a teaching method that he felt could work with learners who did not grow up with the sounds and structures of gamelan in their lives.

Over 30 years of teaching, Joko has developed his own unique style of teaching that emphasizes learning gamelan structure, basic melodies, and then elaboration.

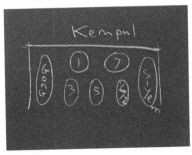

Figure 4.9 Examples of Joko's visuals developed over many years to work with non-Indonesians

Photo courtesy of Karen Howard

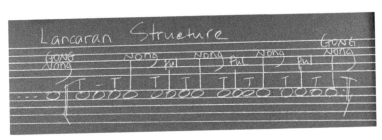

Figure 4.10 Performance route for a particular piece

Photo courtesy of Karen Howard

He did not need to learn in such a manner in Indonesia because it came so naturally, but he now believes in the importance of breaking concepts down into small, manageable steps. He scaffolds his instruction to bring his students to an understanding of the internal structures of gamelan music (Figure 4.13, Figure 4.14). Joko uses the imagery of taking a car apart in order to rebuild it from the ground up to describe his approach to teaching cultural outsiders how to get inside the sonic structure of gamelan.

Q: How do you address the spiritual component of gamelan when teaching students in the U.S.?
A: Music for me is universal, and we just start from there. Music is a part of being a human being, it comes from your heart. This is spiritual to me. The music is not from the instrument, it's from you. I will not allow students to play until they sing in their heart. You have something in common with each other without realizing it. We say the rhythms with our eyes closed and clap on the gong without looking at anybody—that is spiritual. When you play, you know your own part and you need to pay attention to other people. This is very spiritual for me—to feel the music within you and then you share it with everybody. The music is a tool to help us to reach a certain feeling and to accomplish our purpose.

Q: What do you think about gamelan that is taught by cultural outsiders? Is it important to work with someone like you—from the culture?
A: If you want to have a level of confidence and a sense of what (gamelan) is, you need to learn with a culture-bearer, or go to Indonesia, or find somebody who is expert in this field. You might get some of the rhythm, but even something as simple as holding the mallet is important. If you hold the mallet a certain way, there is a different impact on the sound. Sure, there are people that can look at a video to learn, but—does the music have soul? There are people who are living every second with purpose, every word they say has a purpose. Now, it is the same thing if you do gamelan. You must know the reason why you do it. This is part of the way we show respect for other cultures. This is very important. If you want to respect other cultures, you should know how and ask the people who actually deal with it—not just jump in and do whatever you want. We can enjoy and interact, but at the same time there might be things that are not appropriate.

Q: Can you discuss the recontextualization of gamelan music into alternate music settings?
A: Collaboration is important nowadays if we want to know each other. We have created so many differences—ethnicities, musics, religion, cultures. The reason we have differences is to know each other. We can say, "Wow—you are that—can you share it with me? You have this—can we share?" That's the beauty. That's the purpose. We have to maintain respect. We have to look at the similarities rather than the differences. We must find the golden rule within each other's culture. That's powerful. We cannot do just gamelan. I have to be open to many options. We will not survive. Can you imagine if you could only do Western music? No, it is more exciting if more people come to explore your music. That is how cooperation happens.

The interaction of sights and sounds makes gamelan ensembles especially compelling for secondary school students. The musical instruments are often intricately carved and painted brilliantly with scarlet, emerald, turquoise, and gilded with gold leaf. There is no such thing as idle decoration. Every flower or leaf, every bird or serpent, every color has meaning. The universe is replicated in the music and in the design of the musical instruments.

Bali, Indonesia

Having access to a full gamelan may be a goal that takes some time to achieve. A tradition with immediate access for secondary school music students comes from the Indonesian island of Bali. There is probably a greater concentration of orchestras and musicians in Bali than anywhere else in the world. In Bali, it is difficult to draw a line between art music and folk music. The orchestras require virtuosic technique handed down essentially by oral means. The musicians often play several different instruments and begin to learn how to hold the mallets for playing the percussion instruments at the age of four. Sacred music, like that of the theatres, requires that the artists possess a complete mastery of their instruments.

Balinese music requires a high degree of participation on the part of the entire population. The idea of the professional musician is foreign to the Balinese. Underlying Balinese aesthetics is the concept of *ramé* (literally "crowded".) This idea of a crowded sensation indicates the heightened excitement one feels when experiencing coincident multiple layers of meaning, colors, sounds, and events. A well-loved and oft-performed music tradition that expresses this sense of ramé is Kecak. Kecak is Bali's famous chant and dance, which developed from a male chorus performance for ritual trance ceremonies and draws throngs of visitors from around the world. Including up to 200 men dressed in black-and-white checked cloth wrapped around their hips, Kecak performers sit bare-chested around a branched torch that lights the black night with its flickering flames. The men, like a vocal gamelan, are assigned up to eight layers of interlocking vocal chants, primarily using the syllable "tjak," which gives the dance its name (Figure 4.11). The leader assigns other vowel sounds to the rest of the chorus. In the center of the chanters' circle, a dance drama takes place, usually drawn from the Hindu epic Ramayana. When Hanuman, the monkey king, enters the circle, the singers become an army of chattering monkeys, leading to the nickname of Monkey Dance. The Kecak syllables and gestures describe the spells used to drive out evil spirits. The dance of Kecak singers is deceptively simple. The choir remains seated, but the waving of their arms and upper bodies is choreographed to their chanting. While Kecak performances have become popular with tourists visiting Bali, men's choruses continue to perform in the original manner within their Balinese communities during trance or exorcism rituals. Kecak has found its way into contexts outside of Indonesia, with choral adaptations appearing and lesson ideas for school music offered up in publications. Following are suggested recordings for getting to know Kecak.

Suggested Resources for Kecak Performance

- "Kecak," UNESCO/Smithsonian Folkways Recordings.
- "Tjak: The Singers of Peliatan," UNESCO/Smithsonian Folkways Recordings.
- Bakan, M.B. (2010). Monkey business—Performing a simplified version of the Balinese Kecak dance-drama. In W.M. Anderson & P.S. Campbell

Figure 4.11   Basic Kecak vocal patterns. See Suggested Resources at the end of this chapter for the full Kecak story.

(Eds.), *Multicultural perspectives in music education* (Vol. 3, pp. 90–97). New York: Rowman & Littlefield.

Secondary students engaging with complex music traditions such as Kecak are moving forward in growing their understandings of the world around them, and of diverse musical practices. Having students compare the cyclical nature of gamelan and with the vocal polyrhythmic layers of Kecak may deepen aural skills, and may transfer to other musical sounds and settings thereby enriching the musical environment of their lives.

Performing Folkloric Traditions of Puerto Rico in Latin Music Traditions

Secondary students enrolled in a Latin Music Traditions class may find themselves experiencing a wide range of learning experiences. The flexibility surrounding what constitutes a "general" music class allows music teachers the freedom to construct innovative experiences for their students that may include deep listening, dance, and playing piano and percussion in a Puerto Rican folkloric tradition known as Plena.

To explore musical traditions of Puerto Rico, a secondary school music teacher might collaborate with a Spanish teacher to have the classes perform together. A school choir might sing the traditional tunes while the global percussion ensemble provides the rhythmic engine. A piano class might team up with the band to play improvisatory solos during the musical breaks of a song. Regardless of the class setting, some basic sociocultural and sociohistorical information goes a long way toward helping students and their teachers understand a music culture.

Puerto Rico—or Borinquen, its original Indian name—has three important cultural and ethnic threads: Spanish, Afro-Caribbean, and Taíno, which refers to the indigenous culture. In the 1500s, Spanish soldiers took control from the Taíno and fought back Caribs, another indigenous group in the Caribbean. During this time, slaves from West Africa were forced to work along the coastal areas. The mixing of cultures over the centuries resulted in half of Puerto Rico's 500,000 residents having mixed heritages of African and Spanish descent by 1850. Musical influences from all three cultural influences are apparent in folkloric traditions.

Bomba and Plena

Bomba and *plena* are percussion-driven musical traditions. Often mentioned together as though they were a single musical style, both reflect the African heritage of Puerto Rico, but there are basic distinctions between them in rhythm, instrumentation, and lyrics. *Bomba* and *plena* are defining musical sounds of the Afro-Puerto Rican population. These Afro-Puerto Rican musical traditions have been present in New York City and other communities in which Puerto Ricans have settled.

BOMBA

Long before the emergence of *plena* as the voice of the working class, *bomba* was an established tradition on the island. Bomba dates back to the early European colonial period in Puerto Rico. It comes out of the musical traditions brought by enslaved Africans in the 17th century and is considered to be a source of political and spiritual expression.

It is generally accepted that bomba was developed earliest and most strongly in the area of Loíza, a town with a strong African presence on the island's north coast, as a response to the aristocratic music of the local plantation owners. But bomba flourished throughout the island, wherever Africans and their descendants lived and worked the colonial plantations. The term *bomba* refers to a variety of forms of music and dance and to the community event in which it is performed. Originally these dances provided an important social, spiritual, and political outlet for African slaves and their descendants. Bomba was danced during baptisms, marriages, and even political events, but only during feast days and on Sundays. The attire and movements worn by women dancers of the bomba were meant to both imitate and ridicule the plantation ladies.

The music evolved through contact between slave populations from different Caribbean colonies and regions, including the Dutch colonies, Cuba, Santo Domingo, and Haiti. As a result, *bomba* now has 16 different rhythms. *Bombazos* are Puerto

Rican jam sessions where musicians and dancers gather to celebrate, similar to their Mexican counterpart—fandangos.

Bomba music and dance are characterized by two types of call-and-response: between the solo singer and *coro* (chorus) or as a call and response between the dancer and the solo drum (requinto). The solo drummer closely watches the dancer and must be prepared to rhythmically respond to the improvised steps and arm and body movements of the dancer. The solo singer improvises the verse while the audience becomes the chorus, repeating the lead singer's refrain. Bomba instruments include the *subidor* or *primo* (barrel drum), maracas, and *cuá*, two sticks played against the wood of the barrels or another piece of wood. Bomba lyrics conveyed a sense of sadness about life conditions, and the songs served as inspiration for rebellions. But bomba also is for dancing and celebration, helping to create community and identity.

Included in the suggested materials are bomba recordings by U.S.-based group Los Pleneros de la 21, as well as a performance video. Teaching bomba rhythms and dance in secondary music might include introduction of basic rhythms, as found in percussionist Michael de Miranda's video tutorials or a dance tutorial video from members of Los Pleneros de la 21 (see Suggested Resources at the end of the chapter.) Bringing bomba into secondary school performance can include drumming, dancing, and singing.

Suggested Resources for Bomba Performance

* "Baila, Julia Loíza" (Dance, Julia Loíza), Los Pleneros de la 21, Smithsonian Folkways Recordings.
* "Carmelina," Los Pleneros de la 21, in tribute to Marcial Reyes Arvelo at 2005 Smithsonian Folklife Festival (video).
* Fandango-Bombazo (Puerto Rican Jam Session) at 2006 Smithsonian Folklife Festival. At the 2006 Smithsonian Folklife Festival, musicians and dancers from Mexico, Puerto Rico, and other Latino backgrounds came together in an unprecedented, joint fandango-bombazo.

PLENA

Plena developed from *bomba* music around the beginning of the 20th century in southern Puerto Rico. *Plena* comes from the coastal towns and is a medium for sharing stories of the daily lives of ordinary people, historical events, social customs, and religious beliefs. The tales told in *plena* are almost like gossip rather than news and are often humorous and led to the nickname "the newspaper of the people." A combination of Afro-Caribbean and Spanish characteristics, *plena* seems to have made its first appearance in the late 1800s but did not become widely popular until the 1920s.

The four-line stanza and refrain are broken up into call-and-response patterns by solo and chorus. *Plena* has only one basic rhythm set. *Plena* instrumentation has changed greatly over the years, but the main element is the *pandereta* (Figure 4.12), a round hand drum that comes in different sizes. The smallest of them is the *requinto*, which improvises over the rhythm of the other drums. A school performance can feature two folkloric selections—one bomba and one plena—to feature the music culture of Puerto Rico.

Suggested Resources for Performing Plena

- Hector "Tito" Matos and Members of Los Pleneros de la 21 Demonstrate Plena Music (video).
- Fieta de plena (article).

Figure 4.12 Panderetas for plena and guiro

Photo courtesy of Karen Howard

* indicates a slap tone without rebound

Figure 4.13 Basic plena rhythms

Performing Music from French Polynesia in World Music Class

Secondary students enrolled in a World Music Class can delve into the rich percussion traditions from the French Polynesian island of Tahiti. For people in many geographic areas, this remote location in the South Pacific seems unreachable and the musical traditions perhaps unattainable. In fact, Tahitian music is perfect for the phases of WMP. By working through the phases of Attentive, Engaged, and Enactive listening, performance of rapid, interlocking rhythms is easily within reach.

Traditional Tahitian Music

As Christianity spread through Polynesia, traveling missionaries prohibited dancing and many traditional cultural practices. This led to all songs, games, and other forms of social entertainments being strictly forbidden. In Tahiti, French Polynesia, the sacred art of *le tatouage* (body tattoos), dancing, and wearing flower leis during church services were viewed by the missionaries and colonizing French society as negative practices. Tahitians who protested these regulations were exiled.

Traditional music and dance was banned in Tahiti until the late 1800s, when it was allowed just once a year in mid-July. In the 1950s, this July musicking resulted in a group of musicians named Heiva. Within 10 years of the formation of Heiva, many groups formed, eventually leading to a festival by the same name. The festival called Heiva, now known around the world, attracts traditional music groups from throughout Polynesia. Some of the featured music and dance includes indigenized forms of English hymns (*himene*), the folkloric genres of *paoa*, *hivinau*, and *aprima*, and Western-style songs with guitar and ukulele known as *aparima* (hand dance).

TŌ'ERE ENSEMBLE

The *tō'ere* (toe-edd-ee) is a Tahitian percussion instrument made from a hollowed-out log. It is beaten with a *baguette* (a tapered wooden stick) to produce rapid staccato sounds. Typically standing about three feet tall, the tō'ere creates high or low tones depending on where it is hit. The tō'ere is not typically a solo instrument but is usually heard played in groups of three or more. Also included in a traditional Tahitian to'ere ensemble is the *fa'atete* (Figure 4.14). There are numerous rhythm patterns, known as *oteas* (Figure 4.15), that serve as a sonic backdrop for dancers.

Suggested Resources for Performing Music of Tahiti

- "Tamarii Tahiti," Royal Tahitian Dance Company, Smithsonian Folkways Recordings.
- "Toere," Maeva Tahiti Tahitian Folkloric Group, Manuiti.
- "Toere," The Royal Tahitian Dancers and Singers, Viking.

Performing Rhythms of the Brazilian Bateria in Percussion Ensemble

Global drumming ensembles, courses, or units have gained in popularity over the last decade. Performing rhythms from the Brazilian samba school tradition is possible

Figure 4.14 To'ere and fa'atete

Photo courtesy of Karen Howard

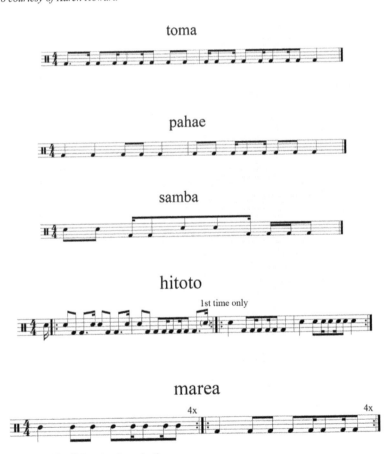

Figure 4.15 Traditional to'ere rhythms

because the necessary instruments have become readily available through percussion websites and educator venues. In addition, quality online tutorials are easily accessible. Putting together a *batucada* (percussion jam session) is a joyful, celebratory way to bring performance into the general music class or a specific world drumming elective course.

The sounds of batucada from Brazil, which was colonized and ruled by the Portuguese from 1500–1822, spans three time zones and several climate regions. The vastness of the Amazon rainforest effectively hindered cultural exchanges with countries along the border. European influence was present in Brazilian musical traditions in the waltz during the mid-1800s and polkas from the 1850s–1880s. This was followed by the music and dance form known as *maxixe* (ma-she-she). Maxixe was the first national urban musical genre, coinciding with the end of slavery at the turn of the 20th century. West African traditions are alive and well in Afro-Brazilian musical practices today. This may be partly because more than four million West Africans of mostly Yoruba and Bantu-Ewe cultural groups were brought to Brazil as slaves, more than to any other single country in the Americas.

Samba: Musical Background

A vibrant musical tradition arising out of the West African presence in Brazil and from which batucada emerged is samba. Samba exemplifies the strong ties between folk music and popular music in Brazil. Local composers of popular music borrowed from folk music to suit fashion and popular trends. A consistent intermingling and borrowing between folk music and popular music is common enough that it is difficult to discern whether any given music is absolutely original.

The musical genre of samba emerged around 1915. The first official samba performance coincided with a massive strike while Brazil was under the rule of Getulio Vargas. Samba music was used to create a national, heterogeneous society. Even with this unifying goal, tensions arose over samba's symbolic value as issues arose between Black and White musicians, mirroring racial tensions within communities.

Contemporary samba has two distinct forms. One form is the samba danced in the rural areas in the *escolas de samba* (schools of samba), which are communities of dancers and musicians. Their mission is exclusively devoted to the arrangement of public *Carnaval* parades. Each samba school has a director who teaches and directs dancing and singing. While the rural samba developed up in the hills, another version flourished in the urban areas. It might be considered as deriving from the previously mentioned maxixe. This version has now become the most characteristic and recognizable kind of Brazilian social dance.

Samba performance is an integral component of the religious celebration known as Carnaval. Carnaval is part of the preparation for the season of Lent and is an ongoing tradition throughout the world as part of wherever the Catholic church played a role in colonization. Carnaval is found in diverse settings in Brazil from rural, informal gatherings to larger, urban organized events. The city of Rio de Janeiro has had the most elaborate Carnaval celebration since the 19th century. The participation of Afro-Brazilians helped to transform the European tradition into a national expression of Brazilian people.

THE BATERIA

The bateria is the percussion band of a samba school. In samba and in Brazilian Carnaval, rhythm represents the spirit of life. Typically, the most powerful rhythmic energy in a Carnaval procession surrounds the bateria. Members of baterias share a rush of adrenaline as up to 400 percussionists drum and move together.

Bateria rhythms always present in duple meter and are played by only percussion instruments. In the first decades of the 20th century, the first samba percussion instruments were made to imitate West African drums. In the 1930s, barrels came into use for the *surdo* (bass drum) and greatly improved the sound. Early samba percussion instruments also included the *pandeiro* (tambourine with head), *agogo* (double metal bell), *caixa* (snare), *chocalho* (shakers), and *reco reco* (loud metal scraper). Over the 1940s and 50s, the *tamborim* (small high-pitched drum) was added, and nylon heads replaced animal skins.

Suggested Resources for Performing Bateria

The bateria (Figure 4.16) works in a similar fashion to an orchestra, with moments in which all instruments are being played, and other times when only certain instruments or groupings perform. There are multiple online tutorials that can guide you through each instrument one at a time. Lessons are available for the most novice player to advanced percussionists. While the following is a list of drums found in a full bateria, secondary music teachers can be creative in substituting instruments at hand if they are unable to acquire or afford the instruments all at once:

- Surdo de Primeira (First surdo)—largest bass drum, responsible for the primary beat (beat 2), played with a soft-headed mallet and a bare hand to dampen the head and change the pitch.
- Surdo de Segunda (Second surdo)—this is the response to the primeira, acting as a counterpoint, higher pitch.

Figure 4.16   A selection of Brazilian percussion instruments from L to R: tamborim, surdo, apito, pandeiro, cuica, reco reco, agogo, repinique

Photo courtesy of Karen Howard

- Surdo de Terceira (Third surdo)—plays in between the primeira and segunda. Each samba school has its own way of inserting the terceira.
- Caixa de Guerra (snare-like drum)—played with two sticks.
- Repique—drum played with one stick and a bare hand, or with two sticks, leads the bateria by signaling breaks and internal cues.
- Repinique—similar function to the repique.
- "Bahia-Cuba," Samba Squad, Independent recording, available on iTunes. Berimbau, agogo bells, surdo, vocals, caxixi.
- "Sambodromo Batería," T.Z. Karp and Y. Varona, West One Music Limited. Apito, repinique, surdo, tamborim, reco reco, caixa.
- "Just Batucada," Voices of the Bateria, OK Records. Caixa, repinique, vocals, cuica, surdo.

Performances Big and Small: There Is Room for Them All!

The array of suggestions for performances and informances of music from eight musical cultures are intended as meaningful and practical means of moving the world's musical cultures into secondary school music settings. All suggestions assume the involvement of students in listening that leads from Attentive to Engaged to Enactive levels of listening and participatory musicking. These experiences that represent three key dimensions of WMP allow students to have substantive understandings of "the way the music goes," what musical material and structures are embedded within the works, how the music is so frequently transmitted and acquired through culturally approved oral-aural means. Students are then skilled and confident, which enables them to want to share the music they have learned in public venues. Even the most exotic music, so far removed from their own families and community experiences, can grow into their sensibilities as developing musicians, and they can make considerable headway in performing the music from the far corners of the world that they have learned by ear, practiced with their voices, in their bodies (in the case of dance traditions such as son jarocho or čoček), and on instruments. A thoughtful, sequential aural and cultural process can better inform the music teacher and students as they work toward creating a sound that is inspired by the recorded sources. Music teachers are in a position to redefine "performance" as it fits their course designs, the students and greater community, and their own musical strengths.

Reference

Campbell, P. S., & Flores, L. S. (2016). Pathways to expressing Mexican musical identity. In H. Schippers & C. Grant (Eds.), *Sustainable futures for music cultures: An ecological perspective.* New York: Oxford University Press.

Listening Episodes

"Bahia-Cuba," Samba Squad, on *Batuque*, Independent recording. Available on iTunes. Vocals, berimbau, agogo bells, surdo, caxixi.

"Baila, Julia, Loíza," Los Pleneros de la 21, Smithsonian Folkways Recordings. Piano, electric guitar, congas, guiro, vocals. www.folkways.si.edu/los-pleneros-de-la-21/baila-julia-loiza-dance-julia-loiza/latin-world/music/track/smithsonian.

"Carmelina," Los Pleneros de la 21, in tribute to Marcial Reyes Arvelo at 2005 Smithsonian Folklife Festival. www.folkways.si.edu/performance-carmelina/latin-world/music/video/smithsonian.

"Čoček Manhattan," Yuri Yunakov Ensemble, Smithsonian Folkways Recordings. Saxophone, clarinet, keyboard, bass, drum set. www.folkways.si.edu/yuri-yunakov-ensemble/cocek-manhattan/world/music/track/Smithsonian.

Fandango-Bombazo (Puerto Rican Jam Session) at Smithsonian Folklife Festival. At the 2006 Smithsonian Folklife Festival, musicians and dancers from Mexico, Puerto Rico, and other Latino backgrounds came together in an unprecedented, joint fandango-bombazo. www.folkways.si.edu/fandango-bombazo/caribbean-latin-world/music/video/smithsonian.

"Just Batucada," Voices of the Bateria, OK Records. Caixa, repinique, vocals, cuica, surdo.

"Kecak," The Library of Congress Endangered Music Project. UNESCO. Smithsonian Folkways Recordings. voices www.folkways.si.edu/kecak/world/music/track/smithsonian.

"Kpanlogo," Kofi Quarshie, Acewonder Ltd. Available on iTunes. Gankoguis, handclaps, vocals, kpanlogo drums.

"Kpanlogo," Nyanyo Addo, Weltwunder. Available on iTunes. Vocals, kpanlogo drums, atokee, axatse.

"Kpanlogo," on *Traditional Drumming and dances of Ghana*. Smithsonian Folkways Recordings. Kpanlogo drums, gankogui, handclaps, vocals, axatse. www.folkways.si.edu/kpanlongo/world/music/track/smithsonian.

Master of Traditional Arts—an ongoing interdisciplinary project produced by Documentary Arts. It focuses on the recipients of the National Heritage Fellowship, awarded annually by the National Endowment of the Arts in the U.S. This website features selected traditional musicians in each state in the U.S. There is a full feature on Yuri Yunakov including several high-energy performance videos. The performance venues include weddings, music festivals, and television shows. Retrieved from www.mastersoftraditionalarts.org/artists/367.

"Mbira—Spirit of the People," Thomas Mapfumo. This 1990 documentary explores mbira traditions, its connection to the Chimurenga revolutionary struggle, and Zimbabwe's transition to independence. With extensive footage from the era, featured are interviews and performances by Thomas Mapfumo and Oliver Mtukudzi. https://youtu.be/5hF2Hstvrfc?list=PLyMF9d8PivLWucTmVZ9hmc8jtTD-pvQjr.

"Nyoka Musango," Thomas Mapfumo, Duke University Press. Available on iTunes. Electic guitars, electric bass guitar, drum set, handclaps, vocals.

"Sambodromo Batería," T.Z. Karp and Y. Varona, on *Carnaval, Carnaval en Brasil*, OK Records. Available on iTunes. Apito, repinique, surdo, tamborim, reco reco, caixa.

"Siquisirí," Son de Madera, Smithsonian Folkways Recordings. Vocals, jarana, guitar. www.folkways.si.edu/son-de-madera/siquisiri-siquisiri/latin-world/music/track/smithsonian.

Son de Madera at the Smithsonian Folklife Festival. This video clip shows a performance from 2009 and clearly features the footwork on the tarima. www.folkways.si.edu/son-de-madera/latin-world/music/video/smithsonian.

Son de Madera performs Son Jarocho. This short video shows the songwriting process for creating lyrics in son jarocho selections. www.folkways.si.edu/son-jarocho/latin-spoken-word-world/music/video/Smithsonian.

"Tamarii Tahiti," Royal Tahitian Dance Company, Smithsonian Folkways Recordings. To'ere ensemble. www.folkways.si.edu/royal-tahitian-dance-company/tamarii-tahiti/world/music/track/smithsonian.

"Tjak: The Singers of Peliatan," UNESCO/Smithsonian Folkways Recordings. Voices. www.folkways.si.edu/the-singers-of-peliatan/tjak/music/track/smithsonian.

"Toere," Maeva Tahiti Tahitian Folkloric Group, 1967/2010, Manuiti. Available on iTunes. To'ere ensemble.

"Toere," The Royal Tahitian Dancers and Singers, Viking. Available on iTunes. To'ere ensemble.

Zimbabwe Mbira—Three melodies played on a 14-note kalimba. Ethnic Folkways Library. Mbiras. www.folkways.si.edu/ackson-zulu/three-melodies-played-on-a-fourteen-note-kalimba/world/music/track/smithsonian.

5

Creating World Music

In Ms. Chintha's World Music Traditions class, the ninth graders are studying art music of Asia. After examining traditional Chinese opera (Xiqu), Japanese Taiko, and Indonesian Gamelan, the students are now exploring raga in the classical music of India. The activities have centered on multiple listening experiences of a recording by Anoushka Shankar on sitar. The listening snippet is brief, featuring a 20-second clip of the fixed section of the raga, and students are listening again and again, with invitations to "map the melody" in its rise-and-fall contour, sing the drone, keep the tala in a hand-clapping and waving motion, and sing silently the raga melody they hear. The Attentive and Engaged listening experiences have run across several days now, so that students can grasp some of the musical essence and participate musically. Ms. Chintha is Indian American, and has meanwhile introduced her students to some of the cultural aspects of India, telling stories of her youth in India, teaching them brief phrases of greeting and etiquette, and bringing in textiles, photos, artifacts, and musical instruments from her personal collection to share with them.

Students have begun learning to play a segment of a raga, first singing brief four- and five-pitch phrases in imitation of their teacher, and then transferring these phrases to guitars. Because note-reading is a curricular expectation, Ms. Chintha follows their learning-by-ear with notation of the phrases, too. With their teacher's guidance, the students learn about the scalar patterns within the raga and, as they progress in performing the raga's melodic material, the recording features again so that students may check themselves, sing along with the performer, and hear the stylistic interpretation of the raga in the fixed melody of the work.

Ms. Chintha wants to press her students not only to perform along with the recording, and to play the melody without the recording, but to edge ever closer to their own fundamental improvisation in the raga. From student imitation of their teacher's phrases, teacher and students perform and imitate phrases that are twice the length, now eight- to ten-pitch phrases, of the earlier exercise. A new exercise emerges now, as Ms. Chintha plays a raga phrase of eight pitches on her guitar, within the time of eight beats, with the expectation that a student improvisation will *follow of the same length. Around the circle they go, Ms. Chintha's musical question followed by individual student answers in their improvisations. The music is improvised, and students are holding to the pitches of the raga that have been learned by listening and through earlier exercises. Ms. Chintha's future lessons include hooking together the fixed melody of the raga, having all students play it together as an ensemble, and then to feature brief but more rhythmically sophisticated improvisations by the individual students.*

A World of Creating

Music is a creative enterprise. Audience members in a nightclub smile as two horn players of a jazz combo banter with each other during their solos in Miles Davis's "So What." In Ghana, Ewe singers and dancers are guided by the spontaneous instruction of the percussionists, specifically the master drummer. In a crowded school auditorium, the choral ensemble called Roomful of Teeth performs "Passacaglia" by the Pulitzer prize–winning composer Caroline Shaw, a gem of a piece that combines traditional choral elements, folk-singing techniques, and aleatoric (chance music) passages all within the printed score. A Persian *tar* (frame drum) player navigates commitment to traditional musical norms and personal creative expression as the *radif* (embellished traditional melody) seems to spontaneously materialize in the fingers and onto the strings of his instrument. Conservatory students in Beijing and Queensland collaborate to compose a new sonic artwork that employs audience participation through the use of their smartphones. All around the world, musicians are actively participating in the creation of new musical expressions, whether through the spontaneous decision making of the performers or the organization of musical sounds to be replicated in future performances. Like the vast world of music-makers, students in secondary school music classrooms deserve opportunities for involvement in creative musical processes like improvisation and composition.

In this fourth dimension of World Music Pedagogy (WMP), Creating World Music encourages music teachers to allow their students to extend their understanding of musical learning by generating their own music. This chapter explores possible avenues to creating music in the style of or inspired by particular world traditions. These suggestions are intended as teaching and learning models for a music teacher's consideration. We encourage teachers to consider the models as pedagogical exercises to be used as they are found, or as jumping-off points for creating new listening experiences that lead to composing and improvising.

Careful listening as described in previous chapters certainly contributes to a creative outcome. Up to this point, working through the first three dimensions of Attentive, Engaged, and Enactive Listening, performance was an end outcome of thoughtfully guided listening. Because the music is now familiar through experience and study, the focus shifts to the creation of new music based upon the studied music, the process of which helps students to internalize musical concepts and structures. This process also aids students in growing a curiosity about the people behind the music, the role it plays in their lives, and how it is transmitted or created within their culture. The first three listening and musicking phases of WMP inform the creative processes of improvisation and composition, from simple extension or elaboration of pieces explored in the classroom to full-blown original works. This progression of listening, to performing, to creating, highlights the key features of WMP.

Before embarking on an exploration of pedagogical issues concerning the creation of world music, it is useful to examine how creative processes are understood cross-culturally, through the lens of ethnomusicology. Ethnomusicologist Bruno Nettl (2015) is clear that there can be misunderstanding or even biases when trying to examine the compositional and improvisational practices in different cultures around the world. He explores the ways that musicians from around the world conceptualize creative processes. One point of discussion is the idea of what is a "new" creation; cultures have different criteria for what constitutes new musical products. In some cultures, improvising on a melody is seen as paying tribute to a previous work (e.g., a solo within a jazz standard) while in other cultures it is seen as the creation of a new work of art (e.g., an Indian raga).

It is also pertinent to consider the distinction between composition and improvisation. These creative acts in some ways are overlapping and rely on similar skills. Improvisation and composition are not two distinct processes or behaviors, but rather parallel and interrelated processes that lie on a continuum of creativity. These creative processes both require experimentation, trial-and-error, and risk-taking, as well as deliberate practice to gain fluency. The primary distinction between these two processes lies in the execution of the music-making. Improvisation is generally performed as an extemporaneous act or being performed in the moment. Alternatively, composition occurs outside of the performance space, where the creator of the music has time to revise and polish the work before performance. However, these descriptions are endpoints on the continuum, and there are modes of creating in the middle that may share elements of both processes. It also should be noted that many secondary music teachers may conceptualize composition as notating new musical ideas on a blank score, with pencil and paper or computer programs; however, composition does not require notation to create works that are enduring over time. The distinctions between composition and improvisation can be fuzzy and are informed by the cultures from which the musical creations originated.

For the developing musician, these creative acts are shaped by powerful listening experiences that inform the student's imagination. When presented with creative tasks within the secondary music classroom, students will be compelled to return to the original sonic material to engage their own understanding. Improvisation and composition are natural extensions of the deep and intense listening experiences; this progression occurs unsurprisingly in many musical cultures around the world—listening begets creation. As this chapter proceeds with sample lessons for a variety of secondary music classrooms, from Advanced Music Theory to songwriting, it will be clear that creative music opportunities are presented alongside intentional listening experiences.

A Starting Point for Creation

Creative tasks in the secondary school music classroom afford the opportunity for many students to explore their musical understanding that they might be deprived of in other performance-centric classrooms. Secondary music courses, especially those outside the scope of traditional large ensembles, allow for these opportunities more freely as instructional time is not dedicated mostly to group performances that are highly visible within the school culture. These opportunities encourage students to develop creative music skills in addition to listening and performing skills—to test their own musical thinking beyond replicating performances.

One of the challenges in facilitating creative music activities is finding an appropriate starting point. Students come into the music classroom with a wide array of experiences, from formal development of musical skills to listening preferences on their personal smartphones, all of which can impact the creative products that they design within the music classroom. In pursuing activities that build on the engagement of musical cultures from around the world, the starting point is clear: students must be given ample opportunity to listen deeply to music of the culture from which they hope to launch their creative expressions. Classroom music activities that encourage deep listening (through Attentive, Engaged, and Enactive Listening) are important to developing the ear, allowing the student to make creative choices that are in line with the music traditions that the class is studying.

One of the resources needed to incorporate creative music activities within secondary music classrooms is time. There must be adequate, even an abundance, of time devoted to the creative activities to allow for students to be successful. First, there must be time dedicated to engaging the sonic material from the musical culture, where students should have multiple exposures to a musical exemplar that is being explored. After students have had the requisite interaction with the musical culture being studied, the music teacher must also provide plenty of time for students to engage in exploration, experimentation, and refinement of their creative products. Students need time to evaluate their work, not only in terms of aesthetic value, but also in style in light of the world music cultures that the students are studying. Music teachers must also provide time for performance of the creative output, allowing these works to come to fruition, as well as opportunity for students and facilitators to provide feedback for each other.

When incorporating creative tasks within the framework of WMP, a music teacher must clarify what musical understanding the students should explore or extend through the compositional or improvisational activities. When embarking on creative activities, it is helpful to the music educator to distinguish between open and closed assignments (Hickey, 2012). With open assignments, very few parameters are given, allowing the student to explore her ingenuity. Alternatively, closed assignments have more conditions on what the creative product should be. For initial explorations into creative processes, music teachers should consider starting with more open compositional assignments so that it allows students to experiment and evaluate their creative work. As students become more adept at creative thinking, stricter parameters on the creative task can be given, such as using the form, rhythm, or tonality from a particular music culture.

Episode 5.1: Creating World Music—Sacred Music of Vietnam

The Socialist Republic of Vietnam, a nation of more than nine million inhabitants, is the result of a turbulent history that spans the past several centuries. In the mid-20th century, Vietnam was engulfed in warfare in an effort to expel the colonial forces of the French as well as prevent occupation by the Japanese, resulting in a partitioned country. Through the 1950s and 1960s, tensions between the North and South Vietnamese states grew and intensified. An international conflict resulted, with Russia and China backing the Communist forces in the North and the United States supporting the South Vietnamese government. After the fall of the southern capital of Saigon in 1975, North Vietnam gained control of the southern state. Shortly thereafter, the two states were merged to create the Socialist Republic of Vietnam. Vietnam was devastated at the conclusion of the war, obliterating many cultural traditions and institutions.

Ritual music from southern Vietnam can be used to teach many musical concepts and skills in a variety of secondary school music classes. This particular recording comes from ceremonies that honor guardian spirits and are used in funerary rites in temple ceremonies of the Cao Dai religion. Caodaism is a monotheistic religion and a blend of the cultural forces that has seeped into Vietnam's complicated history. The Cao Dai belief system is an amalgamation of Confucianism, Buddhism, and Catholicism and espouses that its teachings are an effort to unite all religions or share a common vision of divinity and humanity. Vietnamese ritual music frequently features a slender double-reed instrument with six holes adorned with a wooden bell, called a *ken trung*. This instrument, which is central in Episode 5.1, is the sole melodic instrument in the piece. The melody is created with a free rhythm and not bound by meter, while several percussion instruments accompany. With the interesting use of free rhythm and percussive accompaniment, an episode exploring Vietnamese ritual music would live well in a world percussion ensemble class. It must be remembered that this music is part of a religious ritual, and the facilitator of the music activities must prepare students to treat the material with respect.

Episode 5.1: Celebration of Sounds: Vietnamese Ritual Music

Specific Use: World Drumming Percussion Ensemble

Materials:

- "Bai Trong Lay and Thet," Tu Huyen, Nam Phu, Chin Quon, Sau Phu, and Hai Phat, Smithsonian Folkways Recordings

  Vietnamese Ritual Music with *ken trung* (reed instrument) and percussion

Procedure:

(Attentive)

1 Discuss with students the context of this piece: "This is a ritual piece of music that was used in religious ceremonies."

2 Have students listen for the basic form of the piece, finding sections that change in tempo or mood.

3 Play track (00:01–02:52).

4 "In the next listen, what kinds of instruments do you hear?"

5 Play track (00:01–02:52). Allow additional listens if necessary.

6 Discuss answers. Instruments include ken trung (oboe-like instrument), gong, small cymbals, hollow buffalo horn, drums.

(Creating)

7 Have students create their own piece that celebrates sound. Students can explore the different sounds that can be made on classroom instruments (e.g., pitched and unpitched percussion).

8   "Compositions should have several different sections that change in tempo and instrumentation." While there can be elements of improvisation in their piece, the composition should be able to be reproduced for performance for the class.

The music educator must provide abundant time for students to explore sounds and practice to replicate the piece.

Students in world percussion ensembles get many opportunities to develop their improvisational skills, as they practice new rhythms within the groove of a drum circle; however, these students may have fewer opportunities to compose a piece, making decisions about instrumentation, tone, timbre, and resolution of tension. As in the previous episode, listening to exemplars can inform students how to approach form and instrumentation. These percussionists benefit from time to explore different timbres and sounds that various rhythm instruments make as well as different sounds on one instrument. For instance, the teacher can demonstrate the three main types of sounds on the djembe: bass (hand flat and fingers together, middle of the drum), tone (fingers together, edge of the drumhead), and slap (fingers apart and relaxed, snapping motion toward the center of the drum). Additionally, percussionists can explore unconventional means of using the instruments for their compositions. The teacher will need to devote time for students to practice their creations. Even though there is no need to notate their newly formed compositions, students will want time to practice so that their composition is stable and ideas are fully formed.

Creating, Re-creating, and Preserving

There are different schools of thought regarding the performance of existing music throughout the world. Some performers feel that performances should honor the original source material by replicating every sonic nuance, detail, and movement as faithfully as possible. Culture-bearers are often involved in these types of performances, modeling the typical practices needed to create the iconic sounds of a given music culture.

Another viewpoint on performance practice is in support of the creation of new musical expressions that are inspired by deep listening and learning experiences with musical cultures. An example of this comes from the previously mentioned vocal group, Roomful of Teeth. They perform an original composition, "Otherwise," by founder and director Brad Wells. The piece starts with sounds reminiscent of a Tibetan singing bowl. The vocals then turn clearly toward Bulgaria through timbral changes and switch to an additive meter of 2+2+3+2. It is clear from the strident, straight tone that the composer and singers understand a Bulgarian choral "sound," likely through deep listening experiences, study, rehearsal, and performance practice opportunities. This approach is quite different than that implemented by those who desire to stay close to a performance practice, as heard in most American choral groups. By extending the artistic process to create music inspired by a particular music culture, students are allowed to employ the skills and sociocultural knowledge gained through the previous WMP phases of Attentive, Engaged, and Enactive listening and performance. These two approaches may inform each other, and music teachers often move between them depending on the purpose and intent for a particular composition project.

While learning through listening is present leading up to creating music, teachers often hesitate to follow through with creating in a style inspired by a particular music culture. Concerns of engaging in cultural appropriation can paralyze a well-intentioned teacher who then relies on performance as close to the original as possible—a cycle that leads to frustration when the sound is not exactly so. Music teachers must remember that their classrooms are a recontextualization of the music culture that they are exploring, and as long as they engage the music with a well-informed approach, then their efforts to create within the style of the world music culture should be encouraged.

For music teachers, a sense of identity may also complicate or even discourage creative activities within the music classroom. Some music educators may view themselves primarily as teachers, rather than as performers or composers or improvisers. This is likely a result of Western conservatory-type training where most students are put in tracks (e.g., music education, performance), which often limit the types of experiences that students will encounter. It is far more beneficial for music teachers to develop their identities as expert musicians who participate competently in teaching, performing, composing, and improvising. If teachers adopt this perspective, all students, even those in the conservatory system, are working on the same skills.

The training of music teachers in modes of creativity (or absence of training) can make it complicated for them to navigate the myriad ways in which students create. Many music teachers may be overwhelmed with teaching composition or improvisation in their classrooms because they have had so few experiences with these activities. When the possibly unfamiliar sounds of global traditions enter the learning environment, the complications may increase. There are many strategies to help implement creative activities within the secondary music classroom, as this chapter will soon discuss, but music teachers can also look to how different music cultures compose and improvise within their traditions to develop ideas for the music classroom.

Strategies for Creating World Music

For many music teachers, it is beneficial to describe techniques that promote student learning in compositional and improvisational activities. First, it is important to realize that students enter the classroom with many different skills and musical understandings. Thus, creative tasks that require students to extrapolate musical learning into creative acts must be guided in a way that leads to success. Listening activities are a valuable way to focus student attention onto a musical idea or element that will be useful in the creative task at hand. While the goals of creative tasks may be somewhat abstract (e.g., creating a piece that reflects an emotion), it is the music teacher's duty to make the task as clear and concrete as possible for the students (e.g., creating a piece that is 90–120 seconds long, and contains three sections with different instrumentation with the first and the third having similar instrumentation and tempos).

In the effort to develop students' aesthetic awareness, music teachers should guide their students to produce creative products that have both unity as well as variety. The creative product can be achieved through the use of repetition, variation, and embellishment upon even the simplest musical ideas. In WMP, creative tasks can be framed within the learning of specific melodic or rhythmic motifs that have been encountered in Attentive, Engaged, or Enactive Listening activities. For instance, after students learn about the hijaz scale in Roma music, students create their own elaborate melodies. This process innately allows students to explore their imagination while maintaining elements of unity within their newly formed work.

Episode 5.2: Learning Pathway #1—Marimba Music of Zimbabwe

Within the process of improvising or composing, the students should strive for creating tension and resolving that tension through release. It is important to discuss how tension and release are achieved within the cultures that are being encountered within the classroom; this process will undoubtedly require deep and repeated listening to musical exemplars. As an example, Zimbabwean marimba music creates interest through the layering of intricate and overlapping patterns. Students can adopt this approach of layering sounds on top of each other to create tension and release, even if it is not as sophisticated as the music they have encountered in listening sessions. In the following Learning Pathway, students in a world drumming percussion ensemble develop compositional skills as they design their own short melodies based on Shona proverbs, while still adhering to the overlapping nature of the individual marimba parts.

Episode 5.2: Zimarimba—Marimba Music of Zimbabwe (Learning Pathway #1)

Specific Use: World Percussion Ensemble

Materials:

- "Nyoka Musango," Lora Chiorah-Dye and the Suketai Marimba Dance Ensemble, Smithsonian Folkways Records

  Marimbas, vocals, hosho, claps

Procedure:

(Creating)

1   Review with students the piece "Nyoka Musango," drawing attention to the melodic lines that are layered on top of each other.

2   Play track (00:01–01:05).

3   Using proverbs commonly heard in Shona culture (Figure 5.1), create short melodic ideas using the Shona text. Students can model their short melodies after the singing heard in the recording. This process might start with exact replication of the melody, as it will be quite familiar from all of the previous listening. Encourage the students to change notes here and there

until they create new short melodies that fit within the structure of the piece.

4   Allow students to experiment along with the recording.

5   Play track (00:01–01:05).

6   Combine the new sung melodies with the marimba parts learned previously.

Shona	Translation	Meaning
Kupedza nyota kuenda padziva.	To quench thirst is to go to the pool.	If help is wanted, one should go to an expert or eyewitness.
Charovedzera charovedzera.	One who is used to something is one who is used to something.	We do easily that to which we are accustomed.
Kuziva mbuya huudzwa.	To know one's in-laws means being told who they are.	Wisdom comes from others.
Tsvaga zano iwe une rakowo.	Seek a plan when you have one of your own.	
Kureva ndokunei?	What has speech got?	Looking is also speaking.

Figure 5.1   Selected Shona proverbs

In secondary school music classrooms, students may gravitate toward the skills about which they feel confident while neglecting other skills about which they feel less proficient. For many secondary school students, singing is avoided because they worry about feedback from others in the room. But singing is an important musical skill that all students should develop, even in a world percussion ensemble, as singing is often a part of the world music tradition that is being learned within the class. Before having students singing alone in the midst of class activities, the teacher must create a safe space for the vulnerability that occurs around singing. One strategy to create this safe space is through having a thick texture within the music-making. For instance, in the world drumming percussion ensemble, using the *hosho* (gourd shakers), marimbas, and the recording simultaneously will provide a dense sonority where the students can feel emboldened to use their voices without fear. After students are comfortable within the amalgam of sound, the teacher can move to simpler textures that showcase singing by small groups or individuals; this process works best when gradually moving from whole-class singing to smaller groups. Many musical cultures from around the world, such as the sub-Saharan and Romani examples described in this book, include exuberant singing, dancing, and instrument playing. Students in all kinds of secondary music classrooms should experience these modes of expression and develop their musicianship through world music traditions.

Episode 5.3: Learning Pathway #2—Son de Jarocho From Veracruz, Mexico

Like most teaching, an important element is providing proper scaffolding for student success. When facilitating compositional or improvisational activities, it is incumbent on the music teacher to consider the discrete parts of the creative task at hand and provide support to undertake each element of the creative process. It could be overwhelming for some students to have freedom to make so many musical decisions, but allowing students to experiment with each component of the task could ensure student success. For instance, when beginning to perform improvisatory melodies inspired by world musical cultures, it would be useful to choose activities with limited harmonic choices, perhaps a piece that changes between two common chords; this approach allows students to experiment within limited parameters and to identify what is successful in the sound. "Siquisirí" is a natural choice for exploring improvisation in a guitar class (see Figure 5.2), with its continual use of chords that beginners will know: the A7 chord and D chord.

Episode 5.3: Son de Jarocho from Veracruz, Mexico (Learning Pathway #2)

Specific Use: Guitar class

Materials:

- "Siquisirí," Son de Madera, Smithsonian Folkways Recordings
  Son jarocho piece featuring leona, guitarra de son, jarana tercera, contrabass, and vocals

Procedure:

(Creating)

1   Have students play the accompaniment chords (A7/D) for the song using the strumming patterns learned earlier in Chapter 3. The chordal accompaniment can be passed around the room, each student deciding the strumming rhythm during their turn.

2   Play track (00:21–4:02).

3   Once students are comfortable maintaining the accompaniment on their own or in small groups, students can experiment with melodic improvisation with the recording. Students can take turns playing short improvised melodies over the accompaniment. Scaffold by discussing how the chord-tones of each chord can be important anchors for the melody or by presenting melodic material that is transcribed from the piece (see Figure 5.2 for examples). Students can practice playing these short fragments and embellish or extend them as they see fit. This can be done in small groups or as a class jam session.

4   Play track (00:21–4:02).

5   Once students are comfortable with the melodic material and have had some experience improvising, have half of the students perform the accompaniment while the other half passes the melody throughout the group, with one student playing a question and then the next student playing the answer.

Figure 5.2   Melodic fragments from Siquirisí, which can be the basis for improvisation

Students are more successful when tasks are broken down into manageable steps. In the previous example, melodic excerpts of "Siquisirí" were isolated and presented, allowing students to let these melodies materialize on their fretboard. When introducing patterns like this to novice guitarists, it can be helpful to label finger markings for the class or to translate the notation to tablature. Music teachers need to be flexible in these types of lessons, as guitar students may require time to decipher the notation, put the patterns in their fingers, and finally, to improvise using elements of the pattern. All of these skills do not need to be mastered within one class period, but could be developed over several class sessions. By bringing improvisational activities into the guitar classroom through WMP, guitarists are exploring new skills while continuing to listen deeply and intentionally to world music cultures.

Episode 5.4: Learning Pathway #3—Roma Wedding Music

Theory students should also have opportunities to develop their compositional and improvisatory skills. In fact, these types of experiences allow students to interact with the theoretical concepts within the course material. By incorporating WMP within the theory classroom, students can compose or improvise through the activities inspired by world musical cultures and sounds that may be overlooked from the course design and textbook. As a practical matter, the teacher might allow theory students to improvise on instruments they are most familiar with as a way to promote fluency in the improvisatory process; the teacher will also need to proactively remind students to bring those instruments to class with them.

Alternatively, the theory class could utilize a music lab setting where students each have access to a keyboard; however, the teacher should adjust for students with little keyboard experience, such as suggesting a stable hand position on the keyboard to explore the hijaz scale or giving students several minutes to practice on their own. Just as with other types of secondary music school classes, improvisation in the theory classroom needs to be scaffolded in a way to ensure student success, including developing a safe and inviting classroom where students can take musical risks. In the following episode, the rhythmic intricacies of Čoček Manhattan are broken down so that theory students can practice improvising in a typical Romani meter.

Episode 5.4: Roma Wedding Music
(Learning Pathway #3)

Specific Use: Advanced Placement Music Theory

Materials:

- "Čoček Manhattan," Yuri Yunakov Ensemble, Smithsonian Folkways Recordings

Saxophone, clarinet, keyboard, electric bass, and drum kit

Procedure:

(Creating)

1   Review the asymmetrical meter of the piece, asking students to move or tap to the beat. The beginning of the piece is 2+2+2+3.
2   Play track (00:01–01:13).
3   Review the hijaz scale (see Figure 3.3). Allow students to practice playing through it, ascending, descending, or haphazardly through the scale on their own.
4   After students are comfortable with the scale, have students explore the hijaz scale in the meter of the piece (9/8). As students begin to improvise in this meter, it may be prudent to slow the tempo. The following rhythms could be used to help scaffold rhythmic intricacy as they build their improvisational skills in the scale.
5   Have students improvise along with the recording, even if using more basic rhythms.
6   Play track (1:21–2:26).

Creative opportunities, like composition and improvisation, allow the teacher to relinquish some of the control of the classroom to the students. Students' examination and assessment of their creative work allows them to make democratic decisions by themselves or in small groups. This freedom permits students to identify their learning, both their strengths and weaknesses, and to have ownership of the sounds of the classroom. While these types of activities allow student voice within the musical

Figure 5.3   Scaffolding rhythms for improvisation

activities of the classroom, they also reinforce the need for deep and intense listening. The listening experiences will guide students toward the creative task at hand, especially if music teachers engage the creative processes as approached in different cultures.

Another challenge in facilitating creative music activities is that music teachers are experts in convergent or linear thinking, while these activities promote divergent thinking. In conservatory-style training and hierarchical educational settings, music teachers are groomed to be the authoritative voice on the podium or in the classroom regarding musical decisions: the timing of a cadence, the balance between parts, the shape of a vowel, or the speed of the tempo. In many music-making classrooms, there is only one correct way for the music to materialize. Engaging in music activities like improvisation and composition allows students to foster their own creativity while developing their understanding of world cultures and musical skills. These creative processes encourage divergent thinking, allowing students to explore multiple possible solutions or musical expressions.

Episode 5.5: Creating World Music—Northern India and the Nat-Bhairav Raga

The diverse musical endeavors that take place by Indian people reflect the vastness of the Indian subcontinent. India is situated between the Arabian Sea, Bay of Bengal, and the Indian Ocean and is bordered by the Himalayan Mountains to the north. In the northern and central regions of the country, migrants from across the western and northern borders have settled; this part of the country is frequently called Hindustan.

Hindustani classical music, sometimes called North Indian classical music, has been evolving since the 12th century. Hindustani music is one of two sub-genres of Indian classical music, with the other being Carnatic music, which comes from the southern part of India. Both Hindustani and Carnatic classical music revolve around a system of a melodic *raga* or mode that is played or sung while accompanied by a rhythmic cycle or *tala*.

A *raga* is a set of pitches, presented in a typical order that is adhered to as they appear in melodies. The order of pitches changes if the line is ascending or descending. There are characteristic motifs, or brief phrases, too, that comprise a raga. By using the proper pitches, each with its particular nuance (e.g., a slide into the pitch, or a "shake" like a tremolo), and by proceeding from pitch to pitch in ways characteristic of the raga, the performer sets out to create a mood or atmosphere that is unique to the specific raga. These moods are nuanced in how the intricate melodies are constructed and can convey such complex emotions as yearning, sadness, hope, and eroticism to the trained ear. It is well within the reach of secondary school students, even for students in a piano class, to explore the possibilities of Hindustani classical music within the framework of a particular *raga*.

Northern Hindustani music is highly personalized, as each player creates their own melodies within each performance, guided by their tutelage with gurus as well as an outpouring of their own musical sensibilities. The performance is spontaneous, but built upon the musicians' lived experiences of playing within the parameters of the raga. Thus, while it is improvised in the moment, it is a product of their training and follows culturally created norms.

The *sitar*, the *tabla*, and the *tanpura* are common instruments in Hindustani music. The construction of the sitar has not changed much in the past 600–700 years, with six or seven main strings that run over a curved fingerboard with raised frets. There are also a number of sympathetic strings (most often 11 or 13 strings) that resonate under the fretboard. The frets are movable and can be adjusted depending on the *raga* that is being played. The *tabla* is a two-piece drum, with two barrel-shaped, slightly different sized drums. The intention of the tabla, or any other drum in Hindustani music, is not to maintain a steady beat, but rather to provide a rhythmic counterpoint to the melodic content. The *tanpura* is also a stringed instrument, but unlike the sitar, it does not have frets and has only four or five strings. The tanpura is only used for accompaniment by creating a resonant drone as a stabilizing force of the ensemble.

The sitar player featured in the following episode is Shamim Ahmed Khan, a classical Hindustani composer. Ahmed was born into a family that devoted their lives to Indian classical music. He was introduced to Hindustani vocal music by his father, who was a professional musician in the classical Hindustani tradition. After a debilitating bout of typhoid fever, Shamim Ahmed left studying vocal music to study the sitar, eventually forming a formal student–guru relationship with the celebrated Ravi Shankar. The recording is an instrumental version of a *Nat-Bhairav raga*, which combines two raga versions, the *Nat* and the *Bhairav* (see Figure 5.4). It is considered an early morning *raga*, but it is not identified with a particular season. The *Nat* has a heavy and solemn sonority, while the *Bhairav* is more hopeful. This *raga* is built on D flat, a tonal center that may be uncommon to secondary music students who primarily experience music through notational methods; however, with the use of ear, even novice piano students can improvise melodies inspired by Hindustani music. In the following episode, piano students explore the intricacies of Indian raga while developing their own improvisational skills on the keyboard.

Episode 5.5: Improvising on Indian Raga

Specific Use: Piano Class

Materials:

- "Nat-Bhairev," Shamim Ahmed, Zakir Hussain, and Amanat, Smithsonian Folkways Recordings

  Nat Bhairev raga featuring sitar, tabla, and tanpura

Procedure:

(Attentive)

1 Have students listen to a segment of the raga and note the role of the different instruments (melody, drone, rhythmic interest).
2 Play track (00:01–00:40).

3 Have students listen intently to the melody and identify notes that add interest to the melody line. Students can raise their hand when they hear a note that adds interest to the melodic content.

4 Play track (00:01–00:40).

(Engaged)

5 Have students hum or play along on classroom instruments (guitars, keyboards) to a segment of the raga. Using the notation in Figure 5.4 can help facilitate active performing with the recording, although rhythm will be a challenge in this free metered segment. The music educator can divide the group into two, with half of the group playing the drone.

6 Play track (00:01–00:40). This may require multiple listens to become successful.

(Creative)

7 Discuss with students the improvisational nature of the raga and how performers create them within Hindustani culture.

8 Introduce the Nat-Bhaira raga to the students (Figure 5.4) and practice playing it ascending and descending.

9 Divide students into two groups, with every student at their own keyboard.

Assign one group to maintain the drone on the note of D flat. With the other group, guide students to explore the nature of the Nat-Bhairav raga individually, allowing each student to improvise a short melody. Allow students to pass the melody around, giving each student an opportunity to improvise.

10 Allow groups to switch their roles, from drone to melody.

11 After everyone has had an opportunity to improvise, allow students to discuss how their improvised melodies compared to the recording.

12 Play track (00:01–00:40); students can review their own musical understanding to the exemplar.

*dotted slur indicates long bend

Figure 5.4 Transcription of *Nat Bhairav* raga performed by Shamim Ahmed

Figure 5.5   Pitches of the *Nat Bhairav* raga built on C

Novice piano students may feel confined in their musical expression by learning pieces in only certain keys or by learning music solely through the realization of a notated score. The previous episode allows piano students the opportunities to improvise within a subset of pitches, many of which are outside the standard notes of C hand position. This practice builds agility in the novice pianist to move their hands across the keyboard, as well as dexterity in creating a melody that feels complete and has resolution. For beginners, the teacher may decide to assign pitches to specific fingers (e.g., assigning the first two notes of the *raga* with the left middle and index finger, the right hand assigned to the remaining notes), so that students do not have to change hand position. For more advanced players, students should be encouraged to play the improvised melody in the right hand and offered suggestions where the fingers can cross under or over to continue the line. While proper fingerings can build piano technique, the teacher must remember that the focus of this episode is to play creatively and to build musical understanding through interactions with a particular North Indian music culture.

Providing Feedback in Creative Activities

Music teachers face another challenge when facilitating creative music activities in navigating how to provide feedback to students when they present their creative products. It is important to be supportive and encourage divergent thinking. It is unproductive to label a student's work as "wrong" within this context, but the feedback can be framed in relation to the learning goal at hand. When presented with creative products that do not meet the learning objectives, there is an opportunity to return to the listening examples and to deeply engage with the sonic elements of music, which can provide guidance in what could be more compelling choices within the parameters of the project.

Additionally, the language used in feedback about creative products and process is often abstract (e.g., form, tension, resolution, contrast, interest). The music teacher must clarify the language she uses when discussing compositional or improvisational processes and must present these activities as concretely as possible, while also presenting how these creative processes live within the contexts from which they come. In order to be helpful in guiding students through creative processes, the music teacher must evaluate not only the student work but also how the student is faring within the creative process, and be sensitive to what the student needs to accomplish the creative task. It may be best to allow students to explore avenues of musical thinking that is unconventional, as it may allow the students to learn from their decisions.

Episode 5.6: Creating World Music—Japanese Taiko

The Japanese percussion ensemble known as *taiko* has grown in popularity in secondary school music programs over the last 20 years. The word *taiko* means both any type of drum used in the ensemble and also the ensemble itself. The ensemble format seen and heard today, known as *kumi-daiko*, is a post–World War II phenomenon first documented in 1951. With help from government funding in the 1970s, taiko started to emerge as a means to preserve Japanese cultural heritage and grew in popularity around the country. Many local communities seized the opportunity and funded the creation of their own local taiko groups. Through this initiative, more than 4,000 taiko groups were established in Japan. Some taiko groups focus on preserving local culture and rhythms, whereas others have become national and international sensations through their theatrical performances.

Musician Daihachi Oguchi created the kumi-daiko style and is given much of the credit for the current explosion of interest in taiko. Oguchi was a jazz drummer who happened upon an old score of taiko music. Deciding to perform the old music for the Osuwa shrine, Oguchi infused jazz into the sound as he arranged it. As a jazz musician used to playing with others, he wondered why taiko drums were never played together. He broke with tradition and assembled a taiko drum ensemble.

By including taiko of various sizes, Oguchi utilized a variety of musical voices, which he quickly assigned roles in his arrangements. The high-pitched *shime-daiko* carried the *ji* (backing rhythm.) The *odaiko* (large drum) played a simple rhythm that firmly grounded the pulse. A variety of *nagado-daiko* (long body drum) each had strong riffs that pushed the music along. Because many of his performers were not professional musicians, he also divided the rhythms into easier-to-play parts. In addition, each performer played on several taiko, set up in the fashion of a jazz drumset. Oguchi went on to lead the influential Osuwa Daiko, and spread his exciting taiko style throughout Japan and then throughout the world.

Oguchi composed the piece suggested here in Episode 5.6, "Hiryu San-Dan-Gaeshi," for Osuwa Daiko to perform at the 1970 World's Fair. It paints a sonic story of a dragon god come down from heaven, invited with a rhythmic phrase on

Figure 5.6   New York City–based group Taikoza

Photo courtesy of Marco Leinhard

the taiko. The opening announces the god three times. A *kakeai* (antiphonal section) is then played on the *fue* (bamboo flute) and drum. The third section quickens in tempo and symbolizes the dragon god flying toward the sky. "Hiryu" also includes an instrument developed by Oguchi that was brand new in 1970—the *tetsu-zutsu*, a bell-like instrument consisting of three pieces of pipe of differing diameters welded together. Two of the drum phrases are included in Figure 5.7.

Episode 5.6: Japanese Taiko Drumming

Specific Use: World Percussion Ensemble

Materials:

- "Hiryu San-Dan-Gaesh," O-Suwa-Daiko, Smithsonian Folkways Records Japanese taiko drums

Procedure:

(Enactive)

1. Students review taiko rhythms that they have performed with the recording (see Figure 5.7), playing without the recording.
2. Play track to compare their performance to taiko style.

(Creative)

3. Students, in smalls groups of three or four, create their own rhythms based on the role of their drum to perform for the entire class.

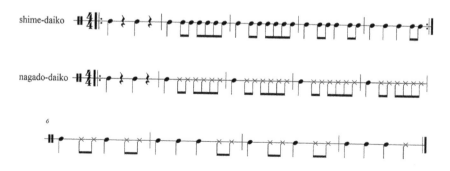

An 'x' notehead indicates playing on the rim

Figure 5.7   Two rhythmic phrases from "Hiryi San-Den-Gaeshi"

Inspiration to Create

Different cultures have varying viewpoints on the source of inspiration for new creative musical works, whether it be a gift from the divine or enlightenment from an ancestor. On the other end of the spectrum, some individuals believe that creativity in music is a product of labor, spending time in the act of creating as well as being embedded within the musical culture. It seems logical that musicians who regularly engage in creative processes would be more successful in composition and improvisation. It is not likely labor alone that molds expert improvisers and composers, but rather an interaction between prolonged creative activity accompanied by a spark in imagination. This spark is likely produced by intensive listening and performing within the musical culture and demonstrates that creating novel music through composition and improvisation is a natural extension of musical understanding.

While most musicians recognize that diligence and practice are important assets in creative processes, students must also be motivated, or even inspired, to produce new creations. It is the music teacher's responsibility to prompt inspiration in the student creative process. By approaching creative activities through the phases of WMP, student imagination can be prompted through deliberative listening practices, where the ear is drawn toward specific musical elements or timbres. New and interesting sounds, or familiar sounds used in new ways, can encourage students toward their own inventions. Additionally, inspiration can be created in students by discussing the context of the music, by allowing students to be introduced to the people behind the music-making, what is important in their lives, and, most importantly for the music classroom, how music is used within their culture. In the following lesson, students can be inspired to create their own musical compositions after engaging with the music of the Syrian National Orchestra and learning their story.

Episode 5.7: Creating World Music—Syrian Music in Times of Conflict

Since the Syrian civil conflict started in 2011, more than 400,000 Syrians have died, with more than 12 million Syrians displaced. The United Nations has called the Syrian refugee crisis the "greatest humanitarian emergency of our era."[1] The civil unrest started as a result of the Arab Spring, a series of anti-government uprisings that occurred in Northern Africa and the Middle East, specifically in Tunisia and Egypt, in 2011. By April of that year, peaceful protests were occurring across Syria in opposition to the government. Fifteen teenage boys from the Syrian city of Daraa were imprisoned and tortured for vandalizing with graffiti in support of the Arab Spring. When one of these boys, 13-year-old Hamza al-Khateeb, was killed from the injuries he sustained from torture, protests against the government turned violent and sparked national outrage. The government, led by President Bashar al-Assad, killed hundreds of protestors and detained many more in an attempt to quell the unrest. By mid-summer, defectors from the military called for the creation of the Free Syrian Army, a resistance group dedicated to ousting Assad from power. As the country became embroiled in conflict, many rebel groups formed to enlist in the fighting, some against the Syrian military and some in support of Assad's regime. Foreign involvement, especially by the United States and Russia, has only further complicated the conflict.

Prior to the civil war in Syria, the Syrian National Orchestra for Arabic Music performed regularly in the Damascus Opera House and employed 90 full-time musicians. This orchestra contains both classical Arabic instruments, such as the *ney* (an

Arabic flute) and the *qanun* (a zither), as well as orchestral instruments that are used in European traditions. Since the war broke out, many of the musicians have fled from Damascus, often as refugees, while others have persevered in the war-torn country. After a five-year absence from music-making, an international campaign was mounted to reunite the Syrian National Orchestra and bring players who had been scattered across the world to perform in Europe in 2016, with performances being streamed live to audiences in Syria as well as a refugee camp in Jordan. The performers who reunited for the event stated that these concerts allowed them to put a human face on the refugee crisis, or as one performer said: "The media tries to show us as savages, as terrorists. But there are different sides to every country in the world; there is the musician and the graphic designer and the coffee-shop worker. We need to show the normal side."[2] In the following episode, a recording of the live performance of "Old Damascus," an homage to the capital city of Syria, is presented to explore several dimensions of WMP including Creating World Music; this recording can be adeptly used in a music composition or music technology class to prompt students to compose music that incorporates the sonic features that are reminiscent of their home and community.

Episode 5.7: Remembrance of Home: The Syrian National Orchestra

Specific Use: Music Composition/Technology

Materials:

• "Old Damascus," The Orchestra of Syrian Musicians, Transgressive Records

 Arrangement for Syrian folk song with orchestral and traditional Middle Eastern instruments

Procedure:

(Attentive)

1 "What part of the world is this music from? What evidence from the music makes you think that?"

2 Play track (00:01–01:15).

3 Discuss answers. The music is from Syria and has many Middle Eastern characteristics (ornamentation, modal melody, use of percussion, groups playing in octaves, instruments to that region including the zither, timbre of flute).

(Engaged)

4 Have students play the melody along with the recording, on keyboard or other classroom instruments.

5 Play track (00:01–01:15).

(Enactive)

6 Play the melody alone, without the recording.

7 Play track (00:01–01:15) to review stylistic characteristics.

(Creative)

8 After discussing the history of this performance, remind students that the melody of the piece is a well-known tune about the old city of Damascus.

9 Have students brainstorm in groups melodies that could represent where they are from (e.g., country, culture, neighborhood) and play their melodies on keyboards or classroom instruments.

10 Once groups can play their melody, student groups should come up with sounds that are emblematic of their musical setting (e.g., timbre of specific instrument, sound effect).

11 Students perform their arrangements of their melodies for the class and describe how the musical sounds represent their community.

In music composition or music technology classes, many students may be intimidated to compose original music because they lack fluency with traditional notation. Music teachers should consider other means of preserving the music that coincide with the educational goals of the class. This practice might include allowing students to record the music on their smartphones, writing descriptive notes of the musical events, and employing graphic notation as a means to facilitate composing activities. Graphic notation is a method for documenting the musical sound by using non-traditional symbols. Students can use regular music clefs (with lines, shading, or chords dissolving into/out of pictures) but can also use more abstract tools like shapes or lines to represent their musical ideas. Graphic notation often intentionally leaves

Figure 5.8   Old Damascus tune

Note: The lines between notes indicate a slide-glissando that is used on the string instruments.

room for performer interpretation. It is important to remind students that the notation, whether traditional or graphic, is only a guide to facilitate future performances and is not the learning goal in and of itself. The musical goals can be achieved by using graphic notation as a means of documenting the sound, or without any notation at all if ample time is supplied.

Episode 5.8: Creating World Music—Joropo Music of the Orinoco Plains

The Orinoco River is one of the longest rivers in South America; it traverses Venezuela and Colombia and has been home to communities of ranchers for centuries. While straddling two different countries, the plains of the Orinoco River have endured histories of slavery, colonialism, dictatorships, civil war, and political unrest. *Joropo* music was created by ranchers and expresses the pride of the regional culture of the plains people. This rhythmic and percussive music is a confluence of Spanish, African, and indigenous musical sounds. *Joropo* music is sometimes synonymous with *musica llanera* (music of the plains), although the latter includes songs that accompany milking and horsemanship activities, in addition to ranching songs. *Joropo* music is often accompanied by flirtatious dancing that includes rhythmic stomping.

The *joropo* tradition evolved from a diverse assortment of instruments and localized repertoire to a more uniform sound. A melodic instrument drives the typical four-person musical groups, most often the *arpa* (harp) or the *bandola* (four-stringed guitar). The inclusion of the harp is a direct musical link to Spain, brought to the New World by the Spaniards centuries ago; with harps left behind by Spanish colonials, Creole communities incorporated their use in their folk music. Accompanying the melody is a trio consisting of *cuatro* (small, four-stringed guitar), *maracas* (a part of gourd rattles), and *contrabajo* (acoustic bass) or *tabla* (electric bass).

Male workers have long sung to accompany their tasks of herding cattle or milking. There is a cultural understanding that this music has a masculine quality about it, and traditionally, only male singers perform *joropo*. More recently, women have broken the gender barrier of performing as singers in this tradition, but they are generally relegated to only singing the more romantic or emotional ballad forms of songs.

The music featured in Episode 5.8 is performed by Grupo Cimarron, a *joropo* ensemble of professional musicians dedicated to presenting the music of the plains in its traditional form. There are two main types of songs in joropo music: the driving *golpe* and the lyrical *pasaje*. The suggested recording is an example of a *golpe* (from the word *golpear*, which means to hit or to strike.) These songs are aggressive and have a distinctive percussive *cuatro* pattern. Within this tradition of music-making, there are known types of golpes (e.g., the *parajillo*) that are distinguished by their chord progressions, melodic content, and metrical emphasis. Typically, in golpes the text is improvised to relate to the situation at hand. The suggested golpe is a traditional *sanrafael*-style golpe. Traditionally, the lyrics of this piece focus on St. Raphael, the patron saint of fishermen; however, in the following example, Ana Veydo, the singer and improviser of the text, presents an homage to the work ethic of the plainswoman and her connection to the land. This exciting piece of folk music can be used to explore improvisation of lyrics within a songwriting class.

Episode 5.8: Joropo Music of Colombia

Specific Use: Songwriting Class

Materials:

- "Un llanero de verdad," Grupo Cimarron, Smithsonian Folkways Recordings

  Joropo llanero featuring bandola and vocals

Procedure:

(Engaged)

1   While listening to the recording, gently hum with the vocal melody of the *llanera*.
2   Play track (01:25–02:11).

(Creating)

3   After reviewing the lyrics of the piece, remind students that these songs have improvised lyrics, which are even mentioned in the song. Have students examine the lyrics for the different topics that the singer brings up over the course of the song.
4   As a class, decide topics that students could improvise that are relevant to their lives, instead of the ranching life.
5   In smaller groups, have students experiment with improvising lyrics over the melody line as the recording plays.
6   Play track (01:25–02:11).
7   With the recording, have students perform their improvised lyrics for the class.
8   Play track (00:01–03:21).

Additional resources on Joropo music listed in Listening Episodes.

Group activities in a songwriting class allow secondary music students to interact with each other as they explore the songwriting process, which is often conceptualized as a solitary experience by secondary students. Through participatory musicking with the recording and classmates, students can delve into the songwriting process by identifying memorable snippets of melodic material, improvising lyrics in real time, and evaluating what musical ideas work and which need to be strengthened. Lessons like this push students to create within parameters that can ensure their success, but they also push students' ability to listen deeply, to perform, and to

Yo soy la que za-pa-te - a, yo soy la que za-pa-te - a, de-ba - jo de una en-ra - ma.

y me son-rien los pa-re - jos, ___ cuan-do me van a ___ sa - car.

soy a - gua de los ja - gu - e - yes, de ___ los ja - gue-yes lu - na

pa - ra en-amo-rar ___ soy lo amar - go del ___ ta - ba - coly cas - ca - bel en - ro - lla.

Translation of text:
I am the one that dances beneath the palm-roofed house
And the men smile at me when they're going to take me out to dance.
I am the water from the springs, the moon to fall in love with.
I am the bitterness of tobacco and of a rattlesnake.
I am the cry of the calf when they're going to lock him up
As well as the sweat of the beasts that come from grazing on the savannah.

Figure 5.9 Melody and translation of verse from "Un llanero de verdad"

Note: The rhythm and pitch approximates the speech like patterns of the singer.

consider music as culture. Through creating music that is inspired by particular world music cultures, students not only immerse themselves within the music, but they become a part of the tradition.

Creating Empathy Through New Imaginings

With all of the demands within the music classroom, to develop so many skills from technical skills in performance to aural learning skills, some music teachers may ask why bother with creative activities. Particularly in the case of teaching the world's musical cultures, teachers may feel the need to stay safe by learning to sing or play the piece only as it was sounded by performers in the origin culture. With a nod again to authenticity, teachers may feel that it is daunting to learn a previously unfamiliar musical style and then to launch into a brand-new creative piece (however connected it is to the style of the studied model piece). However, creative acts like improvisation and composition exhibit and celebrate the musical learning that has occurred within the classroom.

Through composing and improvising, students begin to immerse themselves within the music, to meld with the musical content, and to be inside the music. The learning, and the creative product, become an extension of the student. It can reveal a deeper level of learning than other musical processes that live within the music classroom as it is a personal expression, which is often rare in large music-making ensembles. The creative acts of composition and improvisation allows the student to internalize the musical understanding and to fully engage the musical cultures from around the world. This internalization and deep understanding of the musical culture could translate into empathy toward the people of those musical cultures, as students connect their own expressions with the musical traditions from around the world.

Imaginations Inspired by World Music Cultures: A Showcase of Musical Learning

In this chapter, the creative processes of improvisation and composition have been offered as viable extensions of the musical learning that can occur when engaging with cultural music from around the world. Improvisation and composition are important experiences that students can engage in as an organic extension of the deep and intensive listening that happens in WMP. Moreover, it is important for music educators to understand that composition and improvisation are not separate forms of musical expression, but rather they are parallel processes that display the musical understanding of the student.

Before engaging in creative activities in the secondary music classroom, students must be given generous opportunities to attend to the sonic details of the world music culture. When students have a clear understanding of the sound in their ears, the imagination will spark creative musical products. In order for students to be successful in their creative musical endeavors, music teachers must provide proper scaffolding that breaks down the compositional or improvisational task. By providing students with creative experiences in the style or inspired by world musical cultures, students can develop empathy as they blend their own personal expressions and experiences within a tradition of world music.

Notes

1 Agence France-Presse. (2014, August 29). UN: Syria is biggest humanitarian emergency of our era with three million Syrians now refugees. *The Telegraph*. Retrieved from www.telegraph.co.uk/news/worldnews/middleeast/syria/11062781/UN-Syria-is-biggest-humanitarian-emergency-of-our-era-with-three-million-Syrians-now-refugees.html

2 Khaleeli, H. (2016, June 23). The Orchestra of Syrian Musicians: "When there is violence, you have to make music". *The Guardian*. Retrieved from www.theguardian.com/music/2016/jun/23/syrian-national-orchestra-daman-albarn-when-there-is-violence-you-have-to-make-music

References

Hickey, M. (2012). *Music outside the lines: Ideas for composing in K-12 music classrooms*. New York: Oxford University Press.

Nettl, B. (2015). *The study of ethnomusicology: Thirty-three discussions*. Champaign-Urbana, IL: University of Illinois Press.

Listening Episodes

"Bai Trong Lay and Thet," Tu Huyen, Nam Phu, Chin Quon, Sau Phu, and Hai Phat, Smithsonian Folkways Recordings. Vietnamese Ritual Music with *ken trung* (reed instrument) and percussion. www.folkways.si.edu/tu-huyen-nam-phu-chin-quon-sau-phu-hai-phat/bai-trong-lay-and-thet/music/track/smithsonian.

"Čoček Manhattan," Yuri Yunakov Ensemble, Smithsonian Folkways Recordings. Saxophone, clarinet, keyboard, electric bass, and drum kit. www.folkways.si.edu/yuri-yunakov-ensemble/cocek-manhattan/world/music/track/Smithsonian.

"Hiryu San-Dan-Gaesh," O-Suwa-Daiko, Smithsonian Folkways Records. Japanese taiko drums. www.folkways.si.edu/ensemble-o-suwa-daiko-under-the-direction-of-oguchi-daihachi/hiryu-san-dan-gaeshi/music/track/smithsonian.

"Nat-Bhairev," Shamim Ahmed, Zakir Hussain, and Amanat, Smithsonian Folkways Recordings. Nat Bhairev raga featuring sitar, tabla and tanpura. www.folkways.si.edu/shamim-ahmed/nat-bhairev/world/music/track/smithsonian.

"Nyoka Musango," Lora Chiorah-Dye and the Suketai Marimba Dance Ensemble, Smithsonian Folkways Records. Marimbas, vocals, hosho, claps. www.folkways.si.edu/lora-chiorah-dye-and-sukutai/nyoka-musango/world/music/track/smithsonian.

"Old Damascus," The Orchestra of Syrian Musicians, Transgressive Records. Arrangement for Syrian folk song with orchestral and traditional Middle Eastern instruments. Available on iTunes and Spotify.

"Siquisirí," Son de Madera, Smithsonian Folkways Recordings. Son jarocho piece featuring leona, guitarra de son, jarana tercera, contrabass, and vocals. www.folkways.si.edu/son-de-madera/siquisiri-siquisiri/latin-world/music/track/smithsonian.

"Un llanero de verdad," Grupo Cimarron, Smithsonian Folkways Recordings. Joropo llanero featuring bandola and vocals. www.folkways.si.edu/grupo-cimarron/un-llanero-de-verdad/latin-world/music/track/smithsonian.

Additional Resources on Joropo Music

Members of Cimarron discuss the plain music of Joropo: www.folkways.si.edu/members-cimarron-discuss-llanero-plains/latin-world-spoken-word/music/video/smithsonian.

Members of Cimarron play El Guate, using traditional Joropo instruments including the arpa and the bandola: www.folkways.si.edu/cimarron-performs-el-guate-foreigner/latin-world/music/video/smithsonian.

Vocalist Ana Veydo discusses the role of women in traditional Joropo performance: www.folkways.si.edu/ana-veydo-from-grupo-cimarron-musica-llanera-from-colombia/latin-struggle-and-protest/music/video/smithsonian.

6

Integrating World Music

Mr. Rodriguez has been teaching in his current high school for the past 15 years; five years ago, the school administration decided to change the curriculum schoolwide, where all classes needed to incorporate elements of peace studies within their subject areas. After the initial disruption of changing traditions in the long-standing secondary school music curriculum, teachers within the school embraced change as they implemented dynamic and relevant learning experiences that encouraged students' critical thinking. This change in vision led to more project-based learning and democratic choices by students of what should be included in the course content of a large span of courses in the social sciences and humanities. In Advanced Placement Economics, students not only learned about the fundamentals of the supply-and-demand features of an economic market, but they also explored how those free markets create income disparities and social failures like homelessness and crime, provoking the question in students: "How can we adapt our economic system to be more just and equitable?" Similarly, in science classes, students tackled the relevant issues of climate change in ecology classes and energy supply in physics, while learning the state-standard content for each course. Additionally, educators were collaborating to create projects that would integrate learning from different areas of study. For instance, geography and literature teachers were creating a unit to address the realities of immigration from Central to North America through the voices of migrants in poetry and short stories as well as learning about the terrain and landscape of the path the migrants took. Considerations of peace and justice were thematically making their way into the lives of students through interdisciplinary attention across multiple subjects.

Meanwhile, the music teacher, Mr. Rodriguez, was a talented guitarist and was widely respected by students for the popular songwriting program he established within the music program. On hearing of the curricular changes that were evident in various specialized studies, Mr. Rodriguez decided to develop a course to explore the music of protest and peace campaigns from around the world. He realized that he could survey important music of the Apartheid Era in South Africa, the Civil Rights Movement in the U.S., and the Singing Revolution of the Baltic States. As a group, his students could listen to, perform, and investigate the impetus for the songs, and explore the ways in which the elemental features of the music contributed to its power. The students could create their own songs of protest, too. Mr. Rodriguez discussed the possibilities of a co-taught course with a social studies teacher, and together they discussed how they might explore local community issues with their students for ways of developing multicultural understanding, respect, and support. With guidance from the two teachers, students would discover ways to maintain peace relations through study, discussion, and the composition and performance of songs of protest.

Part of the emerging educational landscape in the 21st century is an examination of how disciplines or subject areas are interrelated and inform one another. The need for interdisciplinary understanding has arisen from the desire to solve complex problems that face our world as well as develop in students the ability to form critical thinking skills that they will use in a yet undefined future. Interdisciplinary learning requires students to synthesize concepts from different fields, which allows them to have a broader understanding and to consider the ethical dimensions of the material. As educational psychologist Howard Gardner (1983) posited, learning that integrates disciplines allows for students with different experiences to engage in the learning of content while utilizing different strengths or developing weaker areas.

By its very nature, music is a multidisciplinary experience. Anthropology, communications, history, linguistics, psychology, and sociology are fields of study that inform musical understanding beyond its sonic attributes. In some secondary school music classrooms, music teachers may give full focus to musical skill-building with nary a nod to how the music fits within its origin culture. For example, secondary school music students can play "Sisquisirí" without ever knowing of the origins of son jarocho, or "Nyoka Musango," the Zimbabwean marimba piece, without a sense of the message of rebellion against the oppressive government tucked into the lyrics, or "Čoček Manhattan" without understanding the legal oppression of Roma musicians. The moments for teaching about a music culture pass, and students go away from the experience with musical skills yet without a revelation of who performs and who listens, or where, when, and why they perform. Also missed is the opportunity to know how the music is received in places of social uncertainties, in the lives of individuals and communities who are mainstream or marginalized, who are expressing joy or sadness or other emotional states in moving ways through the music they make. Teachers present a false reality when they divorce music from its context, when they give sole focus to music listening, performance, and creative work. Music and context are not mutually exclusive, and the learning of music and related disciplines are enhanced by one another. Incorporating the cultural significance of the music makes the learning more meaningful and useful to students.

In the earlier episodes illustrating dimensions of World Music Pedagogy (WMP), provisions of context have been supplied as points of listening, participation, and creative work have been emphasized. Information has trickled in on issues pertinent to geography, history, politics, language, race, ethnicity, and class, partly because musical study is a humanistic endeavor that requires a connection of music with its culture. By situating a listening selection firmly within its culture, students can begin to understand why and how people make music. Guiding the students to sense the bigger picture of a music culture can include the historical origins of a musical example, how the music functions within the culture, or how it is transmitted among members of the community.

With interdisciplinary endeavors, music teachers facilitate learning experiences that may contain elements that are outside of their expertise. These teachers must develop lateral knowledge that will help inform the content of the different fields of learning that will be explored. As music educators Janet Barrett and Kari Veblen (2012) suggested, "teachers' intellectual curiosity, artistic playfulness, willingness to stretch through new experiences, and capacities for inquiry and reflection enable this move into new realms of curricular territory" (p. 366). Barrett and Veblen further suggested that learning environments that encourage collaboration are ripe for this type of learning to flourish. Teachers can reach out to other specialists within their building or community to provide an expert perspective in other subject areas, such as other teachers, parents with extensive knowledge in an area, culture-bearers, professors from local institutions, or community organizations that work in a related field.

Within this chapter, the dimension of Integrating World Music will be further explored. Like the episodes presented in previous chapters, the cultural context of each episode will be provided, detailing how these music examples are important to the musicians who make them. To further inspire the interdisciplinary imaginings of secondary school music teachers, this chapter will also provide examples of true cross-disciplinary experiences. Rather than focus only on how music teachers can integrate music into subjects beyond music, we suggest a multiple-collaborator design that relates other disciplines to the music curriculum and vice versa. These integrative ideas allow music teachers to explore beyond the sonic properties of the music and emphasize the cultural meaning of the music by learning keenly through interdisciplinary means; however, some of these designs may not be suitable for all secondary music classrooms or age groups. While presented as potential courses, these ideas can take the form of a series of lessons, a single unit, or even a fully designed course that encourages integrating between fields of study.

Music and Science

Secondary school music students can tackle complex scientific concepts in interdisciplinary lessons, units, or even a course designed to integrate music and physical science. Although music technology courses for performing, composing, and recording are in evidence, especially in high school programs, they are typically limited to music and rarely explore the scientific method. Yet the integrating of music and science in secondary school music classes can edge further into scientific considerations. Compelling research questions can form the basis for this type of integrating: "What is the physical nature of pitch?", "How does fast music influence human behavior?", "What musically happens to compel listeners to dance?", "What are the complexities involved in tuning a piano, a Persian tar, a Korean kayagum?", "How is it that the initial attacks of such instruments as violin, saxophone, and guitar characterize them, and help listeners in identifying them?", "How early are singing voices culturally conditioned to sound as they do, so that Chinese and Western opera styles are so distinctive?", "How do amps (amplification) work?", and "Through spectral analysis, how do listeners differentiate between the sound of an Egyptian 'ud and a Chinese pipa, or a trumpet played in a Western orchestra, a jazz ensemble, and a mariachi?" As illustrated by these example questions, integration of music and science can live in many secondary music classrooms, including popular music ensemble, guitar class, world music traditions, and AP music theory. Throughout these investigations, students can be involved in forming hypotheses, collecting and analyzing data, and forming conclusions. As in all collaborations, the secondary music teacher may want to coordinate with a scientist—perhaps a colleague who teaches in the building—in designing these types of lessons. When integrating with subjects like science, the students can continue to be involved in deep listening activities and in developing their skills of performing and creative expression.

Building Music Through Science

At the Metropolitan Preparatory School, art teachers are expected to collaborate with STEM (Science, Technology, Engineering, and Mathematics) colleagues in projects that explore the content of both the sciences and the arts. Last year, Mr. Matthews worked with a science colleague to have his students design and build guitars. With the use of the school's 3D printers, students built their own guitars and learned musical skills on their own instruments. This year, he has decided to take the integration one step further. As the literature classes are reading texts from sub-Saharan Africa including Chinua Achebe's Things Fall Apart *and Alan Paton's* Cry the Beloved Country, *Mr. Matthews decided to collaborate with the science department to build a set of Zimbabwean marimbas. With the help of the science faculty, Mr. Matthews planned to engage his students in the physics of acoustics and how the physical materials affected the sounds they produced. Through experimentation, the students decided which parts of the marimba needed to be produced on the 3D printer and which parts needed to be made by hand with different materials (e.g., resonating sound gourds, or PVC tubes as resonators). At the completion of this project, the students learned basic marimba skills and songs that reflect the culture.*

Episode 6.1: Integrating Music and Science— Zimbarimba and Acoustics

A variation on Mr. Matthews's process is provided in Episode 6.1, which has been adapted for a World Percussion Ensemble. This episode continues Learning Pathway #1, integrating Zimbabwe marimba learning with the science of acoustics.

Episode 6.1: Physics of Sound and Zimbabwean Marimbas (Learning Pathway #1)

Specific Use: World Percussion Ensemble

Materials:

- "Nyoka Musango (Snake in the Grass)," Lora Chiorah Dye, Smithsonian Folkways Recordings

  Marimbas, hosho, vocals

Procedure:

(Integrating)

1   Remind students about the context of Zimbabwean instruments and discuss the physical properties of the instrument.
2   Play track (00:01–05:51).
3   Discuss with the students the basic components of sound production, including frequency. Explain to students that frequency is influenced by the physical length of the sound-producing resonator (e.g., string, column of air, bell).
4   Provide students with a marimba (either a Zimbabwean or European; multiple marimbas would be ideal) and have students explore the relationships between the size of the resonator tube and pitches. For instance, same pitch classes should have a 2:1 relationship.
5   Assign students to find the lengths of the resonator tubes for a Zimbabwean marimba that is an octave lower than any that the school own. It will be helpful to remind students that Zimbabwean marimbas are not chromatic, but diatonic on the C scale with the addition of F sharp.

A world percussion ensemble is an ideal secondary music class for the experiences mentioned in the previous episode. Percussionists crave hands-on experiences within the secondary music classroom; the previous episode allows these students to combine their music-making with scientific exploration through hands-on activities. For episodes like this to be successful, it is important for the secondary music teacher to be exceptionally prepared, taking time to properly organize the materials so that each step of the lesson can emerge seamlessly. Classroom management issues, confusion, or chaos could result, especially during transitions, if there is a lack of clarity in student procedures—especially if there are classroom instruments around. It never hurts, especially for novice teachers, to spend a moment to revisit classroom expectations before jumping into hands-on activities, even for secondary music students.

Music and Immigration

Early records of human history have documented the movement of communities from one place to another. By exploring the complex systems that provoke immigration, students can better understand how society should make policy decisions. As communities or individuals move to new places, they bring with them their tangible cultural artifacts and their intangible cultural heritage. To fully understand this complex phenomenon, an interdisciplinary approach must be adopted that includes economic, cultural, religious, political, legal, and ethical considerations. By exploring the musical content of displaced people, secondary students will engage with the stories of people that choose or are forced to migrate. This type of inquiry allows students to examine how international and national forces or policies affect their community; it may also spur students to devise solutions that address immigrants' needs. As in the case of all interdisciplinary approaches to musical study, the topics of migration and music allow students a means for developing their understanding of citizenship and democracy.

Episode 6.2: Integrating Music and Immigration Studies—Son Jarocho in Los Angeles

While the son jarocho style is specifically from the Veracruz region of Mexico, the musical genre traveled with people as they moved across national borders. Son jarocho can be found in Chicano communities across the U.S., in cities such as Los Angeles, Austin, San Francisco, Seattle, and Chicago. In the late 1970s, there was a rebirth of the son jarocho style and a desire to maintain this unique cultural art form. Musicians who continue to expand the son jarocho tradition pay homage to their musical heritage but also use music as a means to reflect the current times.

Las Cafeteras is a group of musicians that emerged on the Los Angeles music scene. They create a fusion sound that combines elements of hip-hop, funk, and folk embedded within the structure of son jarocho. Their sound is unique but represents their East Angeleno (from East Los Angeles) perspectives. The ensemble uses traditional son jarocho instruments in their performance, including the tarima, quijada, requinto, and jarana secondo. The members of the group studied son jarocho style at the Eastside Café, a community learning space in the El Serrano area of Los Angeles. The group expounds on the traditional sounds of san jarocho while advocating for important issues in their community, such as economic opportunity, overincarceration of people of color, and immigration.

As mentioned in Chapter 3 (Episode 3.5), the popular song "La Bamba" (made famous by Ritchie Valens) is a traditional song in the son jarocho repertoire. Las Cafeteras performed their own version of the song on their album "It's Time," where they have reworked the lyrics to express their own experience as Chicanos in Los Angeles. Their version, "La Bamba Rebelde" (rebellious La Bamba), celebrates their Chicano identities. In Episode 6.2, a continuation of Learning Pathway #2, guidance is given using music by Las Cafeteras to explore musical and cultural themes like immigration in a secondary guitar class.

Episode 6.2: Son Jarocho in Los Angeles (Learning Pathway #2)

Specific Use: Guitar Class

Materials:

- "Siquisiri," Son de Madera, Smithsonian Folkways Recordings

  Jaranas, vocals

- "La Bamba Rebelde," Las Cafeteras, Las Cafeteras Music

  Quijada, cajon, marimbolo, vocals, jaranas

- "This Land is Your Land," Las Cafeteras, Las Cafeteras Music

  Reimagining of United States folksong in son jarocho style

  Vocals, jaranas, snare drum, bass, quijada, tarima, accordion

- "If I Was President", Las Cafeteras, Las Cafeteras Music

  Vocals, jaranas, keyboard, drum set

Procedure:

(Integrating)

1 Review the context for son jarocho–style music in the class, reviewing instruments, geography, and approaches to music-making.

2 Play "Siquisirí" to identify the musical and stylistic elements present in the piece; allow students an opportunity to discuss the musical characteristics of the piece.

3 Play track (00:01–04:02).

4 After discussing the origins of son jarocho style, show students on the map where to find the state of Veracruz, Mexico, as well as Los Angeles, California.

5 Explain to students that son jarocho music is currently flourishing in Los Angeles. Ask the students the following questions:

   "Why do you think Los Angeles may be a place where son jarocho is thriving?"

   (People from Veracruz moved there)

   "Why do you think people may have moved there?"

   (Allow students to explore their own ideas of why people immigrate).

6 Explain to students that you will be playing recordings of a current band that mixes son jarocho style with other present popular styles

7 Play tracks or videos by Las Cafeteras

8 Discuss the musical similarities and differences between songs performed by Las Cafeteras and Son de Madera

In the previous episode, providing contextual information to guitarists allows them to more fully understand the cultural importance of the musical tradition. The episode describes how secondary students will come to understand that the son jarocho tradition is not limited to the Veracruz area of Mexico, but migrated to other areas as those who value the musical tradition take it with them. These discussions allow guitarists to identify the musical differences among examples within a musical tradition from different places, the characteristics within a tradition that are essential, and how these considerations impact guitar technique and execution of the music. Having video examples curated from the Internet can be effective in highlighting these differences and similarities. Furthermore, Integrating World Music also allows secondary music students the opportunity to learn that musical traditions are in constant flux, being influenced by musical and cultural forces with which they come into contact.

Teacher Feature: Musical Meaning Through Contextual Understanding—David Aarons

Ethnomusicologist David Aarons Playing Steel Pan

Photo courtesy of David Aarons

David Aarons is a virtuosic Jamaican steel pan player, an ethnomusicologist, and a music clinician who works with teachers and students on a wide span of Caribbean music. While pursuing his doctoral degree in ethnomusicology at the University of Washington, David has been on the faculty of the Smithsonian Folkways Certification in World Music Pedagogy course. David has performed with a number of steel bands in the U.S., Jamaica, and Trinidad and Tobago. He also holds a certificate in steel pan building and tuning from Panland Trinidad and Tobago Instruments Ltd., and has subsequently worked with a number of bands in Jamaica as a pan tuner. His research interests include the music of diasporic communities and return movements, specifically repatriated Rastafari in Ethiopia, as well as religious, community, and popular musics in the Caribbean. As an ethnomusicologist, he presents a perspective on how to include diverse music cultures within the classroom. David expounds on the importance of "place" as a means to inform students about context, people, and musical meaning.

Q: For music educators who are new to engaging world music cultures in the classroom, what are some considerations you would give them as an ethnomusicologist?
A: I think music educators could try to be careful not to present music as being "frozen," or saying "this is what it is." For example, let's talk about steel band. A teacher can show steel band examples like *calypso* or *soca* or music that is traditional in Trinidad and Tobago, but if you go to Trinidad, you will also see people playing Western classical music on steel pan. So, that *is* part of the steel pan culture, too. I think that could be important—it's not just one thing that people are doing. The tradition is evolving. Trying to capture the authentic "one thing," while it seems noble, can be problematic. It's also important to try to understand how the music functions and evolves within that culture.

Q: Can you describe a musical collaboration, whether experienced by you or others, that helped create empathy toward others?
A: I was in Ethiopia, working with Rastafarians who had left Jamaica to go and live in Ethiopia, which changed their entire lives, to fulfill this mission that they were on, to return to Africa. And, at first, I didn't really understand why they were motivated to make that somewhat difficult journey. But while I was there, participating with them in musical contexts, you could see the conviction. You could see the evidence that they were trying to fulfill their purpose in this world. Playing music with them helped me to understand that a little bit more. I don't know if I could have reached that close of an understanding if they had come to me and explained it. There is something to be said about going into their own space, when you go into their rehearsal room, if you go into their tabernacle area where they have worship, and in their own special places that they've created.

Q: It sounds like part of the experience you described was in part due to you going into the space of your collaborators. Do you think music educators can replicate this within their classrooms?
A: I'm not trying to tell you that you need to take your kids out into the field, but it might be worthwhile if possible. Because it's not just about music, but the context in which it happens, and sometimes you need to leave the classroom. But, if bringing in visitors or culture-bearers into the classroom is all you can do, that's good. But then there's the politics of the space that you're bringing them into, which is a classroom, in an institution, and there could be so much baggage in that space. I think it's important because spaces act on us in different ways. And, when people from certain cultures or backgrounds, who may have been wronged by institutions, or who feel intimidated by institutions, come in there, they may not feel comfortable representing themselves. Being aware of this is important. You can't always replicate a space in a classroom,

but perhaps a discussion on space can help to paint a clearer picture for students and make visitors feel more comfortable. Maybe there are things you can do to alter the classroom space as well to make it more suitable.

Music, Race, and Racism

Teachers are sometimes uncomfortable discussing race in the classroom. However, concerns of race and racism are a continuing presence in society and of immense importance to students in developing an understanding of their community, the society of their nation, and interrelationships among people across the world. Some teachers, especially those from a dominant racial group, may see themselves as "color blind," where they believe themselves not to be influenced by race in their decision-making or interactions with people. Still, the perspectives they develop by virtue of their particular experiences may quite naturally be tilted in ways that benefit their own rather than other views.

Some of the outcomes of an exploration of race may include critical thinking as to how cultures develop their understanding of race and racism, developing strategies for creating an anti-racist environment or society, and identifying ways of understanding and interacting with people of different ethnicities. Enter music as a poignant avenue for profound learning. Race and racism are often embedded within the products of musical cultures, which may typify the uneasy relations among races within communities. Music can be a product of a celebration of an ethnic identity, a protest about mistreatment from a dominant race, or even stolen or appropriated for other purposes.

Secondary music classes can investigate the ways in which we think about race as historians and create an understanding of the motivations, choices, and resulting actions around racialization in distinct periods from history and how those understandings are exhibited within music traditions. Beyond the formation of race, secondary music students that explore the intersection of race and music can seek understanding of the ways that people on the margins of political and economic power exercise agency over their lives and find their voices in a region's historical narrative. Students will piece together the story of race, within a guitar class, a piano class, a music theory class, or an integrated course that explicitly looks at these issues.

Episode 6.3: Integrating Music and Race—Racism and the Roma

The Roma migrated to Europe from Northern India over a thousand years ago. As they journeyed their way westward, they faced forced assimilation and oppression. Roma people were the last ethnic group that could be legally used as slaves in Europe; slavery of the Roma was ultimately abolished in Europe in 1860. Roma people are still legally discriminated against in many European countries. In some places, like Bulgaria and Macedonia, it is socially acceptable to be openly discriminatory toward them. This poor behavior is not a new trend, but rather a part of the long history of prejudice against Roma. It is centered around a lack of understanding of a cultural group with its traditional ways of living, its culture-specific language, customs, family lineages, and values. Over the centuries, Roma throughout Europe have dealt with enslavement, illegal evictions, geographical segregation, poor healthcare support, and even legalized prejudicial treatment of Roma children in schools. Not surprisingly, this has resulted in poor school attendance and less academic success for Roma children, leading to more vulnerability and oppression.

Despite these obstacles, Roma have managed to resist total assimilation and maintain a strong cultural identity. The Roma may be victims of racism because others intolerantly see their way of life as travelers who have opted out of society and refuse to conform to local norms. Some Europeans see the Roma as representing an affront to the governing principles of the mainstream culture, rather than as a group striving to provide for its families while retaining important cultural identity. Political and cultural organizations have undertaken the task of raising a political voice among Roma and battling against discrimination.

In 2010, the French government tried to evict tens of thousands of newly arrived Roma back to Eastern Europe, reminiscent of the massive deportations that occurred during World War II. The French people protested this treatment of the Roma and the deportations subsided. While the Roma are still treated unfairly in many parts of Europe, the events in 2010 led to an awareness of the rights of Roma to pursue the "European dream" and to make the marginalized visible. Although the treatment of the Roma has arguably improved in recent years, the influx of refugees into this part of the world creates a new dynamic, where these refugees may be treated as the "new Roma." In the following episode, Advanced Placement Music Theory students explore this important yet complicated issue of race within the study of music featuring the third Learning Pathway.

Episode 6.3: Racism and Roma Music
(Learning Pathway #3)

Specific Use: Advanced Placement Music Theory

Materials:

- "Čoček Manhattan," Yuri Yunakov Ensemble, Smithsonian Folkways Recordings

   Saxophone, clarinet, keyboard, electric bass, drum kit

- "Djelem Djelem," Esma Redzepova, World Village Records

   Unofficial Romani anthem featuring accordion, clarinet, trumpet, and vocals

Procedure:

(Integrating)

1   Review context of the piece and discuss how the Roma are treated in many places in the world.
2   Remind students about the musical characteristics of "Čoček Manhattan."
3   Play track (00:01–03:31) to revisit those characteristics.

4 To further explore understanding of the Roma experience, present "Djelem Djelem." Prompt students: "What emotions are the musicians expressing? How are they presenting those emotions musically?"

5 Play track "Djelem Djelem" (00:01–02:15).

6 Review answers. The song is sad, but hopeful. Musically, this is accomplished by mode, ornamentation (e.g., sliding, trilling), and expressive timing.

7 Explore lyrics with students to further understand the mood of the song.

8 Open a discussion about the local community, examining if there are groups that are treated unfairly. Prompt: "Are there any instances where people are treated differently because of the color of their skin or the language they speak?"

9 Return to Esma Redzepova's version of "Dzelem Dzelem"; have students follow along with the text. Prompt: "As we listen, how does the music make you feel?"

10 Discuss students' reactions.

Advanced Placement Music Theory students are often the most experienced and skilled musicians within secondary music programs; the rigorous curriculum attracts curious and committed secondary musicians. Learning experiences like those described in the aforementioned episode are essential for students in theory courses. While the focus of the class may be the mechanics of tonal harmony, context is important to fully understand the value of the music found within its sonic properties as well as its cultural value. Providing context for theory students not only draws attention to how harmonic devices can be valued from within their specific culture, but also pushes students to consider the experiences of other people, perhaps creating building blocks toward empathy. Teachers must be reminded that they do not have to give all of the integrated information within one class session; just like all dimensions of WMP, the learning and listening can be spaced out over multiple lessons.

Music and Citizenship

Musicians around the world have used music as a vehicle to articulate the role of citizens in society. Integrating citizenship education with music learning can provide students with deep learning about multiple disciplines. The goal of citizenship education is to produce well-informed, productive members of society. In citizenship classes, students explore the rights and civic privileges that are afforded to citizens from a governing body. Often, students learn about the institutions and the mechanisms that produce and preserve citizens' rights. As a consequence of this learning, students develop critical thinking skills in regard to the preservation of human rights and democratic institutions. Students also explore their own roles and responsibilities in the maintenance of a just and civil society. As a result of these discussions, students debate about the nature of democracy, the difference between personal and collective freedoms, the rejection of discrimination, and understanding the role of a global citizen. When teaching about citizenship within the secondary classroom, it is important for the democratic principles that are being learned to be on display for the students to engage; educators should not approach this material in a top-down, teacher-centered fashion, but rather present the concepts for students to form their own critical understanding.

Although some teachers may be enticed to use overly nationalistic music to demonstrate the concepts of citizenship of a home country, the incorporation of world music learning and understanding its context can lead to illustrating the citizenship concepts. Moreover, when learning about citizenship in the classroom, students should be given the freedom to express their understanding—music can be one avenue for discussions about democratic ideas and civil responsibilities. As an illustration of learning music and citizenship in an integrated fashion, consider the Tropicalists in Brazil and their approach to musical free speech in the face of governmental censorship. This exploration can be experienced in a variety of secondary music classrooms, including a popular music ensemble.

Episode 6.4: Integrating Music and Citizenship Education— Tropicalism in Brazil

During the 1960s, many countries throughout the world experienced social unrest and protests; Brazil was no different. Prior to a military coup, student organizations led protests to democratize university education by allowing more students to attend. During the political instability, protestors adopted more socialist and populist ideas, such as universal literacy programs or sanitation reform campaigns. These student protestors also developed their own cultural products that allowed them to make artistic works that call for social change. After the military coup, civil rights were eroded significantly. Student organizations were disbanded on campuses, and any political statements against the regime were prohibited. While the government was actively censoring the views of the government's critics, artists were still given some flexibility to express their views.

It is from this context that the *Tropicalia* artistic movement emerged. Led by Brazilian musicians Gilberto Gil, Caetano Veloso, Gal Costa, Tom Ze, and the group Os Mutantes, Tropicalists wanted to form a new Brazilian aesthetic that was a departure from the nationalistic and traditional forms used by the leftist student movement. This cultural movement got its name from the work of Oswald de Andrade, who posited that Brazilians were in a unique position to "cannibalize" the cultural influences around them, including indigenous and colonial forces, to create a new, improved culture. The Tropicalists wanted to fuse musical art forms, including traditional Brazilian sounds, psychedelic rock, and avant-garde performance art. For these artists, this was a way to subvert cultural imperialism while promoting their own visions of the future of Brazilian music. Because of their unconventional musical creations, with irregular time signatures, unorthodox song structures, elements of musique concrète, and peculiar performance costumes and demeanor, as well as their involvement in anti-government protests, the Tropicalists became the target of governmental harassment. In 1969, after disregarding censorship laws and making several highly visible provocative performances that criticized the government, Gilberto Gil and Caetano Veloso were imprisoned for two months, although there is no official record of why they were detained. Subsequently, the two musicians were forced to seek exile in the United Kingdom. After his exile, Gil eventually served in the Brazilian government as the Minister of Culture from 2001 to 2008. He was the second black person to ever serve in a presidential cabinet in Brazil. In learning about the Tropicalist movement, secondary music students explore the role of artistic expression as a right of freedom of speech. This material can be included in existing secondary music classrooms, as depicted in Episode 6.4 in a Popular Music Ensemble.

Episode 6.4: Gilberto Gil and the Tropicalists

Specific Use: Popular Music Ensemble

Materials:

- "Aquelo Abraço," Gilberto Gil, Phillips LP
  Guitar, bass, vocals, kettledrum, cowbell, whistle, and cabasa
- "Batmacumba," Gilberto Gil, Caetano Veloso, and Gal Costa, Phillips LP
  Psychedelic rock song featuring guitar, bass, vocals, tambourine, and bongos
- "Panis Et Circensis," Os Mutantes, Phillips LP
  Avant-garde rock song featuring brass, guitar, organ, vocals, trumpet, tambourine, bass, and drumset

Procedure:

(Integrating)

1 Discuss with the students the musical context of the Tropicalist movement. Importantly, describe how the Tropicalists were an artistic movement that incorporated avant-garde performance techniques, African rhythms, psychedelic rock characteristics from the U.S. and the UK, and traditional Brazilian forms like samba.

2 Explore the tracks "Panis Et Circensis" and "Batmacumba" to identify how these different influences are present in the pieces.

3 "Listen for unusual musical elements to be present in these rock songs."

4 Play track "Panis Et Circensis" (00:01–03:39).

5 Review answers (unrelated musical introduction, sound effects at end of song, virtuosic trumpet solo/tonguing technique).

6 Play track "Batmacumba" (00:01–02:35).

7 Review answers (unusual form, no verses or chorus, unusual use of text).

8 Provide complete translations of the text and allow students to explore the lyrics. "Batmacumba" has little meaning, although *macumba* is equivalent to Brazilian voodoo. "Panis Et Circensis" explores the complacency of many Brazilians in the wake of the military takeover of the government and is a genius satire of the bourgeois (e.g., translated lyrics include "I sent the lions to my neighbors' yard/But all the people having dinner inside/Are very busy with their food/Until they die").

9   A brief review of the historical context of this music should be presented, specifically that critiques of the government were not tolerated. Additionally, Gilberto Gil and Caetano Veloso were imprisoned and exiled for their music and participation in protests.

10   Play track "Aquelo Abraço" (00:01–04:45).

11   Discuss with students that Gilberto Gil wrote this song between his imprisonment and his exile out of the country. The text discusses all the things he will miss about his country.

12   Allow students to discuss the differences in musical characteristics between this piece and the other Tropicalist songs. Permit multiple listens to identify stylistic similarities and differences.

13   Conclude learning about the Tropicalists by having a discussion about freedom of expression. Prompting questions for the discussion could include: What kind of expression should be against the law? What about hate speech? What is the role of the citizen to protect these types of freedoms? Should people be imprisoned for musical expressions? Would you be willing to be exiled for something that you believe in?

By integrating music learning and citizenship education, as portrayed in the preceding episode, secondary music students can identify the context of the popular music trends and how musical artists are responding to the social issues of their time. Many popular music ensembles employ informal learning practices that reflect the musical development of performing artists in popular genres. These practices include immersive listening to models, peer-to-peer transmission of skills, student agency in song selection, and self-teaching techniques. In the previous episode, multiple exemplars are provided, allowing ensemble members to choose what songs may be most aesthetically alluring or most relevant to their lives. If students are invested in repertoire selection, motivation will be fostered, even as technical challenges are encountered.

Experiencing the dimensions of WMP within a popular music ensemble can highlight the sonic features of musical cultures as well as engender students' abilities to learn musical skills through an oral-aural process, in much of the same way as popular musicians learn. WMP showcases this sequence from listening to performance and should be encouraged by the teacher's guidance; however, the teacher should also provide space for students to learn through informal practices as well.

Music and Indigenous Peoples

Integrated lessons within secondary music classes that focus on Indigenous peoples and music allow students to explore the intellectual and cultural traditions of many groups around the world. By learning about Indigenous peoples, students can increase their understanding, awareness, and respect for Indigenous culture. Integrated lessons or units work best if they are taught from an understanding from within the lived experience, with the aid of a culture-bearer or some other partnership, rather than exogenously (i.e., exclusively from an outsider's point of view); this perspective allows for an honest view of the full effects of colonialism on Indigenous communities. Hopefully, through this type of learning, students can help forge better relationships between Indigenous and non-Indigenous people within their community. Integrated material like this reminds students that many lands have been taken away from native peoples and that their history, culture, and continued presence on that land is important.

An interest in designing such a class will necessarily require sensitivity and considerable caution. There are strict norms within Indigenous cultures concerning musical ownership (e.g., who is allowed to perform musical material from a given culture, or in what contexts the music can be performed), so that the study of the music of North American Indigenous groups, and of the Sami *Joik*, the Hawaiian *hula*, and the Samoan *sa sa* requires a careful read of what is and is not appropriate. The use of sacred music must also be carefully considered, as in when and whether to feature music of Buddhist, Christian, Hindu, Jewish, and Muslim practices, both because of the sensitivities within the origin culture of the music as well as due to strictures of curricular policy within state-funded schools. Music teachers can stumble into quandaries despite well-intended interests in celebrating the music and people, and may unknowingly break the codes of conduct of the musical cultures. Culture-bearers, local musicians, and members of local communities can be helpful to teachers in navigating tricky issues. Music teachers do well to select recordings of Indigenous musicians carefully, reading the liner notes, and checking print and electronic media for guidance as to what should or should not be experienced and studied. At times, Indigenous musicians may suggest that music may be listened to but not performed and recordings be used that have been approved and permitted by the group (as in the case of the Native American collection within Smithsonian Folkways Recordings). Popular music by Indigenous musicians is typically open for use since it is meant to be consumed by a wider audience outside of the Indigenous community, as opposed to ritual music that has special meaning and rules for ownership within the community.[1]

Episode 6.5: Integrating in Action—Indigenous Matters in North American Popular Music

Buffy Sainte-Marie is an activist musician from the Piapot Plains Cree First Nation in Canada. Sainte-Marie wrote the song "Bury My Heart at Wounded Knee" in the early 1990s and takes its title from a book that was published in 1970; the book was one of the first histories of American westward expansion in the 19th century written through a critical lens, and it recounts the abuses of the American government on its native people. In South Dakota, the village of Wounded Knee is the site of a massacre where more than 200 Lakota men, women, and children were killed or injured in 1890. While the title of the song reminds listeners of this past atrocity, the content of the song discusses the events that happened in 1973, known as the Wounded Knee Incident. Residents of the Pine Ridge Reservation were growing dissatisfied with the leadership of tribal president Richard Wilson, who was seen as exploiting communal lands for political capital, using reservation resources for his own intimidation tactics, and acquiescing to federal organizations in making decisions that affected tribal people. After an unsuccessful attempt to impeach Wilson from his office, tribal chiefs along with activists from the American Indian Movement decided to occupy the town of Wounded Knee with the demands of removing Wilson from power and to renegotiate the relationship between the U.S. government and the reservation, wanting to be a sovereign and independent nation. Federal forces, including Federal Marshals and the

FBI, set up roadblocks, surrounding all thoroughfares into or out of Wounded Knee. The confrontation quickly escalated as both sides began to arm themselves; the federal forces brought in armored vehicles and helicopters. Both sides engaged in violence and both endured casualties. After a local reservation resident, Lawrence "Buddy" Lamont, was killed by a government sniper, the elders of the community moved to end the siege. Federal authorities took control of the town after 71 days.

While the song alludes to earlier abuses by the U.S. government, Sainte-Marie's song centers on the poor treatment of people on tribal lands as the government was exploiting their land for use by energy companies. Despite the song being more than 25 years old, the topic of the song is reminiscent of the 2016–2017 standoff between the Standing Rock Sioux and the U.S. government over the proposal to build an oil pipeline near sacred lands.[2] In her verses, Sainte-Marie alluded to several events that occurred around the Wounded Knee incident. In one verse, "Annie Mae" is mentioned, which refers to activist Annie Mae Aquash, who took part in the occupation of Wounded Knee and was found murdered a few years later. Her body was identified, but the original federal investigation suggested that she had died of exposure, which later was to be discounted as there was physical evidence that she had been shot in the head. The inclusion of this story within the song illustrates the skepticism of native people to the colonial powers that still exist and influence their daily lives. The song also mentions Leonard Peltier, who was convicted and is still serving time for murdering federal investigators, despite questionable evidence and testimony. In a songwriting class, as illustrated in Episode 6.6, secondary music students explore important issues for Indigenous people while developing listening, performing, and composing skills.

Episode 6.5: "Bury My Heart at Wounded Knee"

Specific Use: Songwriting Class

Materials:

- "Bury My Heart at Wounded Knee," Buffy Sainte-Marie, EMI Records
  Guitar, vocals, bass, keyboard, electric guitar, drum set

Procedure:

(Integrating)

1 Provide students with the historical and cultural background to the song "Bury My Heart at Wounded Knee." This may take a bit of time to unpack the issues of Native American rights, criminal justice, and environmental rights.

2 Play track (00:01–05:12).

3 Discuss with students the musical techniques that are employed that reinforce the main ideas of the piece (including the incorporation of Native American singing techniques).

4 Have students play the chords with the recording.

5 Play track (00:23–01:00).

6 Students write their own lyrics to the chord progression that they have been playing. Lyrics can center on issues that are important in their neighborhoods or within the school itself.

It should be noted that the transcription (Figure 6.1) is faithful to the recording, and playing the notes and chords as transcribed will allow students to play along with the recording. However, the chords are somewhat unusual for beginning guitar players who may be in a songwriting class. Lowering the key by a half-step would allow students to play fairly common chords on the guitar (D, C, A, G, B minor, F flat major). Another modification for beginning students is to have them only play the bass notes of the chord, allowing students to learn to move around the fretboard with ease. As music teachers embark on these important discussions about colonial forces and native peoples with their students, it is advisable to give students the complete lyrics, whether projected on a screen or in a handout. This practice will allow students to more fully comprehend the meaning behind the text.

Music and Gender

Musical study provides a rich opportunity for understanding how gender is embedded into cultural life and norms. In exploring gender within the secondary school music curriculum, the design can be the identification of influences of gender and sexuality within songs and instrumental pieces as well as the ways that such music can contribute to an understanding of society and culture. A journey into gender studies in high school courses allows students to recognize the contributions of women and sexual minorities (e.g., LGBTQ) to music, as well as to acknowledge the oppression endured by these groups historically and the struggle for recognition, validation, and equitable treatment. High school students can reckon with fundamental understandings of the intersections between and among gender, sexuality, race, class, and ethnicity. This content can be easily included in a variety of secondary school music classes, such as class piano, songwriting, world percussion ensemble, and world music traditions. As with all interdisciplinary content in this chapter, integrating music and gender studies requires intentional listening experiences and participatory music-making for students to fully interact with the material.

Interdisciplinary content that explores gender could include the history of women in the world, while examining musical expressions of women from diverse cultures. Students can explore how gender norms impact culture, as well as the deeper historical content about the history of women. A major emphasis can be comparisons between historical periods and current events affecting women today, such as the terrorism of women by Boko Haram, education for girls in Afghanistan, or the Women's March in Washington, D.C. to demonstrate for human and women's rights. On learning some concepts relative to a history of gender, including women's (and men's) rights, and applying them to the history of the family, students can select themes from among politics, economics, religion, culture, ideals, and sexuality to explore in greater detail. Assessments can include an individual research project

Figure 6.1 Verse and chorus of "Bury My Heart at Wounded Knee"

Figure 6.2   Protesters at the Women's March in Washington, D.C.

Photo courtesy of Michelle Alexander

comparing women's experiences in two cultures. Content for this type of course can include listening and learning the music of current musicians who are making statements about the status of women around the world, like Pussy Riot in Russia or Oumou Sangare in Mali.

Episode 6.6: Integrating Gender and Music—South Korean K-Pop

After several armed conflicts throughout the 20th century, South Korea has become a nexus of cultural influences, as traditional Korean culture is impacted by Chinese, Japanese, European, and American influences so that a more contemporary Korean culture has emerged. K-Pop, or Korean Pop, is an amalgam of influences, and video productions of the music relies on elements like precise choreography and memorable fashion choices. The music of K-Pop is similarly a combination of genres, mostly identifiable as pop while also incorporating elements from hip-hop, techno, rock, rap, and R&B characteristics. K-Pop groups are called "idol groups" because they are cultivated by entertainment agencies, who find talented young people and offer them an exclusive contract. New idol groups are then put through an extensive training program, where they are sequestered with their other bandmates to learn requisite skills like dancing, singing, and foreign languages; this practice is sometimes criticized by media outlets, as many of these newcomers are children.

In K-Pop music, it is common for the singers to vacillate between Korean and English, and even sometimes Mandarin—this approach is to appeal to a broader market audience as well as have an international feel to the production of this music. More recently, most K-Pop groups have English names. The values that are espoused within K-Pop music convey a progressive, multicultural perspective. In the performance of K-Pop music, the different members of the group are each parts of the song to be showcased. While the musical product is not very different from pop music in other parts of the world, the stylized attention to dance and fashion have made K-Pop a commercial success both inside and outside of South Korea. K-Pop has helped South Korea create the rise of *Hallyu* (Korean Wave), where there has been an increased interest and economic investment in Korean culture.

In Episode 6.6, K-Pop is explored through the lens of examining gender. The song "I Don't Need a Man" by the group *miss A* displays many of the common attributes of K-Pop music, including the mélange of musical genres with the inclusion of a rap at the end, stylized dance moves, the inclusion of English phrases within the text, and allowing each performer time to be in the spotlight. While the target audience for this music is young adolescents, the subject matter of this song explores gender within society today.

Episode 6.6: K-Pop and Feminism

Specific Use: Piano Class

Materials:

- "I Don't Need a Man," miss A, AQ/JYP/KT

  K-Pop song that explores gender roles in modern times

Procedure:

(Integrating)

1   Review with students the elements of the K-Pop musical style.
2   Listen to track or watch video (00:01–03:50).
3   Discuss the musical elements of the song and how it relates to K-Pop style.
4   Ask students about the themes of the lyrics and what the overall message is. Prompt students: "What do these performers say about being a girl (or woman) in society today?"

5   Listen to or watch track (00:01–03:50).

6   Continue to discuss what messages about gender the performers are conveying with this song. Allow students to agree or disagree based on their experiences.

7   Ask students if they believe the performers are honestly portraying their feelings about gender as this musical product is a commercial effort and knowing that these performers have been groomed to be entertainers. Prompt question: "Is this a true critique of how women are treated within society or a way for the music company to capitalize on female empowerment?"

8   Continue discussion by examining other popular songs that explore gender.

Additional Resources

1   Janelle Monae, "Q.U.E.E.N.," Wondaland Records

2   Beyoncé, "Run the World (Girls)," Columbia Records

Music as Protest

Music is an integral part of protests in response to war, social injustice, the hardships of poverty, government corruption, and other forms of oppression. All revolutions are fortified by people singing, playing instruments (especially drums and brass instruments that are capable of considerable projection), and a kind of collective movement in the marching forward to a unified beat. This material is ripe for students to understand the world around them more completely, to understand the complex systems that create conflict within societies and how to voice opposition within them. Exploring protest music is feasible for many secondary music classrooms, including guitar class, piano class, songwriting class, popular music ensembles, and gospel choirs.

It is not uncommon to find particular musicians or songs that have become integral to social movements. Examples of the capacity of music to strengthen protests include the anti-apartheid movement in South Africa, the Civil Rights Movement in the U.S., and the anti–Vietnam War movement. While music has not been credited as the singular source to affect change in the world, there is acknowledgment of the powerful contributions of music to states-of-mind. Music-making can allow for sharing social states-of-mind and building a sense of community, shared purpose, and solidarity—perfect conditions for a protest mentality.

Protest songs have a long history with struggles related to human rights agendas. Musical responses to social marginalization come from musician-activists including Pete Seeger and Woody Guthrie in the U.S., and particularly powerful protest songs such as Abel Meeropol's anti-lynching anthem "Strange Fruit." Much musically expressed protest of injustice in the last 30 years has been done through international hip-hop traditions. Whether rapping about political corruption, endangering the environment, mistreatment based on religion, or mistreatment based on sexuality, hip-hop has become an avenue to voice frustration over marginalization and oppression. In a class where protest music is studied, many world music cultures can be explored.

Episode 6.7: Integrating Music as Protest—Fighting Apartheid in South Africa

When considering the potent influence of music as protest against the status quo, a poignant example is the struggle of the South African people against apartheid in the 20th century. After centuries of colonization and policies that allowed removal of land from black South Africans by whites, a legalized "apartheid" (meaning separateness) was implemented by the Afrikaner National Party with more than 300 laws, such as requiring all people to carry racial identification cards, designations where races could live, and anti-miscegenation laws. Black South Africans were forcibly moved to designated townships. Access to education and employment opportunities were very limited. Black South Africans protested the unfair and heinous treatment, but the Afrikaner establishment would not acquiesce, imprisoning leaders of the vocal movement for change.

International pressure for change in government policies increased after hundreds of black South African school children who were peacefully protesting were killed during the Soweto Township Uprising. The official count of black victims is 176, but some present believe that up to 700 students were killed by police forces, with another thousand injured. The death of resistance leader Steven Biko in police custody also drew attention from the international community. The United Nations Security council voted to embargo arms sales to South Africa and denounced the apartheid policies.

Over the next several years, the economic state of South Africa suffered a downturn, as many countries experienced a worldwide recession. Several countries applied sanctions on South Africa for their continued human rights abuses and the use of apartheid. In order to appease the external economic influences, the National Party administration of Pieter Botha instituted some reforms, such as an end to the criminalization of interracial relationships and marriage. These changes were far from substantive, and pressure continued for change. Botha was succeeded by F. W. de Klerk, whose administration removed most of the laws that were the legal basis for the apartheid system. A new constitution was instituted that enfranchised all races within South Africa. For several years, a truth and reconciliation campaign ensued to mend the fractious relationships between different groups. In the following episode, the story of the struggle against apartheid unfolds for students in a World Music Traditions class, as several key songs are explored and experienced.

Episode 6.7: Protest Music Against Apartheid in South Africa

Specific Use: World Music Traditions

Materials:

- "Nkosi Sikelel'i Afrika," Ladysmith Black Mambazo, Gallo Record Company

  A cappella singing

- "Beware Verwoerd! (Ndodemnyama)," Miriam Makeba, RCA Victor

  Vocals, guitar, bass, djembe, body percussion
- "Meadowlands (Mielieland)," Nancy Jacobs & Her Sisters, (2004). Gallo Record Company

  Piano, drum set, guitar, bass, vocals
- "Senzenina," Lalela Cape Town Choir, (2014). Lalela Music

  A cappella singing
- "Sobashiy'abazali" (We Will Leave Our Parents"), African Cream Freedom Choir, African Cream Music

  Vocals, bass drum, whistling

Procedure:

(Integrating)

1   The story of the fight against apartheid in South Africa can be recounted by the music that was used to protest against injustice. The sampling of songs discussed here are just "the tip of the spear" of a vast catalogue of music that chronicles the resistance to apartheid in South Africa. Certainly, a whole course on just this subject is possible, but it also could live in secondary music classrooms as a unit or a series of lessons. Any of these selections can be experienced in the music classroom in a wealth of activities from Attentive Listening activities to performing and creating activities.

Nkosi Sikelel'i Afrika

Originally written as a hymn at the end of the 19th century by a teacher at a Methodist school in Johannesburg, Nkosi Sikelel'i Afrika became the unofficial anthem for the fight against the apartheid government. Originally written in the Xhosa language, the song became very popular in churches throughout South Africa, as the hymn contains both Western and Indigenous South African characteristics. This song was an important pillar during the decades-long fight against apartheid, as it was often sung at the beginning and ending of meetings. It was the official anthem of the African National Congress (ANC). It was associated with the campaign to end apartheid, and as such banned by the government.

With the renunciation of the apartheid government in 1994, Nelson Mandela proclaimed that Nkosi Sikelel'i Afrika would be merged with the existing South African national anthem "Die Stem van Suids-Afrika"; it was a symbol of reconciliation and honoring all cultures and people within the country. The current anthem contains multiple languages to reflect the diversity that is contained within her borders. The first stanza is in Xhosa and Zulu, the second is in Sesotho, then contains a portion of the former anthem in Afrikaans, with the final stanza in English.

Beware Verwoerd! (Ndodemnyama)

This song became popular in response to the "good neighborly" reforms of apartheid in 1950 under the direction of Prime Minister Hendrik Verwoerd, the chief architect of the apartheid system when the government systematically began to strip the rights away from black South Africans. The song's melody and rhythm seems to be buoyant and uplifting, with the text seeming repetitive and simple. The translation of the words, however, say that Verwoerd should be cautious of the "black man." The words "pasopa Verwoerd" mean "look out, Verwoerd" and use a derivative of Afrikaans language, instead of the more vernacular Xhosa. This use of the Afrikaner language was to send a direct message to the police and government officials, in which the singers are cautioning the white power structure of the might of the black man. At this point in the fight against apartheid, the resistance was not armed, but this song telegraphed the eventual victory for equality.

The song was composed by Vuyisile Mini, who had composed many of the freedom songs used in the struggle against apartheid. Mini was a member of various choral ensembles and loved classical music; he knew the power of music to unite people. He used songs as a way to organize people against unjust laws. In 1951, he joined the ANC, an organization that combatted apartheid through non-violent tactics until the Sharpeville massacre (see following discussion). In an act of defiance, he was arrested for trespassing in a "whites only" part of a railway property and lost his job in a battery factory because of his imprisonment. After he was released, he worked as a labor organizer and continued his work with the ANC. He was arrested several years later with two other prominent members of the ANC and was found guilty of 17 acts of sabotage as well as colluding to murder a police informant; Mini was sentenced to death. He was hanged in 1964, singing this song as he was led up to the scaffold.

Outside of South Africa, the song was made famous by Miriam Makeba on her collaborative album with Harry Belafonte. Makeba had success in South Africa during the 1950s, singing with several bands and theatrical productions, becoming well-known by both white and black audiences. She also was featured in an anti-apartheid film, *Come Back, Africa*, that had to be filmed in secret, as the government would have been unreceptive to the messages being promoted in it. Even though her appearance in the film was brief, approximately four minutes, she gained international recognition for her performance, which led to invitations to perform abroad in New York and London. It was in London that she met Harry Belafonte, who helped mentor her toward producing her solo records.

In 1960, shortly after the Sharpeville massacre (see Sobashiy'abazali discussion), when trying to travel outside of the United States, Makeba was notified that her passport had been cancelled, effectively putting her in exile. While she had attempted to maintain a low profile in political matters and avoided making statements in opposition to the apartheid government, the Sharpeville massacre had emboldened her to become an advocate for justice and a voice for freedom. She visited Kenya in 1962 to testify on the United Nations Special Committee against Apartheid, advocating for a ban on arms sales to South Africa, as they would likely be used against its citizens, including women and children. As a consequence, South Africa revoked Makeba's citizenship, leaving her stateless. Belgium, Guinea, and Ghana each granted her a passport in response. She continued her advocacy for South African people through her music throughout her career.

Meadowlands (Mielieland)

In the 1950s, Sophiatown was a vibrant cultural hub for black South Africans just outside of Johannesburg. This area was originally a "whites only" area until a sewage facility was housed near the settlement and white South Africans no longer wanted to live there; blacks and other "coloured" people were given permission to live there in the early 20th century. Slum clearance laws perpetrated by the National Party barred new arrivals to the inner city of Johannesburg from owning land. Some black landowners, burdened with high mortgage payments, allowed these newcomers to live on their land. By the standards of the National Party, Sophiatown was becoming unacceptably overcrowded. In 1954, the Native Resettlement Act was passed, which forced black and coloured residents to move from Sophiatown to a newly constructed township, Meadowlands, located in Soweto. These new homes had no toilets, running water, or electricity. The residents of Sophiatown protested and did not move. In 1955, 2,000 armed policemen forcibly removed 60,000 residents from Sophiatown and destroyed their homes. Some residents of Sophiatown continued to resist, using explosives and guns to stave off the removal to Meadowlands. By 1960, Sophiatown had been completely destroyed. Many residents had lost everything they owned at the hands of the government. The treatment of the residents of Sophiatown was a touchstone for the fight against apartheid, and its aftermath caused organizations like the ANC to organize against the unjust treatment of black people.

This song was originally written by Strike Vilakazi and is a clear protest of the treatment of blacks during this time period. The song is deceptively upbeat and sunny, and the text essentially denotes that residents are excited and happy to move to the new Meadowlands. However, the song is meant to be ironic. In 1962, this song was covered by the white South African musicians, Archie Coker and the Meteors. It is unclear if the choice to cover this song was an act of solidarity against the apartheid regime in power, or if it was an effort to capitalize financially on the struggle of these people by appropriating this freedom song.

Senzenina

This freedom song reached the height of popularity in the 1980s. The title can be translated as "What have we done?" It is in both Xhosa and Zulu languages; these languages are both Bantu languages and can be considered dialects of each other. This song has a mournful characteristic and was often sung at funerals during the fight against apartheid. While the original composer is not definitely known, the song has been considered to be a hallmark of the fight against apartheid and has been compared to "We Shall Overcome," the unofficial anthem of the Civil Rights Movement in the United States. This powerful song concludes with the text, "It is a sin to be black/ It is a sin in this country."

Sobashiy'abazali (We Will Leave Our Parents)

During the struggle against apartheid, many people, including important organizations like the ANC, wanted to change the nation through non-violent means. However, many black South Africans began to reconsider their non-violent efforts as the apartheid regimes escalated the violence against black citizens. In 1960, organizations across South Africa staged a non-violent protest of the pass laws, where people of color were required to carry a pass-book with them to travel in certain parts of the city. In Sharpeville, hundreds of people protested this law by leaving their pass-books at home or burning them and reporting to the local police station. When they arrived, they were met with a line of heavily armed police officers. By mid-afternoon, thousands of protesters had arrived at the police station, chanting freedom songs and slogans. With little or perhaps even no provocation, a policeman on top of an armored car opened fire onto the protestors. There was no warning or chance for the crowd to disperse before lethal force was used. Sixty-nine people were killed in the massacre, with another 189 wounded.

As a result of this violence, protestors began to question if they should militarize against the brutal forces of the apartheid regime. ANC leaders, including Nelson Mandela, created the uMkhonto we Sizwe (MS), which was a militant wing of the ANC that took on campaigns of sabotage against the government. Young people left South Africa, for neighboring states, to train in military techniques and to organize campaigns against the apartheid regime. This song was a nostalgic, yet hopeful tune as it lamented the separation from family caused by the training, but hoping for a new day.

Additional Materials

Amandla! A Revolution in Four-Part Harmony. (2002). Dean, S. S., Markgraaff, D., & Hirsch, L. (Producers), & Hirsch, L. (Director). South Africa: ATO Productions.

Come Back, Africa. (1959). Rogosin, L. (Producer & Director). USA: Rogosin Films.
Cry Freedom. (1987). Clegg, T. A. (Producer) & Attenborough, R. (Director). USA: Universal Pictures.
"Anti-Apartheid Freedom Songs Then and Now" by Tayo Jolaosho. Cover story from Smithsonian Folkways Magazine.

The wealth of musical learning that can occur through exploring the rich music of South Africa is vast. In the previous episode, students in a World Music Traditions course encounter only five pieces of music from the decades-long resistance against the apartheid government; but by learning about these particular songs, students uncover different facets of the story that eventually led to truth and reconciliation in a divided country. Secondary music teachers can certainly include more, but they must consider balancing the curriculum with interactions with other music traditions as well. When employing lessons like these in a World Music Traditions class, it is paramount that the teacher allows students to experience these pieces not only through Attentive Listening, but also Engaged Listening, Enactive Listening, and Creating World Music. While the teacher can certainly tell the story and share the music, students will connect with the music if they are singing, moving, and playing with the recordings. No special equipment is required, as students can learn a vocal part by ear or tap drum patterns on their desk. The contextual information of this music is certainly serious, and space should be afforded by the teacher for students to discuss their feelings and understandings of the material. By providing the cultural context of world music traditions, students learn that the sounds of music have meaning and shape the world around them.

Interdisciplinary understandings of music are there within the grasp of a music teacher's imagination to design and develop within current curricular offerings in secondary school music programs, as well as through new courses that can give full attention to themes, fields, and disciplines. The opportunity for secondary school music students to connect their listening and performance skills to diverse fields of study allows them to have a fuller understanding of the cultural meaning of music. Through integrating content in an interdisciplinary manner, paired with intentional listening and participatory musicking with exemplars from a variety of musical cultures, secondary students will find new ways to understand the world.

Music as Activism

Music teachers have a responsibility in teaching music and working with the power of music to support student learning of music and of the world at large. For instance, it is an act of conscience to include learning activities from musical cultures that have been left out of the Western canon of art music. The inclusion of music from diverse musical cultures is a meaningful act in promoting the value and beauty of musical material from those cultures as well as a recognition of those people. How educators design their curriculum, including what musical cultures to explore with students, is a political action. Some may advocate that the wealth of learning in the music classroom should be focused on the study of music as an aesthetic experience that is devoid of need for contextual understanding, and that music is consequently apolitical. There is a long-standing philosophical view of music-as-music, in that the true value of music lies only in the sonic properties that are allayed to the listener. Author and Nobel Laureate Toni Morrison decried this notion of apolitical aesthetics:

> All good art is political! There is none that isn't. And the ones that try hard not to be political are political by saying, 'We love the status quo.' We've just dirtied the word 'politics,' made it sound like it's unpatriotic or something. That all started in the period of state art, when you had the communists and fascists running around doing this poster stuff, and the reaction was 'No, no, no; there's only aesthetics.' My point is that there has to be both: beautiful and political at the same time. I'm not interested in art that is not in the world.
>
> (Nance, 2008, p. 50)

Morrison articulates that our attention should be focused on more than the substance of art—in the case for musicians, the sonic properties of the music—but to focus also on the music-makers and the environs from which the music comes.

A by-product of a multicultural music education is empathy for others—empathy for classmates, for neighbors, for people on the other side of the planet. This happens through close and intimate encounters with diverse musical cultures. Since communities are created through music-making, the act of listening to and making music from across the world is a means of bridging differences, finding commonalities, and growing multicultural understandings. This creation of community is an integral part of WMP and is precisely why participatory music-making, performance, and creative composition and improvisation are paramount for the learning of music within its sonic potentials. An understanding of the cultural context of music, of its cultural meaning, is vital, and thus the models for integrating are offered as a means of growing empathy and building community.

Together, the various dimensions of WMP, when applied to one musical selection, or to several songs or musical works within a cultural practice, allow students to learn the music and learn about the moving power of music to build communities, to call for justice, to mourn tragedy, to topple regimes, and to celebrate the human spirit. It seems a natural extension to maintain that a combination of pedagogical techniques can not only foster empathy toward people of the world's cultures but also orient students to understanding the problems that people in those cultures endure. Through candid discussions and sensitive facilitation, music teachers can lead students to examine how systems and institutions maintain the status quo, a normalcy that continues to oppress certain people. With intimate experiences with world music cultures, students foster interest in and empathy toward diverse populations of people, many of whom have been systematically oppressed. Acknowledgment of social problems is a first step in changing the status quo, while secondary school students can also progress from a meaningful episode in the integration of music and culture to become actors with agency in the pursuit of social justice.

With an emphasis on social justice in our music classrooms, educators need to be clear what the aims of that justice are. Many campaigns in multicultural education have centered on establishing "community" where barriers are seemingly obfuscated and everyone has equal participation. However, this is likely a simplistic approach because part of social justice work should be inclusion of all while still acknowledging, or even celebrating, differences. In this regard, poet, feminist, and social activist

Audre Lorde (1990) summarized this idea by saying, "our future survival is predicated upon our ability to relate within equality . . . we must recognize difference . . . and devise ways to use each other's difference to enrich our visions and our joint struggles" (p. 122). Social justice through multicultural music education must be more than equal access to participate within the classroom. These experiences that develop empathy and expose the gross inequities in many parts of the world should embolden our students to act to become activists who question the status quo and deliver solutions to social ills. But, students must be led by example. As education philosopher Maxine Greene (1978) described:

> if teachers today are to initiate young people into an ethical existence, they themselves must attend more fully than they normally have to their own lives and its requirements; they have to break with mechanical life, to overcome their own submergence in the habitual, even in what they conceive to be the virtuous, and ask the "why" with which learning and moral reasoning begin.
>
> (p. 46)

It is through this disruption of routines and performance schedules that secondary school music teachers can begin to work toward social justice within classrooms. Integrating content from beyond the sonic properties allows the unseen to be seen and the unheard to be heard. The result of this kind of education is transformative. As Allsup and Shieh (2012) described, "at the heart of teaching others is the moral imperative to care. It is the imperative to perceive and act, and to not look away" (p. 48). Music teachers who engage their students through the dimensions of WMP, and who follow through to the integration of music across disciplines and subjects, are opening young minds to a world outside of their normal experiences. With deliberate integration of the information about the people and places who make the music, music educators can inspire students to care and take action.

Notes

1 There are commercially available recordings of Indigenous groups performing their music. While the recordings may have been collected ethically, it is strongly suggested that music teachers ascertain permission to use Indigenous music in their classrooms. Again, this type of learning will be best suited under the direction of a culture-bearer.

2 Smith, M. (2017, February 23). Standing Rock protest camp, once home to thousands, is razed. *The New York Times*. Retrieved from www.nytimes.com/2017/02/23/us/standing-rock-protest-dakota-access-pipeline.html

References

Allsup, R., & Shieh, E. (2012). Social justice and music education: The call for a public pedagogy. *Music Educators Journal, 98*(4), 47–51.

Barrett, J. R., & Veblen, K. K. (2012). Meaningful connections in a comprehensive music curriculum. In G. E. McPherson & G. F. Welch (Eds.), *The Oxford handbook of music education, volume 1*. New York: Oxford University Press.

Gardner, H. (1983). *Frame of mind: The theory of multiple intelligences*. New York: Basic Books.

Greene, M. (1978). *Landscapes of learning*. New York: Teacher College Press.

Lorde, A. (1990). Age, race, class, and sex. Woman redefining difference. In R. Ferguson, M. Gever, T. Minh-ha, & C. West (Eds.), *Out there: Marginalization and contemporary cultures* (pp. 281–288). Cambridge, MA: MIT Press.

Nance, K. (2008). The spirit and the strength: A profile of Toni Morrison. *Poets & Writers, 36*(6), 47–54.

Listening Episodes

"Aquelo Abraço," Gilberto Gil, Phillips LP. Guitar, bass, vocals, kettle drum, cowbell, whistle, and cabasa. Available on iTunes and Spotify.

"Batmacumba," Gilberto Gil, Caetano Veloso, and Gal Costa, Phillips LP. Psychedelic rock song featuring guitar, bass, vocals, tambourine, and bongos. Available on iTunes and Spotify.

"Beware Verwoerd! (Ndodemnyama)," Miriam Makeba, RCA Victor. Vocals, guitar, bass, djembe, body percussion. Available on iTunes.

"Bury My Heart at Wounded Knee," Buffy Sainte-Marie, EMI Records. Guitar, vocals, bass, keyboard, electric guitar, drum set. Available on iTunes.

"Čoček Manhattan," Yuri Yunakov Ensemble, Smithsonian Folkways Recordings. Saxophone, clarinet, keyboard, electric bass, drum kit. www.folkways.si.edu/yuri -yunakov-ensemble/cocek-manhattan/world/music/track/smithsonian.

"Djelem Djelem," Esme Redzepova, World Village Records. Unofficial Romani anthem featuring accordion, clarinet, trumpet, and vocals. Available on iTunes.

"I Don't Need A Man," miss A, AQ/JYP/KT. K-Pop song that explores gender roles in modern times. Official video: www.youtube.com/watch?v=EkSOOiMDGiY. Track available on iTunes.

"If I Was President," Las Cafeteras, Las Cafeteras Music. Vocals, jaranas, keyboard, drum set. http://lascafeteras.com/videos/.

"La Bamba Rebelde," Las Cafeteras, Las Cafeteras Music. Quijada, cajon, marimbolo, vocals, jaranas. http://lascafeteras.com/videos/.

"Meadowlands (Mielieland)," Nancy Jacobs & Her Sisters, (2004). Gallo Record Company. Piano, drum set, guitar, bass, vocals. Available on iTunes and Spotify.

"Nkosi Sikelel'i Afrika," Ladysmith Black Mambazo, Gallo Record Company. A cappella singing. Available on iTunes and Spotify.

"Nyoka Musango (Snake in the Grass), Lora Chiorah Dye, Smithsonian Folkways Recordings. Marimbas, hosho, vocals. www.folkways.si.edu/lora-chiorah-dye-and-sukutai/ nyoka-musango/world/music/track/smithsonian.

"Panis Et Circensis," Os Mutantes, Phillips LP. Avant-garde rock song featuring brass, guitar, organ, vocals, trumpet, tambourine, bass, and drumset. Available on iTunes and Spotify.

"Senzenina," Lalela Cape Town Choir, (2014). Lalela Music. A cappella singing. Available on iTunes.

"Siquisiri," Son de Madera, Smithsonian Folkways Recordings. Jaranas, vocals. www.folkways.si.edu/son-de-madera/siquisiri-siquisiri/latin-world/music/track/smithsonian.

"Sobashiy'abazali" (We Will Leave Our Parents)," African Cream Freedom Choir, African Cream Music. Vocals, bass drum, whistling. Available on iTunes.

"This Land is Your Land," Las Cafeteras, Las Cafeteras Music. Reimagining of United States folksong in son jarocho style. Vocals, jaranas, snare drum, bass, quijada, tarima, accordion. http://lascafeteras.com/videos/.

Additional Resources and Recordings

Amandla! A Revolution in Four-Part Harmony. (2002). Dean, S. S., Markgraaff, D., & Hirsch, L. (Producers), & Hirsch, L. (Director). South Africa: ATO Productions.

"Anti-Apartheid Freedom Songs Then and Now" by Tayo Jolaosho. Cover story from Smithsonian Folkways Magazine.

Come Back, Africa. (1959). Rogosin, L. (Producer & Director). USA: Rogosin Films.

Cry Freedom. (1987). Clegg, T. A. (Producer) & Attenborough, R. (Director). USA: Universal Pictures.

"Run the World (Girls)," Beyoncé, Columbia Records. Available on iTunes and Spotify.

"Q.U.E.E.N.," Janelle Monae, Wondaland Records. Available on iTunes and Spotify.

7

Surmountable Challenges and Worthy Outcomes

Veteran secondary school music teacher Mr. McBride teaches at a public school that is also a Spanish Immersion Magnet, meaning "every student learns Spanish." Nearly all of the teachers and support staff in the school speak Spanish. Mr. McBride is the only white male in the building, and he is not fluent in Spanish. While his music curriculum has always been what can be considered "multicultural," it is actually predominantly bicultural via implementation of Latino folk traditions and music. He engages his students in lessons designed with attention to the phases of World Music Pedagogy, including Attentive, Engaged, and Enactive Listening experiences, as well as opportunities to participate in Creating World Music based on these deep listening episodes.

Nearly 35–40% of the school population are native Spanish speakers. Mr. McBride's intention is to ensure that his Latino students, whether first or second generation, continue to build a relationship with their home countries' musical traditions. He discovered that more than 75% of his Latino students claim Mexican heritage. He continued looking at ways to build his students' experiences in Latino music traditions. Through these efforts, he became aware of another music teacher in his town and her connections in the Mariachi world, particularly to the Las Vegas, Nevada school district.

Mr. McBride connected with the new Middle School orchestra director and others who wanted to begin Mariachi in the school district and further meet the needs of both the fifth- to eighth-grade students (ages 11–14) and the Latino students with the largest growing population coming from Mexico. His efforts to support Spanish-speaking populations are truly divided across Latin American music cultures per the school's focus and his professional mission.

He initially asked to start a Mariachi program some three years earlier, but he was unsuccessful in getting support at a time with decreasing state funding. A second challenge was the amount of training he personally needed to direct the ensemble by himself, or the task of finding someone to assist in directing the ensemble or to teach the instruments with which he had the least experience.

More than 25 students joined the first year of Mariachi and rehearsed weekly after school. Over half of the enrolled students were Latino. This meant the ensemble met the needs of both the Latino students and their families, as well as the non-Latino students who did not necessarily speak Spanish or know about Mariachi music. The first year's efforts gained momentum via a district grant for purchasing instruments and training resources for the students. Along with community performances, the ensemble and grant connections became a means of marketing by reaching both Latino and non-Latino families. While Mariachi speaks mostly to Mexican and Mexican American culture, the school district showed strong support for the musical endeavor.

Mr. McBride's colleague received some Mariachi training prior to starting the ensemble with him, and she directed most of the rehearsals, leading the violins and guitars while he directed the trumpets. Another colleague performed on the newly purchased vihuela (stringed guitar-like instrument), co-taught the guitars, and helped with student and family communications. Mr. McBride assisted with rehearsals and handled administrative duties for the finances and performances. When asked how he made a non-traditional ensemble happen successfully in his secondary school, he replied, "With a lot of human resources, and a willingness to go beyond the norm of my own cultural expectations, and keep asking. When one door closes, look for the window."

Mr. McBride's efforts to create innovative learning experiences allowed his secondary students to use music as a means to express parts of their identities, to learn something of fellow students' cultural identities, and to receive emotional benefits from participating in the music-making. Students of this age listen to and participate in music to fill an emotional need, to be entertained, and to relieve stress. For secondary school students, music functions as a way to formulate and negotiate their identities.

Throughout this book, deep listening has been presented as the route into the wide world of musical cultures: the means by which music can be learned by secondary school students who open their ears, join in participatory ways to perform it, create new expressions with linkages to learned styles, and understand its multicultural meanings. The five dimensions of World Music Pedagogy (WMP) focus on developing the holistic musician, developing ear, mind, and spirit. Attention has been focused on ways to bring students into close contact with music of many cultures, using recordings to launch the learning experiences, and applying listening rather than extensive note-reading to learn musical expressions that largely know no notational system but that are transmitted orally and received aurally. For secondary school music students, the musical, social, and cultural benefits of teaching and learning the world's musical cultures are indisputable, and the teaching-learning practices suggested by WMP are straightforward means of meeting music education goals.

It is clear that secondary school music programs have traditionally followed artistic and pedagogical practices that emanated out of Western Europe and are continued through a predominantly white and Eurocentric perspective. This dependence upon the "old world" ways of using European art music to set straight the music curriculum in contemporary practice appears to be holding despite the presence of indigenous, immigrant, and diverse populations of students who may have other interests and experiences in music, and who bring their own valuable means of transmission and teaching, learning and acquisition, and cultural understanding through music.

The way forward to develop the musical sensitivity and critical thinking of secondary school music students lies in helping them to understand music as a global phenomenon through innovative course designs and instructional strategies and techniques, as presented through the phases of WMP and the chapters of this book. This learning is made possible by music teachers who embrace diverse musical practices and demonstrate an awareness and concern for the sociocultural and socio-historical features of the music and its origin culture. Music teachers with a genuine interest in facilitating student learning experiences do well to increase their own understanding of music in culture, and to keep an open mind in creating new para-digms for music education practices that allow musical and cultural diversity to flow into curriculum and instruction.

At a recent international symposium, music teachers and ethnomusicologists reflected on the 50 years since the Tanglewood Declaration. One of the most oft-cited findings from this seminal meeting in 1967 was that:

> Music of all periods, styles, forms, and cultures belongs in the curriculum. The musical repertory should be expanded to involve music of our time in its rich vari-ety, including currently popular teenage music and avant-garde music, American folk music, and the music of other cultures.
>
> (p. 139)

It seems worth noting that the participants at Tanglewood were almost exclusively white men. In 1967, this did not raise protest, but it certainly would garner criticism in today's society, even though it is still the norm. While the Tanglewood Symposium was focused on music education in the U.S., its findings have impacted curricular considerations on an international level. Music teachers in Finland are exploring hip-hop music, Tanzanian music educators are considering including traditional music into schools alongside Western European practices, and other educators around the world are seeking out effective means for creating music courses that embrace and celebrate a vast palette of music cultures. At times, there is a quick response of "but what of Western classical music?" Practicing WMP in no way suggests or supports the removal of Western European art music or long-standing conventional ensembles from schools, but instead advocates an equalization of the playing field of repertoire selection and the modeling of pedagogical practices.

The palette of possibilities for enriching and diversifying secondary school music programs is large, and the episodes suggested here are by no means exhaustive but rather illustrative of how teaching and learning can be diversified in middle and high schools. While the dimensions of WMP can be applied to music of any genre or culture, the world of music beyond the West is ripe for selection and use. Certainly, teachers can facilitate WMP experiences for students with a Beethoven symphony, a Bartok piano étude, a Schubert string quartet, or a Rossini aria. But since the world is there awaiting discovery, why would teachers not draw on music cultures that stretch their students' ears and minds toward unfamiliar people, places, and sounds?

The movement to globalize the musical education of secondary school students is long and ongoing. Yet, for all of the expansion of repertoire now available for integration into a music curriculum, more attention must be paid by music teachers to the musicians and their sociocultural surrounds, or to an understanding that music can be taught and learned with not only musical but also multicultural and sociohis-torical aims in mind. By selecting music with meaningful texts, historical symbolism, and cultural signifiers (signals to a particular cultural identity), music teachers can craft opportunities for their adolescent students to take on the challenges inherent in analysis, performance, and creative work.

While we work from our own U.S. perspectives on music education, we recognize the extent to which the work of diversifying curricula pairs well with those found in contemporary educational systems in international settings. The following section highlights strategies for overcoming surmountable challenges faced by music teachers who are intent on offering innovative educational experiences designed with WMP for their secondary students and celebrates the worthiest of outcomes of such pedagogical endeavors.

Strategies for Success

As with all music teaching, particular strategies can assist secondary school music teachers in the delivery of efficient, exciting, and effective lessons based on the phases of WMP. In the following section, we address several challenges that may arise when diversifying a music curriculum and creating innovative learning experiences. Pedagogical considerations and strategies are offered in order to easily surmount these challenges, leading to musical outcomes worthy of celebration for teachers and their students.

Positionality and Reflection

What are music teachers to do when faced with the myriad of movements, policies, philosophies, and theories regarding the globalization of music curricula? Reflection on one's own beliefs about repertoire, pedagogical strategies, and the role of music in secondary school can lead to the development of a critical consciousness. This reflexive practice must include acknowledgment of one's own positions within systems of inequality to understand how oppression works on many levels. Becoming aware of the societal and education norms that reinforce privilege and marginalization, inside and outside of the secondary music classroom, is an important process for each music teacher to undertake. Taking the time, again and again, to contemplate the intersections of these identities in ourselves (including racial, gender, sexual, and political) as music teachers and as members of society, can foster a meaningful environment for education that reflects a contemporary, globally minded society.

Making Diversity Matter

The meaning of equity in education has changed considerably over the last several decades. While some societal movements emerged out of war, others were born through racial, ethnic, and class struggles. Important historic events of the last century are highlighted as they respond to multicultural, intercultural, and ethnocultural ideals and challenges. While these movements reflect a U.S. historical perspective, readers in other countries will no doubt connect to important historical and social movements in their own communities.

The intergroup education movement in the U.S. emerged in the 1930s and 1940s to deal with anti-Semitism and racial tensions. Much of this movement was focused on the reduction of prejudice and the promotion of understanding among diverse groups. This time period reflects the early stages, slow but steady in its development, of an acknowledgment that school curricula helped students erroneously believe that all culture groups shared the ideals of the dominant culture. Therefore, curricula needed to reflect the true nature of the society for which it was created.

These efforts led to the development of "ethnic studies," which slowly started to appear in secondary music classes in the form of global music recordings, Latin percussion instruments, and folk dances from multiple countries. In the latter part of the 1960s, programs took on an insurgent nature, featuring subversive agendas intended to disrupt the existing educational paradigms. The development of black studies was to challenge Eurocentric intellectual and cultural hegemony in the academy and liberate African American and African culture from white dominance. This movement directly challenged the unwritten conclusion that Western values and norms applied to all teachers, their university preparation, and the courses that they designed and delivered to their students.

The lack of a consistent definition of multiculturalism and multicultural education leads to multiple interpretations, thereby allowing space for critics to view multicultural education as an idea without theoretical foundations. Music teachers have been working to establish a multicultural approach to music education that honors the core beliefs of multiculturalism. Scholars in multicultural music education explore the exclusion of students based on race, ethnicity, class, or gender and explore ways to reform curricula with the goal of giving all secondary school music students an equal opportunity to engage in quality music experiences consisting of rich and diverse musical traditions and perspectives.

Over the last 20 years, it seemed that a decoupling of music education pedagogical practices and repertoire from its Eurocentric focus was inevitable, with an increase in the numbers of courses such as global drumming ensembles, songwriting classes, and digital beat-making. The core principles of recognizing and including cultural diversity in repertoire and approach seemed obvious and acknowledged. Yet, there has been a backlash against particular efforts to globalize and diversify music curricula. Despite efforts to honor diversity within communities and throughout the world, the term "multicultural" is not always celebrated. Calls for minority groups to fit in with dominant cultural practices have become more common and have been reflected in the narrowing of curricular options. As mentioned previously, a frequent critique of multiculturalism is its inability to address institutionalized inequalities such as racism and discrimination. While multicultural education typically has grown out of civil rights struggles, it has not challenged the power systems that allow inequitable situations to persist. Rather, it emphasizes difference with the intent to foster appreciation and respect. The teaching scenarios suggested throughout these chapters work to shift the traditional paradigm of secondary school music course content and pedagogical approaches.

Efforts to infuse ideas from multicultural education into music curricula have been well-intentioned, but often hover at the surface. The integration of content such as a song from a particular culture, or a map, is not a sufficient means to experience and understand music of a culture, or to know the people and traditions of that culture. This basic level of instruction does not help students reduce prejudice or develop globalized values. Varied approaches to multicultural music education exist, with some receiving sharp criticism for what is perceived as a trivialization of diversity through surface-level learning experiences. Further criticism has claimed that multiculturalizing course design overemphasizes the impact of curricular change and underutilizes or ignores a wider scope of social constructs, including racism, sexism, discrimination, and related matters of power and privilege.

Anti-racism pedagogy seeks to disrupt unequal power relations that stem from privilege and to create equity through and in education. Hess (2015) offered the following definition of anti-racism as it applies to music education:

> Anti-racism is an action-oriented anti-stance that allows for the systematic critique of liberalism, the application of intersectional analysis, and the voicing of counternarratives within society. It also employs critique as a key analytical tool, systematically critiquing unequal power relations, colorblindness, and systemic racism, as well as challenging institutions that facilitate these unequal power relations.
>
> (p. 72)

WHITE PRIVILEGE

Secondary school music teachers who are intent on implementing anti-racism pedagogy are ready to challenge the privilege of class and whiteness as it has appeared in the selected repertoire, course offerings, and teaching approaches to date. These music teachers note the frequent absence of these topics in the design and delivery of secondary school music programs and wish to change the conversation while experiencing meaningful music-making. These teachers also examine the marginalization of certain music cultures in the world and the role that racial privilege plays in inclusion, access, and representation in music courses.

Among music teachers, culturally responsive teaching (CRT) and pedagogy has gained well-deserved attention over the last quarter century. Gay (2010) described this approach as "using the cultural characteristics, experiences, and perspectives of ethnically-diverse students as conduits for teaching them more effectively" (p. 107). Among music teachers, there has been much exploration of ways to create musical experiences that address the cultures that are represented in their classes through innovative course offerings such as songwriting, digital production, world percussion ensemble, and hip-hop culture (Lind & McKoy, 2016). These teachers also incorporate diverse listening experiences into long-standing course designs such as music theory, piano class, or guitar ensemble. The challenge remains for secondary music teachers to ensure representation of a diversity in music cultures even when their student populations are not diverse.

Terms and labels evolve and will continue to do so. All of these movements include shared concerns for recognition, relief from oppression, the uplifting of marginalized peoples and cultures, and the removal of inequity. Initiatives that fall under the umbrella term "social justice" emphasize appropriate understanding of indigenous, immigrant, refugee, and other marginalized culture groups.

Authenticity and Context

Much has been made here of the matter of authenticity in the treatment of world music cultures in secondary school music. Who has the right and authority to define what is authentic? Why is authenticity not considered an issue when dealing with music from the Western European art music tradition? Regardless of where a music selection originates from, there are common considerations across discipline-specific situations, including appropriateness of text, range, tessitura, fingering, meter, rhythmic complexity, number of parts, or accompaniment. Secondary school music teachers have a responsibility to figure out ways to fit musical selections into the context of their classes, even if they are in unfamiliar languages, normally combined with dance, or traditionally played on indigenous instruments. The integrity of the existing school music environment combines with the original context of the music selection to create a syncretic hybrid that ideally honors both settings.

Our final consideration of the recontextualization of music for use in a secondary school music setting reveals a challenge for music teachers: how necessary and how possible is it to re-create the original cultural context? Music teachers have the authority as pedagogical experts who understand secondary school students to select repertoire from a variety of musical genres and cultures as well as the understanding of how best to present it in its new school context. From pop song mash-ups, to songs in different languages, or a group of musicians who relocate from one country to another and create a performing ensemble in their new setting, there is an ever-present current of change within traditional practices. This shifting of cultural circumstances and settings is a healthy norm rather than a worrisome exception and should not deter music teachers from creating courses including and celebrating world music cultures.

One example of a musical form leaving its original context in the hands of experts is the change that occurred in the genre of African American spirituals. When African American spirituals first started to appear on secondary school concert programs, there was resistance from some in the Black church community against this different type of setting. Piano and other instrumental accompaniments for the spirituals in concert performance seemed contrived to fit the school setting. Eventually, musicians created arrangements that honored the original character of the songs, but altered the nature to fit the new performance environment.

Another example of a change in traditions is in the genre of *tuk* bands from the Caribbean country of Barbados, which originally featured singers in a prominent role accompanied by triangle and drums. Over time, with the fife in the lead role instead of voice, the art form almost died out. After Barbados achieved independence, the government supported the resurrection and reconfiguration of the art into a new role—a tourism attraction. Tuk bands now appear in secondary school curricula in Barbados and are part of the entertainment circuit for visitors to the island. The tuk tradition was recontextualized for a new purpose in order to sustain the tradition and to share cultural practices with outsiders.

Yet another example of successful and meaningful movement of a music from one setting to another is found in the Wagogo region of central Tanzania in East Africa. Around the capitol city of Dodoma, a long-held musical tradition called *muheme* was for generations connected to female circumcision, a highly controversial practice also found in cultures outside of Tanzania. After laws were passed in the 1990s banning the practice on girls, the music—so rich in cultural tradition, knowledge, and history—was recontextualized into two different formats. A secular form of muheme was created for public functions and festivals, and a church muheme developed for sacred functions. The new formats allowed the transmission of cultural heritage to continue, albeit in a dramatically changed context.

The previous examples describe recontextualization of music outside of a school setting. What should secondary music teachers consider when moving a piece of music *into* a school setting? Of great importance is a consideration of what is practically possible to accomplish given the time, age, and ability of the students as well as the level of experience of the music teacher in the given music culture.

Once the parameters for a piece are defined, teachers need to decide what changes, if any, need to be made in order to create a meaningful, musical learning experience for the particular students and the particular class. Possible changes from an original context could include: range, stylistic ornaments, text, dance moves, rhythmic movement, length, instruments, and instrumentation. Even though the setting may be in a new context, consideration must be given to the mode of presentation. A Caribbean playground game taught in an elementary music classroom is very close in nature to the original—same age group, same playful nature—an easy switch to make. A traditional Bulgarian women's work song rearranged for secondary guitar class is a large leap, but still with educational merit. If the arrangement is crafted by a musician with a working understanding of both contexts—Bulgarian women's work songs and guitar ensembles—then an appropriate and respectable hybrid could be created that helps the students understand performative and cultural aspects of another culture while continuing to progress in their own culture of a school music course.

Where does this leave the music teacher who is hoping to create a respectful, musical experience that honors the practical realities of the secondary school setting while helping to reflect the integrity of the musical tradition represented in the performance? It is understandable and necessary to sensitively and thoughtfully adapt music of the world's cultures in ways that keep the underlying character and features intact. Specific conditions can lead creative teachers to make contextual adaptations to music based on the vision and direction to be pursued. It is not uncommon to experience false starts and stumbling blocks when adapting music for a secondary school setting. This should not discourage music teachers from continuing to try. Even a simple presentation, and possible misrepresentation of features of a particular musical culture, is important because it creates a space for other musics in the school music canon and is an important learning experience for a music teacher. Teachers who experience initial missteps in the planning process can improve with practice, much like their students will improve their musical skills and increase their cultural competence over time.

Music teachers with an eye and ear for representing a truly diverse, global society in the repertoire performed and environment created in their classes will continue to find ways to adapt global musics to make it fit within their situations. While some musical traditions should not be tampered with (e.g., religious music, particularly Native American music, copyrighted material), others might be more amenable to adaptation but miss the mark with reinforcement of negative stereotyping, and yet others might successfully straddle the crossroads between the cultures of school music and the culture of origin.

NAVIGATING THE MURKY WATERS OF CULTURAL APPROPRIATION

Enmeshed with matters of authenticity and context is the troubling practice of cultural appropriation, which can be defined as the use of a culture's traditions, rituals, symbols, and practices by members of another culture that has had power over or participated in marginalizing the other. A challenge for music teachers is the navigation of cultural traditions without crossing a line into an experience that can be viewed as exploitative of the culture. Music teachers interested in cultural authenticity must understand the power positionality invoked by a dominant culture taking elements from a culture group that has been oppressed by that same dominant group. Careful and intentional design of reflective practice and learning experiences can help to navigate this complicated dynamic. If students in a secondary school global percussion ensemble perform the Zimbabwean tune "Nyoka Musango," one of the Learning Pathways featured throughout the book, it does not equal cultural appropriation. The episodes have been designed in such a way as to include the students in a process of deep listening to the sonic features and deep exploration of the people and culture behind the music.

Meaningful Collaboration With Culture-Bearers

The benefits of collaborating with culture-bearers have been emphasized throughout these chapters. The process of searching out a culture-bearer, meeting to discuss and plan what the visits will entail, facilitating the classes or workshops, and following up after the visits are complete requires extra preparation from the music teacher. Challenges may arise including (a) funding these short- or longer-term visits, which can be realized through school- and district-wide grants, parent-teacher organization funds, and other private funding possibilities, and (b) determining which artist may best serve curricular needs. It is important to consider whether an individual from a given culture is truly a genuine artist and capable communicator.

Continuing to Develop One's Own Musicianship

Ethnomusicologist Mantle Hood (1959) wrote about the concept of bimusicality and the necessity to strive for continued experiences that draws one more deeply into the musical tradition, in order to best understand it from an outsider's perspective. Bimusicality as Hood intended refers to the intentional work that it takes to work past the dominance of one's familiar musical culture to become fluent in a different music culture.

During the secondary school years, students might hear a performance given by a peer who traveled to another culture to study, or work in-depth with a culture-bearer closer to their home community. For example, picture a cello student going to Brazil as part of a cultural exchange and returning to offer a recital of which one-half is cello repertoire and the other half traditional Brazilian percussion and samba music. For some in the audience, hearing such different performance practice can be a revelatory experience. This sort of revelation may even lead to a musical obsession by way of a sense of urgency to learn as much as possible about a new music—a leap to action to start the process.

Music teachers might also take advantage of opportunities to learn from and perform with musicians and groups outside of their main performance areas, such as a salsa band, a jazz combo, a mariachi, a gospel choir, a Japanese taiko group, a West African percussion ensemble, a Bulgarian women's choir, a rock band, or an international folk music group. These interactive experiences with new and different rhythmic structures, melodic contours, harmonic formations, and dance traditions might nurture a desire for further study, perhaps leading to travel to the culture of origin. While some music teachers develop a passion for a particular music that drives them to study, others feel a sense of responsibility to represent a diverse repertoire with their students and to honor musical cultures from a global perspective.

Secondary music teachers should not feel that they have to achieve a professional level of expertise with a music culture in order to bring it to their students. There are many areas of a music teacher's work that do not require a professional level of musical proficiency in order to teach well, but instead require a sound understanding of pedagogy. Instrumental teachers are responsible for the instruction of instruments that they know how to play (outside of their main instrument) with only a basic level of proficiency, and more importantly, a solid understanding of good pedagogical techniques to help students learn and eventually surpass their teachers. Choral directors help their students sing in languages they do not personally speak, but for which they have learned the phonetic rules. Composers who lived centuries before have their repertoire performed, and their musical and life histories are discussed with a familiarity that makes them seem still present.

The process of learning new musical traditions as a university student, or as a practicing music teacher, is critical in shaping a teacher's approach to secondary school music pedagogy. It can inform the teaching of global musics by making known the difficulties that arise in the learning process. An example of this comes from a music teacher who traveled to Ghana and shared memories of her first weeks of study with a music culture that was brand new to her and far outside of Western art music conservatory training:

> I remember clearly how challenging it was to pick out the different rhythms that were sounding simultaneously. Sometimes the three bell parts blurred together, other times the complementary drum parts made sense to my ear, but then would run away from my grasp. The struggle and the sense of my own uncertainty helped me later to help others learn this music, because I had experienced some of their very challenges and could anticipate them. I now hear this music from the inside, and know comfortably just how the parts link with one another.

These types of learning experiences can lead to meaningful relationships between an adult student and teacher, with the secondary school students directly benefitting from these encounters.

Hood (1960) asserted that this type of deep study leads to the development of "some sort of understanding of and an insight into not only music and the related arts but also language, religion, customs, history—in other words, the whole identity of the society of which music is only one, but one very important part" (p. 58). These experiences with a new music culture can free a musician from reliance on a conductor and from notation.

Ethnomusicologist Jeff Titon (1995) wrote of using bimusicality (or perhaps a more fitting term is multimusicality) as a learning strategy. The more that music teachers study new music traditions, the more they may come to realize that they need to change the way they hear music. Titon (1995) referred to a "subject shift" that happens when deeply studying a music that is new and different—"figuratively stepping outside oneself to view the world with oneself in it, thereby becoming both object and subject simultaneously" (p. 288). The music teacher who traveled to Ghana shared her experience with this concept of subject shift:

> I traveled with my teacher to his birth village. He came over to me and handed me sticks and whispered in my ear that I was to go to the *atsimevu*, the master drum, and lead an ensemble in a recreational piece. I could hear my heart in my ears. I played the opening, and then the Kinka groove started. I managed to sneak a look and saw that people had started to dance. I had a moment where I could see myself objectively and watched my hands moving, and watched the people responding to the signals that I played, and yet I was in the music at the same time.

This type of performative experience can lead to what Titon (1995) calls "subject breakthrough," those moments when we are "wrenched out of our ordinary identity and learn something about our informants and ourselves" (p. 290). When studying music of a culture different from one's own, we may wonder how the music and the context in which it is performed could ever cross over into a secondary classroom setting. The reality of a school environment is indeed removed from the very contexts in which these other musics normally take place. This process allows a re-evaluation of the nature of authenticity.

We can think of the musical goal for secondary students involved in WMP not as imitation but as respectful interpretation. Music teachers need to be brave and persistent in their pursuit of broader musical understanding for their students and themselves. They need to be willing to make mistakes, to inquire, to study, and to practice alongside their students. It may be easier to imagine the process of a music teacher working toward multimusicality as two-fold: first the aesthetic features (e.g., the ability to listen to, appreciate, enjoy, and understand music) and then performance, considered a higher level of achievement perhaps involving memorization and then reproduction of music.

Secondary school music teachers can cite festival obligations, concert requirements, or audition procedures as reasons for sticking to certain types of repertoire. But even more probable is a lack of experience in global music cultures. Where does this leave their secondary music students, who deserve to know diverse musical practices?

It is neither recommended nor necessary to rush to learn too many music cultures simultaneously. Time and patience are the allies of music teachers. The first step must be to decide on the genre of focus. The selected musical culture helps guide the steps to follow. Perhaps there is a personal interest in traditional Irish music; local Irish festivals happen in most large cities and can offer inspiration for repertoire and possible connections for lessons and collaborations. Some communities have Irish pubs that feature local and touring bands. Attending festivals, taking workshops, seeing local bands, and extensive listening and watching as suggested in WMP contribute to a growing understanding of the music, while seeing it in context helps with cultural questions. There may be pre-existing arrangements for traditional tunes, but after a time a music teacher could try her hand at arranging. She could bring an expert fiddler to class to raise excitement among the students and school community while she gets the chance to watch, learn, and eventually with determined practice, emulate.

During a visit to a high school popular music class, music student Antoine (Figure 7.1) was asked what he might suggest to secondary school music teachers who feel underprepared to teach a wide array of music cultures. Antoine responded immediately with a question:

> What is the problem with any other forms of music in which a person is just telling you how he feels? It's neither good or bad. Instead of saying, "This is the music that touches me. I'm going to cut myself off from these other things," people should be saying, "I understand this. I relate. It's all music. This is my thing, and that's yours. I understand that."

In his last year of high school, Antoine already demonstrates an openness to musical genres and a curiosity toward the people who listen to, create, and perform them. His attitude is an example of the type of empathy that can evolve through experiences in innovative music courses that inspire a sense of wonder at the world.

Figure 7.1 High school student musician Antoine Ferguson

Photo courtesy of Karen Howard

Creating a New Course or Ensemble

Stepping forward to take on the creative, logistical, and pedagogical challenges of creating a new secondary music course or ensemble can certainly seem daunting. Secondary school music students Gabby and Mac (Figure 7.2) shared their perspectives on what an innovative new course, Indonesian Gamelan, meant to their musical lives. Gabby, a longtime choir member, explained the similarities and differences between gamelan under the guidance of instructor Joko Sutrisno and more traditional ensembles such as band and choir in her school experience:

> I learned how to play all of the instruments without the use of any notation. That never happens in other ensembles. The main structure of the pieces was outlined on the board, but we had to memorize it right away in order to hear our places within the sound.

Mac's observations reflected the difference in Joko's role:

> Learning gamelan was like any other ensemble in that we would meet to practice our pieces. However, the way we learned the music was completely different. Joko would first teach us the structure of the piece by writing it on the chalkboard and then demonstrating the patterns for each instrument. In this way, he had a much more involved role in our understanding of the piece, in addition to the fact that he led the ensemble by being a part of the ensemble.

Figure 7.2 Joko Sutrisno rehearsing with student gamelan ensemble. Gabby (center), Mac (2nd from R)

Photo courtesy of Karen Howard

Gabby imagined that the inclusion of music from diverse cultures in a secondary music curriculum could be intimidating for teachers:

> Particularly when you are afraid you don't feel like you possess the knowledge and skills to teach that kind of music. However, I think taking the time to research and learn about how to go about teaching it is worth the time. Gamelan has challenged my musical abilities in ways I didn't expect. From someone who was trained to follow a conductor exactly, and read only what was on the page, it was challenging for me to have to *feel* the music more than I read it. I was forced to listen across the ensemble to make sure I was fitting exactly where I was supposed to, and I had to listen to the beat very carefully in order to know where the transitions and ends of songs were.

While it is true that teachers face challenges when creating course content or new course designs incorporating the techniques of WMP, Gabby and Mac express the rich benefits that secondary students gain from the learning experiences such innovative courses offer. Although acquiring an Indonesian Gamelan for a school may seem a unique opportunity that is out of reach for a music teacher, these opportunities can and do arise. In Gabby and Mac's situation, the gamelan arrived as a result of a musician who moved to a smaller house and was looking for somewhere to house her instruments. Gabby and Mac's music teacher saw it as a chance to provide safe storage for the instruments in exchange for using them with her students.

Finding sufficient funding sources to start a global percussion ensemble, or to create a recording studio for digital music production, or to acquire instruments for small rock band work takes resilience and persistence from music teachers. Becoming involved with a school's parent-teacher organization can create meaningful relationships with the community and increase the likelihood of support for innovative requests. Grants can be researched online, and while certainly highly competitive, many school districts have assistance for teachers who are interested in crafting such proposals in order to increase their chances at success. Another consideration is sharing instruments with another school, perhaps one group using a set of steel pans for the first semester, and then another program using them while the first group moves on to a different music culture.

Another important issue is that of the overall music schedule. It is one that every secondary music teacher must grapple with continuously during a teaching career. There are many pieces to the puzzle of a master school schedule. Conflicts with other courses the students want or need may, at times, interfere with both course times and the ability of students to enroll in music courses. While a music teacher may not always have the power to change schedule matters that impact their course offerings and student enrollment, a teacher should work collaboratively and proactively with those who create the schedule to offer the best possible courses and time options for students.

Enrollment numbers are an important consideration. Many middle and high school administrations will not allow music classes to run if a minimum of students have not registered. For secondary music classes that are outside of the traditional large performance-centric model (e.g., band, choir, and orchestra), this issue is more pronounced. Choirs, bands, and orchestras can have as many as 80 students or more in one class period, only needing one teacher to staff the class, whereas classes outside the traditional ensembles become hampered by having more students than is educationally viable (e.g., having more students than instruments in guitar, steel band, or stations in a piano lab). While innovative secondary music classes may appear to have lower enrollments when compared to traditional ensembles, the confident teacher will advocate to their administration that enrollment can increase if the school will provide additional materials so more students can participate.

Music teachers wanting to promote innovative secondary music courses, like a digital music production course or a songwriting class, need to articulate the benefits of the implementation and inclusion of these new classes. When presenting a new course proposal to school administrators, music teachers should emphasize the ways in which the course is innovative, works toward equity, and when designed with WMP criteria in mind, can help students develop empathy toward others. Music teachers do well to find common ground between their aspirations for the music program and the goals of the school administration.

Student recruitment for existing and new course innovations is yet another important consideration for secondary music teachers. Ensemble teachers may be concerned that the inclusion of diverse secondary music courses might lead to the siphoning of students away from existing ensembles. As has been emphasized here, music teachers should remember that many secondary students are not attracted to the large ensemble format, or feel that those experiences are not relevant to their lives. By offering a diversity of music classes, different parts of the student population will be interested in participating in new kinds of music-making, be it learning about music technology or playing Brazilian Bateria. It should be the goal of secondary music teachers to corral as many students into their classes as possible so that they may share the vast and rich musical traditions available to them.

It is helpful to work to recruit students well before the time arrives to register for classes. Music teachers can promote the types of music teaching and learning found in the different classes and ensembles. For example, if a music program is adding a mariachi, as Mr. McBride did, having a local mariachi come perform at an assembly or even during lunch periods could pique the interest of secondary school students. Secondary music teachers can create a short video to promote their elective classes, particularly those courses that may seem ambiguous to secondary students (e.g., popular music ensemble, world percussion ensemble, world music traditions). These short clips depicting diverse secondary music classrooms can be broadcast during the morning announcements or posted on the school's website. A successful video will need to be well-produced, so music teachers may benefit from consulting the Audio/Visual specialist in the building, parent volunteers who have video editing skills, or possibly the best resource of all, students with technological know-how, in order to produce a quality advertisement. In the video, exuberant student music-making needs to be the focal point, with different genders, races, and ethnic groups represented in order to demonstrate that all are welcome to participate in these courses.

While an informative video may attract students' interest, the essence of recruitment lies in developing personal relationships. Music teachers who are involved with the goings-on of their schools will easily develop rapport with students who are not already enrolled in their music classes. This could happen during lunch room supervision, by spending time in the halls before or after school, by sponsoring a club or after-school activity, or by attending school sports events. Even a small gesture can be effective: chatting with a student about a T-shirt featuring a favorite band or musician, asking what they like about that particular music, and taking the opportunity to share that there is a songwriting class during second semester. By being a friendly and genuinely curious presence, who demonstrates a desire to get to know students, music teachers may find more students enrolling in their courses. However, if the sole motivation to get to know these students is recruitment purposes, the interactions will feel shallow or even contrived.

Another important consideration for secondary teachers is making connections with their "feeder" schools: the elementary and middle schools in the local area that eventually make up the student body. Connections can help a teacher meet and recruit the incoming students who may not know of the musical possibilities within the secondary music program. Music teachers can facilitate a "tour day" where different groups representing the music program (e.g., a group of songwriters from songwriting class, the gospel choir, a contingent from the marching band, the World Percussion Ensemble) travel to multiple feeder schools within a day to highlight the class options at the secondary level. Music teachers should interact with their music colleagues at the feeder schools to facilitate meaningful interactions, allowing time for a question-and-answer period, perhaps participating in a short episode of music-making together. The elementary music teachers can help identify students with particular musical interests or untapped potential who are good candidates for the secondary music program. Successful secondary music teachers stay involved in the recruitment process by creating ways to compile information about potential students, construct procedures to follow up, and delegate recruitment responsibilities to parent volunteers or responsible students. Healthy music programs, regardless of the size of the school population, are the result, in part, of proactive music teachers maintaining positive relationships with feeder schools.

PERFORMANCES

Courses that are not band, choir, or orchestra may be perceived to be less musically and academically rigorous than long-standing large ensembles. Music students in piano class, guitar class, songwriting classes, and music theory are rarely given opportunities to perform outside of class or demonstrate their musical growth. This is a missed opportunity and likely persists as a matter of institutional traditions, rather than pedagogical reasons. It is imperative that all secondary music students have the opportunity to perform and showcase their musical skills for each other and for audiences. As described in Chapter 4, secondary music teachers can provide a variety of performance options from informances that engage the audience through demonstrations to a more standard formal concert.

RANGE OF ABILITIES

Outside of the traditional large ensemble, music students will likely have greatly varying levels of experience, even within the same class. For instance, there may not be enough students enrolled in an introductory theory class, covering basic music literacy (e.g., clefs, key signatures, intervals, scales) and Advanced Placement Music Theory to run two separate classes; these two classes may be combined within one class period to satisfy the minimum requirement that allows the course to run. This practice relies on an adept and flexible music teacher to provide meaningful instruction to both groups simultaneously while keeping them engrossed in the music learning. In many differentiated classrooms, the music teacher will allow the advanced students to help the less skilled students: guitarists who have been studying for several years may help the novice guitarists with their hand positions and fingerings. The adept music teacher will find opportunities, through the use of WMP, to provide authentic participatory musicking experiences that allow all students to engage with the sound and perform together; while there can be gaps in understanding or skill between groups, students will quickly learn from one another and delight in building community in and through the music.

Secondary School Innovations in Music Education

The practice of privileging certain established courses over new and innovative designs leaves important musical traditions out of the mainstream of the secondary school music program. This musical "tradition" leaves music teachers with the complex challenge of deciding which music cultures to include. If the student population in a given school setting has a clearly dominant culture group, then it would make perfect sense to try to represent that culture somewhere in the chosen repertoire. However, a student population can also be predominantly white, black, Latino, Asian, predominantly homogenous though a minority culture, or simply predominantly diverse. Considerations of the teacher's expertise, the size of the school population, and the identification of underrepresented music cultures in the school and community-at-large can help lead to meaningful choices. The course designs and implementations within existing courses suggested throughout the book are meant to inspire music teachers to be creative when infusing WMP into their curricula. Starting a Popular Music Ensemble, co-teaching a class with a colleague from another subject area, or combining classes such as guitar and piano for in-class performing opportunities are excellent opportunities to grow musical skills and expand musical and cultural horizons.

Secondary school students are capable of great insights about the benefits they receive from innovative music courses crafted with attention to the phases of WMP, as noted earlier with Gabby and Mac. High school senior Antoine (Figure 7.1) was working on a new composition at the keyboard during a break in his newly offered music elective course, "Popular Music in America." When asked what benefits he perceived from new music course designs, he offered:

> It creates an environment that you don't really see except in schools where the focus on music isn't just the traditional kind. It's the kind that people in the community can see and think, "Yeah, that's the thing I do. Tell me more about my history!" My experience of any music in a school environment, or choir or band, seems geared to something you can take to college. But, this class, if you want to make music that I make, it's possible. You can take those experiences to other education environments. It creates an environment in which I can make and do music that I like and not feel bad about it. It's not considered a bad thing here. It's freeing and expressive.

While Antoine shared his impressions, Ubah and Asho (Figure 7.3), both recent immigrants from Somalia, sat on the other side of the classroom having their first-ever experience with an instrument (acoustic guitar), learning to strum the chords for a rock song. This creatively designed course is in tune with contemporary youth culture, offers new curricular content, and acts as an entry point for teenagers who have recently immigrated with no prior musical experience, which is often a barrier for participation in secondary music.

Figure 7.3   High school guitar students Ubah Ahmed (L), Asho Mohamed (R)

Photo courtesy of Karen Howard

Enacting an Equity Pedagogy: Toward a Global Empathy

While there are those working toward progressive and global pedagogical strategies, many secondary school music experiences focus exclusively on an older paradigm. The Western art music chapter of history is certainly important, but it is time that it is made a *part* of music education rather than the framework for its entirety. By incorporating ethnomusicological strategies and practices into course designs, secondary school music teachers can grow students' understanding of music and its creators, performers, and enthusiastic participants. Features found in other cultures can transfer into a school setting in ways that make space for all students, rather than the select few who continue through upper secondary school. A few publishers of pedagogical materials have been keen to diversify the music intended for listening, singing, playing, moving, and creating. However, much of the material that has emerged over the last 30 years has been geared toward younger students. Secondary school music materials need increased representation of world music cultures. Pre-service music teachers require broader musical experiences during their university years, and practicing teachers need continued learning experiences, including practice with pedagogical strategies for working with world music cultures.

The ultimate aims of secondary school music curricula should not limit the cultural experiences, but rather, as music education philosopher Keith Swanwick (2003) described, allow music teachers "to break out of 'restricted worlds of culturally defined reality' and promote 'imaginative criticism', bringing procedures and criteria out in to the open" (p. 116). Working toward a teaching philosophy that makes room for people, their cultures, their stories, and their sounds can be challenging, as expressed by music education historian Marie McCarthy (2009):

> The transition from endorsing one set of values based on a limited number of musical traditions to one that seeks to value all musics, regardless of social, cultural, or historical circumstances, requires monumental change in the assumptions and structures that underlie curriculum.
>
> (p. 31)

Returning one final time to the voices of secondary music students, Mac and Gabby both had strong feelings about the importance of including ensembles in school music that lead to meaningful learning and performing experiences with a wider range of musical traditions. Gabby shared:

> Not only do the members of the group get to expand their musical knowledge, but audience members will as well. I remember leaving an event where our gamelan group performed and overhearing an audience member say that it wasn't like anything they had ever heard before. I think that people . . . simply aren't aware of the different types of music that exist in other cultures. By performing more world music in ensembles, you can help people discover a musical interest that they didn't even know they had.

Mac addressed what he viewed as a lack of exposure to a variety of music cultures:

> People—and even musicians—these days seem to have skewed perceptions of music because of the overwhelming presence of Western European tradition in it. Half the people I talk to about Gamelan tell me they really don't like it because it

just sounds like clanging metal. I understand everyone will have their opinions, but to completely discredit a way of music, especially as a musician, I think is simply narrow-minded thinking. People have to understand that there are so many different styles and traditions of music, and none of them are invalid just because people aren't used to them. Music is one of the many mediums of culture, and I have never come across an instance where exposure to different cultures is bad. I have, however, learned of many occasions where insularity and apathy have resulted in very unfortunate outcomes.

Our secondary music students can know music more deeply by understanding its instruments, voices, and the sociohistorical contexts and functions within culture. By engaging in thoughtful experiences with the cultural, historical, and social significance of music, students may enrich their understanding of themselves, their classmates and teachers, their communities, and their broader global society. These students can come to know the sonic structures and social meanings of music in its culture of origin. Through a teaching and learning process that engages WMP with its emphasis on deep listening, understanding the full context of a music culture, performance, creativity, and integration with other disciplines, secondary students can grow their cultural understanding and empathy toward their fellow students and their broader community both near and far.

The aims of WMP, living at the nexus of music education with ethnomusicology, intersect with our current times and carry the potential for music teachers to create musical experiences as diversely expressed throughout the world. WMP is about music as sound, about the musicians who make the music, about the values held by those in the culture, and how they perform and learn. Through participatory musicking, performance, creative experiences, and musical learning integrated with other subject areas, music teachers help students to better understand music's role and function within the culture of origin, and then within the culture of secondary school. Music education through WMP can open teachers' and students' eyes, ears, and minds to a growing empathy and consideration of their local and broader global communities while nurturing the potential for a life-long, active relationship with music.

References

Gay, G. (2000). *Culturally responsive teaching: Theory, research, and practice* (2nd ed.). New York: Teachers College Press.

Hess, J. (2015). Upping the "anti-": The value of an anti-racist theoretical framework in music education. *Action, Criticism, and Theory, 14*(1), 66–92.

Hood, M. (1960). The challenge of "bi-musicality". *Ethnomusicology, 4*(2), 55–59.

Lind, V. R., & McKoy, C. L. (2016). *Culturally responsive teaching in music education: From understanding to application.* New York: Routledge.

McCarthy, M. (2009). Re-thinking "music" in the context of education. In T. A. Regelski & J. T. Gates (Eds.), *Music education for changing times: Guiding visions for practice* (pp. 29–37). New York: Springer.

Swanwick, K. 2003. *Music, mind, and education.* New York: Routledge.

Titon, J. (1995). Bi-musicality as a metaphor. *Journal of American Folklore, 108*(429), 287–297.

Appendix 1
Learning Pathways

Learning Pathway #1

Watch Out! Snake in the Grass! "Nyoka Musango" and Zimbabwean Marimba

Specific Use: World Percussion Ensemble

Materials:

- "Nyoka Musango," performed by Lora Chiorah-Dye and the Suketai Marimba and Dance Ensemble (2000). *Sarafini in transit: Music of African Immigrants.* Smithsonian Folkways Records

Procedure:

(Attentive)

1   "What instruments do you hear?"
2   Play track (00:01–01:05).
3   Review answer: *hosho* (gourd shaker), handclaps, vocal lines, marimbas.
4   If students did not hear all instrument, allow another listen.
5   Play track (00:01–01:05).
6   Review instruments in the piece.
7   "The entrance of the marimbas are staggered. Listen to the first, second, and third marimbas enter. As they enter, is each line higher or lower than the one that precedes it?"
8   Play track (00:01–00:20).
9   Review answers. The second marimba is higher than the first. The third marimba is higher than the preceding two.
10 Have students listen for the bass line. "Listen for the lowest note in the bass line. Find a word that describes the tone of that low note.
11 Play track (00:01–01:05).
12 Review words that students use to describe the low bass note. Words like "buzzy" or "vibrant" may be used to describe the tone of the bass note.
13 Have students track the bass line pattern and tap when the low bass note is sounded at the beginning of each pattern. This may take multiple listenings to the track to accomplish successfully.
14 Play track (00:01–01:20).
15 Have student continue to tap on the low bass note with one hand. With the other hand, they should tap the handclaps (or the teacher could divide the class into two groups, one tapping on the bass note and one on the handclaps).

16 Play entire track (00:01–05:50).

17 Assess students' ability to synchronize with the bass line, the handclaps, or both.

(Engaged)

1 Play track to determine what is heard (marimbas, vocals, claps, hosho).

2 Figure out where each marimba part enters by playing the beginning of the track repeatedly (e.g., marimba 1: 00.00–00.05, marimba 2: 00.06–00.10, etc.).

3 Figure out the outline of each part without all of the repeating notes through repeated listening.

(Enactive)

1 Transfer the melody with repeating notes to marimba or xylophones using the recording to check for style and musical accuracy.

2 Discover where and how many repeating notes are present, or present notation of one part at a time.

3 Listen to the recording again to determine how the parts line up in the cycle with each other.

4 Present notation for all four parts when the students seem ready.

5 Play opening (on marimbas or guitars) with all four parts in the same order that they appear in the recording.

Nyoka Musango

Thomas Mapfumo

Figure 3.9 Opening of "Nyoka Musango"

Figure 3.9 (Continued)

(Creating)

1 Review with students the piece "Nyoka Musango," drawing attention to the melodic lines that are layered on top of each other.

2 Play track (00:01–01:05).

3 Using proverbs commonly heard in Shona culture (Figure 5.1), create short melodic ideas using the Shona text. Students can model their short melodies after the singing heard in the recording. This process might start with exact replication of the melody, as it will be quite familiar from all of the previous listening. Encourage the students to change notes here and there until they create new short melodies that fit within the structure of the piece.

4 Allow students to experiment along with the recording.

5 Play track (00:01–01:05).

6 Combine the new sung melodies with the marimba parts learned previously.

Shona	Translation	Meaning
Kupedza nyota kuenda padziva.	To quench thirst is to go to the pool.	If help is wanted, one should go to an expert or eyewitness.
Charovedzera charovedzera.	One who is used to something is one who is used to something.	We do easily that to which we are accustomed.
Kuziva mbuya huudzwa.	To know one's in-laws means being told who they are.	Wisdom comes from others.
Tsvaga zano iwe une rakowo.	Seek a plan when you have one of your own.	
Kureva ndokunei?	What has speech got?	Looking is also speaking.

Figure 5.1 Selected Shona proverbs

(Integration)

1   Remind students about the context of Zimbabwean instruments and discuss the physical properties of the instrument.

2   Play track (00:01–05:51).

3   Discuss with the students the basic components of sound production, including frequency. Explain to students that frequency is influenced by the physical length of the sound-producing resonator (e.g., string, column of air, bell).

4   Provide students with a marimba (either a Zimbabwean or European; multiple marimbas would be ideal) and have students explore the relationships between the size of the resonator tube and pitches. For instance, same pitch classes should have a 2:1 relationship.

5   Assign students to find the lengths of the resonator tubes for a Zimbabwean marimba that is an octave lower than any that the school own. It will be helpful to remind students that Zimbabwean marimbas are not chromatic, but diatonic on the C scale with the addition of F sharp.

Learning Pathway #2

Son Jarocho from Veracruz, Mexico

Specific Use: Guitar Class

Materials:

- "Siquisirí" (2009). By Son de Madera. On *Son de Mi Tierra*. Recorded by Son de Madera. Smithsonian Folkways Recordings

Procedure:

(Attentive)

1 "What instruments do you hear?"

2 Play track (00:01–01:10).

3 Review answers (guitars, vocals).

4 "The ensemble in the recording is made up of stringed instruments of various sizes—they are all similar to the familiar guitar. Does the first instrument play a melody line or chords? What about the second and third instruments to join in?"

5 Play track (00:01–01:10).

6 Discuss that the first instrument is a solo melody line, the second instrument joins with chords, the third with a melodic bass line.

7 Show pictures or videos of son jarocho instrument, playing by themselves.

8 "What is the relationship between the vocal part and the guitarra de son (the higher melodic instrument)?"

9 Play track (00:01–01:10).

10 Discuss how the vocal line and the guitarra de son interact back and forth throughout the song.

11 "What is the meter of this music? Can you tap it quietly?"

12 Play track (00:01–01:10).

13 The meter is 3/4, although the introduction uses a variety of meters.

14 Have students listen to the *leona* part (the lowest part) and listen for rhythmic motives (Figure 2.1).

15 Play track (00:01–01:10).

16 Discuss what students heard in the *leona* part (e.g., quarter note bass line).

17 Have students listen to the *leona* part for the entire track to identify recurring rhythmic motives in the bass line.

18 Play track (00:01–4:02).

19 Discuss the recurring rhythmic motives; students can chant or clap the motives if they are unable to notate them. The teacher can then present examples (see Figure 2.2) on the board and have students perform.

Figure 2.1 Examples of *leona* rhythmic patterns in bass line

Materials:

* "La Bamba," José Gutiérrez and Los Hermanos Ochoa, Smithsonian Folkways Recordings
* "La Bamba," Son de Madera, Smithsonian Folkways Recordings
* "La Bamba," Richie Valens, Classic Records

Procedure:

(Engaged)

1 Through multiple listenings, compare and contrast the Gutíerrez and Ochoa Brothers recording with the Son de Madera version.
2 Listen again to check the list of similarities and differences.

(Enactive)

3 Listen to the Valens recording to discover the rhythm of the guitar strum pattern.
4 Play guitar or ukulele chords (I, V) with the discovered rhythm pattern along with these two traditional versions. Figure out a rhythm to strum or use a composite of the audible strum rhythms such as:

5 Listen to the recording of Siquisirí by Son de Madera to identify the rhythm of the strum pattern. This rhythm is referred to as *sesquialtera*, meaning a ratio of 3:2.

6   Play track.

7   Using guitars or ukuleles, practice playing the chords (A major, D major) using the *sesquialtera* rhythm.

8   Play along with the recording.

(Creating)

1   Have students play the accompaniment chords (A7/D) for the song using the strumming pattern. The chordal accompaniment can be passed around the room, each student deciding the strumming rhythm during their turn.

2   Play track (00:21–4:02).

3   Once students are comfortable maintaining the accompaniment on their own or in small groups, students can experiment with melodic improvisation with the recording. Students can take turns playing short improvised melodies over the accompaniment. Scaffold by discussing how the chord-tones of each chord can be important anchors for the melody or by presenting melodic material that is transcribed from the piece (see Figure 5.2 for examples). Students can practice playing these short fragments and embellish or extend them as they see fit. This can be done in small groups or as a class jam session.

4   Play track (00:21–4:02).

5   Once students are comfortable with the melodic material and have had some experience improvising, have half of the students perform the accompaniment while the other half passes the melody throughout the group, with one student playing a question and then the next student playing the answer.

Figure 5.2   Melodic fragments from Siquirisí, which can be basis for improvisation

Materials:

- "Siquisiri," Son de Madera, Smithsonian Folkways Recordings
  Jaranas, vocals
- "La Bamba Rebelde," Las Cafeteras, Las Cafeteras Music
  Quijada, cajon, marimbolo, vocals, jaranas
- "This Land is Your Land," Las Cafeteras, Las Cafeteras Music. Reimagining of U.S. folksong in son jarocho style
  Vocals, jaranas, snare drum, bass, quijada, tarima, accordion

- "If I Was President," Las Cafeteras, Las Cafeteras Music
  Vocals, jaranas, keyboard, drum set

Procedure:

(Integration)

1   Review the context for son jarocho style music in the class, reviewing instruments, geography, and approaches to music making.

2   Play Siquisirí to identify the musical and stylistic elements present in the piece; allow students the opportunity to discuss the musical characteristics of the piece.

3   Play track (00:01–04:02).

4   After discussing the origins of son jarocho style, show students on the map where to find the state of Veracruz, Mexico, as well as Los Angeles, California.

5   Explain to students that currently son jarocho music is flourishing in Los Angeles. Ask the students the following questions:

"Why do you think Los Angeles may be a place where san jarocho is thriving?'

(People from Veracruz moved there)

"Why do you think people may have moved there?"

(Allow students to explore their own ideas of why people immigrate)

6   Explain to students that you will be playing recordings of a current band that mixes son jarocho style with other present popular styles.

7   Play tracks or videos by Las Cafeteras.

8   Discuss the musical similarities and differences between songs performed by Las Cafeteras and Son de Madera.

Learning Pathway #3

Roma Wedding Music

Specific Use: Advanced Placement Music Theory

Materials:

- "Čoček Manhattan" (2001). By Yuri Yunakov Ensemble. SFW Recordings. On New York City: Global Beat of the Boroughs: Various Artists

Procedure:

(Attentive)

1. "What instruments do you hear in this piece? Specifically, listen for what instrument plays the solo."
2. Play track (00:25–1:55).
3. Discuss answers (saxophone, clarinet, accordion, drum set, guitar, bass guitar). Allow an additional listen to identify all instruments.
4. Play track (00:25–1:55).
5. Review instruments.
6. "What instruments are featured in the first section? What instruments are featured in the solo section?"
7. Play track (00:25–1:55).
8. Review answers. Beginning section: saxophone, clarinet, and accordion are playing melody in unison. Solo section: saxophone while the guitar and accordion accompany. Bass and drum set play throughout the clip.
9. "What is the meter of the piece?" Guide students to tap silently with music.
10. Play track (00:25–1:55).
11. Discuss answers. The piece is in 9/8 time.
12. "Is the meter divided evenly into three beats or is there some other subdivision?
13. Play track (00:25–1:55).
14. Review answers. The overriding metrical pattern is $2 + 2 + 2 + 3$. There are some moments where it varies, but maintains the overall 9/8 meter.
15. "We will listen to recording once more and please put the beat somewhere on your body or tap quietly on your desk."
16. Play track (00:25–1:55).
17. Assess students' ability to tap on the proper beats.

Materials:

Two different versions of a dance known as "Čoček" are suggested:

- "Gypsy Dance," Esma Redzepova, Smithsonian Folkways Recordings. *Gypsy Dance* features the self-proclaimed "Queen of the Gypsies" Esma Redzepova from Macedonia
- "Cocek Manhattan," Yuri Yunakov Ensemble, Smithsonian Folkways Records. Yuri Yunakov is a Turkish-Bulgarian Roma and puts a contemporary spin on his version of a Čoček

Procedure:

(Engaged)

1 After working through the steps of Attentive Listening with both selections, compare and contrast the orchestration and general feeling of the groove.
2 Play track.
3 Have students tap the underlying rhythm (2+2+2+3) while listening.
4 Play track.

(Enactive)

5 Play track again. The teacher models the basic dance step while listening.
6 Teach a basic version of the dance. Add a variation once the students have mastered the steps. (See Čoček Dance Steps)
7 Use both suggested recordings of different čočeks for dancing using the same steps.
8 Transcribe a Čoček melody to play on instruments or have the students learn to mplay a section of the melody by ear.

Čoček Dance Steps

Formation: Open circle, hands held (or not) down low

Meter: 9/8

Introduction: This depends on the recording. Let an even number of phrases pass, or until vocals enter if there are any.

The rhythmic phrase is 2+2+2+3. In folk dance terms, this phrase can be referred to as "quick quick quick slow." Beats 1, 2, and 3 subdivide into groups of "2" while beat 4 subdivides into a group of "3."

Measure	Beats	Steps
1	1	Lift Right foot
	2	Step straight back on Right
	3	Lift Left foot
	4	Step straight back on Left
2	1	Lift Right foot
	2	Step back with the Right
	3 & 4	Step twice in place with the Left and Right, changing the weight
3	1	Lift Left foot
	2	Step across in front with the Left—turning to face Right of center
	3	Step forward with the Right foot
	4	Step forward with the Left foot, turning to face the center to start the sequence again.

Styling tip: lifting of the foot is subtle. Imagine a puppet string lifting your knee to raise your foot. As the foot is lifted, bring the standing heel off the ground and then lower it again to touch the ground on the beat.

(Creating)

1 Review the asymmetrical meter of the piece, asking students to move or tap to the beat. The beginning of the piece is 2+2+2+3.

2 Play track (00:01–01:13).

3 Review the hijaz scale (see Figure 3.3). Allow students to practice playing through it, ascending, descending, or haphazardly through the scale on their own.

4 After students are comfortable with the scale, have students explore the hijaz scale in the meter of the piece (9/8). As students begin to improvise in this meter, it may be prudent to slow the tempo. The following rhythms (Figure 5.3) could be used to help scaffold rhythmic intricacy as they build their improvisational skills in the scale.

5 Have student improvise along with the recording, even if using more basic rhythms.

6 Play track (1:21–2:26).

Figure 5.3   Scaffolding rhythms for improvisation

Materials:

- "Čoček Manhattan," Yuri Yunakov Ensemble, Smithsonian Folkways Recordings

  Saxophone, clarinet, keyboard, electric bass, drum kit
- "Djelem Djelem," Esme Redzepova, World Village Records

  Unofficial Romani anthem featuring accordion, clarinet, trumpet, and vocals

Procedure:

(Integration)

1   Review context of the Romani piece and discuss how the Roma are treated in many places in the world.
2   Remind students about the musical characteristics of "Čoček Manhattan."
3   Play track (00:01–03:31) to revisit those characteristics.
4   To further explore understanding of the Roma experience, present "Djelem Djelem." Prompt students: "What emotions are the musicians expressing? How are they presenting those emotions musically?"
5   Play track "Djelem Djelem" (00:01–02:15).
6   Review answers. The song is sad but hopeful. Musically, this is accomplished by mode, ornamentation (e.g., sliding, trilling), and expressive timing.

7 Explore lyrics with students to further understand the mood of the song.

8 Open a discussion about the local community, examining if there are groups that are treated unfairly. Prompt: "Are there any instances where people are treated differently because of the color of their skin or the language they speak?"

9 Return to Esme Redzepova's version of Dzelem Dzelem; have students follow along with the text. Prompt: "As we listen, how does the music make you feel?"

10 Discuss students' reactions.

Appendix 2
List of Audio/Video Recordings

Chapter 1

"Hot Cheetos and Takis," (Video, August 9, 2012) Y. N. Rich Kids. 13twentythree, retrieved from https://youtu.be/7YLy4j8EZIk

"Kodo" (2012). On *Yoshida brothers best, Vol. two*. Sony Music Corp. Available on iTunes.

Chapter 2

"Čoček Manhattan," Yuri Yunakov Ensemble, Smithsonian Folkways Recordings. Saxophone, clarinet, keyboard, electric bass, and drum kit. www.folkways.si.edu/ yuri-yunakov-ensemble/cocek-manhattan/world/music/track/Smithsonian.

"Ko tzu fei," Wong Kuen, Smithsonian Folkways Recordings. Classical Chinese piece played on the ti-tzu (flute). www.folkways.si.edu/wong-kuen/ko-tzu-fei-pigeons-flying/ music/track/smithsonian.

"Nyoka Musango," Lora Chiorah-Dye and the Suketai Marimba and Dance Ensemble, Smithsonian Folkways Records. Marimbas, hosho, body percussion, vocals. www. folkways.si.edu/lora-chiorah-dye-and-sukutai/nyoka-musango/world/music/track/ smithsonian.

"Siquisirí," Son de Madera, Smithsonian Folkways Recordings. Son jarocho featuring leona, guitarra de son, jarana tercera, contrabass, and vocals. www.folkways.si.edu/ son-de-madera/siquisiri-siquisiri/latin-world/music/track/smithsonian.

"Smoky Lum/Maggie's Pancakes/Dancing Feet/The Mason's Apron," The Tannahill Weavers, Green Linnet Records. Scottish Reel featuring fiddle, whistle, bones, guitar, and highland bagpipes. Available on iTunes and Spotify.

"The Sun Will Never Go Down," Sweet Honey in the Rock, Flying Fish Records. African American spiritual, a cappella singing. Available on iTunes.

"Ua lata mai le aso fa'amasino," Le Patiloa, Smithsonian Folkways Recordings. Guitar, bass, vocals. www.folkways.si.edu/le-patiloa/ua-lata-mai-le-aso-faamasino/world/music/track/smithsonian.

"Ya Hbibi Malek Sahi," Abdeskan Cherkaoui, Smithsonian Folkways Recordings. Middle eastern oud with vocals. www.folkways.si.edu/abdeslam-cherkaoui/ya-hbibi-malek-sahi-lover-why-are-you-forgetful/music/track/smithsonian.

Chapter 3

"Cocek Manhattan", Yuri Yunakov Ensemble, Smithsonian Folkways Recordings. www.folkways.si.edu/yuri-yunakov-ensemble/cocek-manhattan/world/music/track/smith sonian.

"Everyday People", Sly and the Family Stone, Epic Records.

"Gypsy Dance", Esma Redzepova, Smithsonian Folkways Recordings. www.folkways.si.edu/esma-redzepova-and-usnija-jasarova/gypsy-dance-cocek/world/music/track/smithsonian.

"La Bamba", José Gutiérrez & Los Hermanos Ochoa, Smithsonian Folkways Recordings. José Gutiérrez, Felipe Ochoa, and Marcos Ochoa, raised on farms in Veracruz, are considered to be three of the most accomplished modern-day son jarocho performers featuring the traditional regional Vercruz arpa (harp) and guitars called jarana and requinto. www.folkways.si.edu/jose-gutierrez-los-hermanos-ochoa/la-bamba/latin-world/music/track/smithsonian.

"La Bamba", Son de Madera, Smithsonian Folkways Recordings. The members of the group Son de Madera are key figures in the current revival of son jarocho. www.folkways.si.edu/son-de-madera/la-bamba-the-bamba/latin-world/music/track/smithsonian.

"La Bamba", Richie Valens, Classic Records.

"Nyoka Musango" (Snake in the Grass), Lora Chiorah Dye, Smithsonian Folkways Recordings. www.folkways.si.edu/lora-chiroah-dye-and-sukutai/nyoka-musango/world/music/track/smithsonian.

"People Everyday", Arrested Development, Smithsonian Folkways Recordings. Early 1990s hip-hop tune featuring positive messages in the lyrics. www.folkways.si.edu/arrested-development/people-everyday/african-american-spoken-american-history-poetry-prose/track/smithsonian.

"People Everyday" (In the Style of Arrested Development), Sunfly Karaoke Ltd. Available on iTunes.

Rare footage of Romani band in Macedonia, 1968. www.folkways.si.edu/rare-footage-of-romani-band-in-macedonia-1968/music/video/smithsonian.

"Ušti Ušti Baba", Esme Redzepova, Smithsonian Folkways Recordings. A classic čoček by the self-proclaimed Queen of the Gypsies. www.folkways.si.edu/esma-redz-epova-and-usnija-jasarova/get-up-father-ustli-ustli-baba/world/music/track/smithsonian.

Chapter 4

"Bahia-Cuba," Samba Squad, on *Batuque*, independent recording. Available on iTunes. Vocals, berimbau, agogo bells, surdo, caxixi.

"Baila, Julia, Loíza," Los Pleneros de la 21, Smithsonian Folkways Recordings. Piano, electric guitar, congas, guiro, vocals. www.folkways.si.edu/los-pleneros-de-la-21/baila-julia-loiza-dance-julia-loiza/latin-world/music/track/smithsonian.

"Carmelina," Los Pleneros de la 21, in tribute to Marcial Reyes Arvelo at 2005 Smithsonian Folklife Festival. www.folkways.si.edu/performance-carmelina/latin-world/music/video/smithsonian.

"Čoček Manhattan," Yuri Yunakov Ensemble, Smithsonian Folkways Recordings. Saxophone, clarinet, keyboard, bass, drum set. www.folkways.si.edu/yuri-yunakov-ensemble/cocek-manhattan/world/music/track/Smithsonian.

Fandango-Bombazo (Puerto Rican Jam Session) at Smithsonian Folklife Festival. At the 2006 Smithsonian Folklife Festival, musicians and dancers from Mexico, Puerto Rico, and other Latino backgrounds came together in an unprecedented, joint fandango-bombazo. www.folkways.si.edu/fandango-bombazo/caribbean-latin-world/music/video/smithsonian.

"Just Batucada," Voices of the Bateria, OK Records. Caixa, repinique, vocals, cuica, surdo.

"Kecak," The Library of Congress Endangered Music Project. UNESCO. Smithsonian Folkways Recordings. voices www.folkways.si.edu/kecak/world/music/track/smithsonian.

"Kpanlogo," Kofi Quarshie, Acewonder Ltd. Available on iTunes. Gankoguis, handclaps, vocals, kpanlogo drums.

"Kpanlogo," Nyanyo Addo, Weltwunder. Available on iTunes. Vocals, kpanlogo drums, atokee, axatse.

"Kpanlogo," on *Traditional Drumming and dances of Ghana*. Smithsonian Folkways Recordings. Kpanlogo drums, gankogui, handclaps, vocals, axatse. www.folkways.si.edu/kpanlongo/world/music/track/smithsonian.

Master of Traditional Arts—an ongoing interdisciplinary project produced by Documentary Arts. It focuses on the recipients of the National Heritage Fellowship, awarded annually by the National Endowment of the Arts in the U.S. This website features selected traditional musicians in each state in the U.S. There is a full feature on Yuri Yunakov including several high-energy performance videos. The performance venues include weddings, music festivals, and television shows. Retrieved from www.mastersoftraditionalarts.org/artists/367.

"Mbira—Spirit of the People." Thomas Mapfumo, This 1990 documentary explores mbira traditions, its connection to the Chimurenga revolutionary struggle, and Zimbabwe's transition to independence. With extensive footage from the era, featured are interviews and performances by Thomas Mapfumo and Oliver Mtukudzi. https://youtu.be/5hF2Hstvrfc?list=PLyMF9d8PivLWucTmVZ9hmc8jtTD-pvQjr.

"Nyoka Musango," Thomas Mapfumo, Duke University Press. Available on iTunes. Electic guitars, electric bass guitar, drum set, handclaps, vocals.

"Sambodromo Batería," T.Z. Karp and Y. Varona, on *Carnaval, Carnaval en Brasil*, OK Records. Available on iTunes. Apito, repinique, surdo, tamborim, reco reco, caixa.

"Siquisirí," Son de Madera, Smithsonian Folkways Recordings. Vocals, jarana, guitar. www.folkways.si.edu/son-de-madera/siquisiri-siquisiri/latin-world/music/track/smithsonian.

Son de Madera at the Smithsonian Folklife Festival. This video clip shows a performance from 2009 and clearly features the footwork on the tarima. www.folkways.si.edu/son-de-madera/latin-world/music/video/smithsonian.

Son de Madera performs Son Jarocho. This short video shows the songwriting process for creating lyrics in son jarocho selections. www.folkways.si.edu/son-jarocho/latin-spoken-word-world/music/video/Smithsonian.

"Tamarii Tahiti," Royal Tahitian Dance Company, Smithsonian Folkways Recordings. To'ere ensemble. www.folkways.si.edu/royal-tahitian-dance-company/tamarii-tahiti/world/music/track/smithsonian.

"Tjak: The Singers of Peliatan," UNESCO/Smithsonian Folkways Recordings. Voices. www.folkways.si.edu/the-singers-of-peliatan/tjak/music/track/smithsonian.

"Toere," Maeva Tahiti Tahitian Folkloric Group, 1967/2010, Manuiti. Available on iTunes. To'ere ensemble.

"Toere," The Royal Tahitian Dancers and Singers, Viking. Available on iTunes. To'ere ensemble.

Zimbabwe Mbira—Three melodies played on a 14-note kalimba. Ethnic Folkways Library. Mbiras. www.folkways.si.edu/ackson-zulu/three-melodies-played-on-a-fourteen-note-kalimba/world/music/track/smithsonian.

Chapter 5

"Bai Trong Lay and Thet," Tu Huyen, Nam Phu, Chin Quon, Sau Phu, and Hai Phat, Smithsonian Folkways Recordings. Vietnamese Ritual Music with *ken trung* (reed instrument) and percussion. www.folkways.si.edu/tu-huyen-nam-phu-chin-quon-sau-phu-hai-phat/bai-trong-lay-and-thet/music/track/smithsonian.

"Čoček Manhattan," Yuri Yunakov Ensemble, Smithsonian Folkways Recordings. Saxophone, clarinet, keyboard, electric bass, and drum kit. www.folkways.si.edu/yuri-yunakov-ensemble/cocek-manhattan/world/music/track/Smithsonian.

"Hiryu San-Dan-Gaesh," O-Suwa-Daiko, Smithsonian Folkways Records. Japanese taiko drums. www.folkways.si.edu/ensemble-o-suwa-daiko-under-the-direction-of-oguchi-daihachi/hiryu-san-dan-gaeshi/music/track/smithsonian.

"Nat-Bhairev," Shamim Ahmed, Zakir Hussain, and Amanat, Smithsonian Folkways Recordings. Nat Bhairev raga featuring sitar, tabla and tanpura. www.folkways.si.edu/shamim-ahmed/nat-bhairev/world/music/track/smithsonian.

"Nyoka Musango," Lora Chiorah-Dye and the Suketai Marimba Dance Ensemble, Smithsonian Folkways Records. Marimbas, vocals, hosho, claps. www.folkways.si.edu/lora-chiorah-dye-and-sukutai/nyoka-musango/world/music/track/smithsonian.

"Old Damascus," The Orchestra of Syrian Musicians, Transgressive Records. Arrangement for Syrian folk song with orchestral and traditional Middle Eastern instruments. Available on iTunes and Spotify.

"Siquisirí," Son de Madera, Smithsonian Folkways Recordings. Son jarocho piece featuring leona, guitarra de son, jarana tercera, contrabass, and vocals. www.folkways.si.edu/son-de-madera/siquisiri-siquisiri/latin-world/music/track/smithsonian.

"Un llanero de verdad," Grupo Cimarron, Smithsonian Folkways Recordings. Joropo llanero featuring bandola and vocals. www.folkways.si.edu/grupo-cimarron/un-llanero-de-verdad/latin-world/music/track/smithsonian.

Chapter 6

"Aquelo Abraço," Gilberto Gil, Phillips LP. Guitar, bass, vocals, kettle drum, cowbell, whistle, and cabasa. Available on iTunes and Spotify.

"Batmacumba," Gilberto Gil, Caetano Veloso, and Gal Costa, Phillips LP. Psychedelic rock song featuring guitar, bass, vocals, tambourine, and bongos. Available on iTunes and Spotify.

"Beware Verwoerd! (Ndodemnyama)," Miriam Makeba, RCA Victor. Vocals, guitar, bass, djembe, body percussion. Available on iTunes.

"Bury My Heart at Wounded Knee," Buffy Sainte-Marie, EMI Records. Guitar, vocals, bass, keyboard, electric guitar, drum set. Available on iTunes.

"Čoček Manhattan," Yuri Yunakov Ensemble, Smithsonian Folkways Recordings. Saxophone, clarinet, keyboard, electric bass, drum kit. www.folkways.si.edu/yuri -yunakov-ensemble/cocek-manhattan/world/music/track/smithsonian.

"Djelem Djelem," Esme Redzepova, World Village Records. Unofficial Romani anthem featuring accordion, clarinet, trumpet, and vocals. Available on iTunes.

"I Don't Need A Man," miss A, AQ/JYP/KT. K-Pop song that explores gender roles in modern times. Official video: www.youtube.com/watch?v=EkSOOiMDGiY. Track available on iTunes.

"If I Was President," Las Cafeteras, Las Cafeteras Music. Vocals, jaranas, keyboard, drum set. http://lascafeteras.com/videos/.

"La Bamba Rebelde," Las Cafeteras, Las Cafeteras Music. Quijada, cajon, marimbolo, vocals, jaranas. http://lascafeteras.com/videos/.

"Meadowlands (Mielieland)," Nancy Jacobs & Her Sisters (2004). Gallo Record Company. Piano, drum set, guitar, bass, vocals. Available on iTunes and Spotify.

"Nkosi Sikelel'i Afrika," Ladysmith Black Mambazo, Gallo Record Company. A cappella singing. Available on iTunes and Spotify.

"Nyoka Musango (Snake in the Grass)," Lora Chiorah Dye, Smithsonian Folkways Recordings. Marimbas, hosho, vocals. www.folkways.si.edu/lora-chiorah-dye-and-sukutai/ nyoka-musango/world/music/track/smithsonian.

"Panis Et Circensis," Os Mutantes, Phillips LP. Avant-garde rock song featuring brass, guitar, organ, vocals, trumpet, tambourine, bass, and drumset. Available on iTunes and Spotify.

"Senzenina," Lalela Cape Town Choir (2014). Lalela Music. A cappella singing. Available on iTunes.

"Siquisiri," Son de Madera, Smithsonian Folkways Recordings. Jaranas, vocals. www. folkways.si.edu/son-de-madera/siquisiri-siquisiri/latin-world/music/track/smith sonian.

"Sobashiy'abazali" (We Will Leave Our Parents)," African Cream Freedom Choir, African Cream Music. Vocals, bass drum, whistling. Available on iTunes.

"This Land is Your Land," Las Cafeteras, Las Cafeteras Music. Reimagining of United States folksong in son jarocho style. Vocals, jaranas, snare drum, bass, quijada, tarima, accordion. http://lascafeteras.com/videos/.

Index